Unlocking the Bible Story flows from the pen of a pastor who understands how important it is to encourage God's people to read and discover the power of the Bible. Colin Smith has written a practical tool to facilitate the wonderful adventure of reading and understanding the Bible. **I recommend that every pastor and church consider deepening their Bible knowledge by utilizing this tool** that has produced incredible results in the church Pastor Smith leads.

WILLIAM HAMEL
PRESIDENT, EVANGELICAL FREE CHURCH OF AMERICA

"...touches the deepest concerns of our hearts."

DR. GREGORY L. WAYBRIGHT,
PRESIDENT TRINITY INTERNATIONAL UNIVERSITY

Colin Smith's *Unlocking the Bible Story* is a significant work. In fact, I'm convinced it will make a lasting contribution to God's people regardless of age or ethnicity.

At first glance the Bible appears to many people as a puzzle, with parts that are not easily assembled. Here is **a simplified explanation for understanding and learning to love the scriptures.** My colleague, Colin Smith, capably serves up a pleasing and satisfying literary meal that merits thoughtful consumption in our day of biblical starvation.

HOWARD G. HENDRICKS,
DISTINGUISHED PROFESSOR
CHAIRMAN, CENTER FOR CHRISTIAN LEADERSHIP
DALLAS THEOLOGICAL SEMINARY

Unlocking the Bible Story explores the mountain peaks of Scripture, helping us trace the Bible's story line from beginning to end. I promise, it does unlock the Bible, showing us the unity of God's revelation. Best of all, it shows that Christ is the central theme, as the Biblical narrative moves from one event to another. Excellent for those who want to "get into" the Bible.

ERWIN W. LUTZER,
SENIOR PASTOR MOODY CHURCH

"Excellent for those who want to "get into" the Bible."

This is a satisfying and insightful overview of Scripture that tells "the old, old story" in a fascinating way. Even seasoned Bible students will find their eyes opened and their hearts warmed as they read it.

WARREN WIERSBE
AUTHOR AND CONFERENCE SPEAKER

UNLOCKING THE BIBLE STORY
VOLUME 2

Colin S. Smith

Moody Press
Chicago

All Scripture quotations, unless otherwise indicated, are
taken from the Holy Bible, New International Version®. NIV®.
Copyright © 1973, 1978, 1984 by International Bible Society.
Used by permission of Zondervan Publishing House. All
rights reserved.

Scripture quotations marked NASB are taken from the New
American Standard Bible®, © Copyright The Lockman
Foundation 1960, 1962, 1963, 1968, 1971, 1972, 1973, 1975,
1977, 1995. Used by permission.

Scripture quotations marked NKJV are taken from the New
King James Version. Copyright © 1982 by Thomas Nelson, Inc.
Used by permission. All rights reserved.

ISBN: 0-8024-6544-7

1 3 5 7 9 10 8 6 4 2

Printed in the United States of America

For Karen,

*whose love, patience, loyalty, and courage
mean more to me than words can tell.*

CONTENTS

Acknowledgments 9

Introduction 11

1 Suffering 17

2 Resurrection 29

3 Revelation 41

4 Wisdom 53

5 Holiness 65

6 Comfort 79

7 Servant 91

8 Calling 105

9 Heart   119

10 Tears   131

11 Glory   143

12 Shepherd   155

13 Breath   169

14 Alien   183

15 Love   195

16 Faith   207

17 Hope   221

Reading the Bible In One Year   235

Acknowledgments

What makes a sermon memorable? Every week thousands of sermons are preached. Many make only a slight and short-lived impression, but some leave their mark forever. The preachers and teachers who have left a lasting impression on my life are those who communicate the greatness and the glory of God.

My own vision of the greatness of God has been stretched as I have worked on the chapters of this book. That's what happened to Job through his suffering, and to the prophets as God revealed what He was doing in the momentous days in which they lived. My hope and prayer for this volume is that God will use it to give you a fresh glimpse of His glory that will feed your soul and lead you to worship.

It is now ten years since I heard Eric Alexander preach on Isaiah's vision at the Evangelical Ministry Assembly in London. His vivid presentation of the awesome glory of God was powerful then and has lived in my memory ever since. I am especially grateful to him for his observation that those who stood in the presence of God could not look directly on His glory. His insights were the foundation for my own reflections on Isaiah's vision.

Other Bible teachers have contributed to my understanding of various themes found in this book. I was helped by Don Carson's lectures on Ezekiel given to pastors of the Evangelical Free Church of America. His presentation of the glory of God and the flying platform in Ezekiel's vision opened up that book for me.

I am also grateful to Stuart Briscoe for his description of wisdom as "life skills," which I have used in chapter 4. Stuart spoke on "the fear of the Lord is the beginning of wisdom," in England in 1994. That was when we first met and led, through his kindness, to our first visit to America.

The timelines in this volume are again based on dates in Walter Kaiser's book *A History of Israel* (Broadman & Holman). They illustrate how God's words through the prophets relate to events that were taking place at the time, many of which we discovered in volume 1 of *Unlocking the Bible Story*.

It has again been a joy to work with the publishing team at Moody, and I am especially grateful to Jim Vincent for the editorial skill and insight that he has brought to this project. My younger son David also worked with me on this volume. Our three weeks together in researching this book are a special memory for us both, and I greatly appreciate the enthusiasm with which David gave himself to this task.

I am again deeply conscious of my debt to many pastors, friends, and colleagues whose ministry I have appreciated over the years. I have spoken about some of them in the acknowledgments in volume one. If there are others whose influence on these chapters I have forgotten, then I hope that they will forgive my oversight.

Finally, I again owe an unpayable debt of gratitude to my wife, Karen, without whose love, support and encouragement, I would never have been able to complete this task. This volume is gratefully dedicated to her.

INTRODUCTION

"I've been in church for years. I don't feel that I have a good grasp of the Bible. But I wish that I did."

I've lost count of the number of times I've heard a comment like that. Churches are filled with many people who know stories from the Bible but do not know the story of the Bible. Others who do not attend church may find it difficult to know where to begin in the Bible. When you know some stories without knowing the story of the Bible, it's like having a handful of pearls with no string to link them together. *Unlocking the Bible Story* will give you the string, and show you how the pearls of God's truth fit together.

The Bible is one story. Thus it begins with two people in a beautiful garden and ends with a vast crowd in a magnificent city. All the way through, it points us to Jesus Christ. *Unlocking the Bible Story* will show you the big picture and help you to discover the breathtaking sweep of the whole Bible story.

These volumes began as a series of sermons preached over a period of two years at Arlington Heights Evangelical Free Church in Illinois. I had been planning to teach the story of the Old Testament, and when the chairman of our elder council suggested the idea of encouraging the congregation to read the Bible in a year, the two ideas came together and ignited a spark.

We presented the challenge to the congregation and offered the gift of *The One Year Bible* to everyone who would make a commitment to read it. We promised that every Sunday the preaching would come from the Bible book we were reading, and would show how each part fits into the whole. We ordered four hundred Bibles. But the response was overwhelming. Fourteen hundred people made the commitment!

Now, two years later, I am deeply moved by many testimonies of how this journey through the Bible has touched and changed people's lives.

"Though I have been a believer [most] of my life, I have never continuously read through the Bible from beginning to end. I have studied different passages and books, which was great, but they did not give me comprehensive message of the Bible...I especially appreciate understanding the Old Testament and find it enriches my understanding of who Christ is." —Hyacinth, a corporate human resources manager

"The most significant benefit of these two years of unlocking the Bible has been seeing how God's plan is so intricately woven through the Bible. Many of the...

stories...of the Bible used to seem disconnected and now are wonderfully brought together. What an encouragement."—Jeff, an engineer

"The messages of *Unlocking the Bible Story* [have] given me a new way to talk to seekers about the Bible as a whole and how it impacts them."—Liz, a nurse and mother

What has happened for these folks can happen for you!

There are two ways to use *Unlocking the Bible Story*. You may choose to read the Bible in a year, and use these volumes (this is volume two of four) as a roadmap for your journey. At the end of this book you will find a Bible reading plan based on *The One Year Bible* published by Tyndale House. You may want to use this approach.

Alternatively, you can use *Unlocking the Bible Story* as an aerial photograph, to gain a big-picture perspective on the Bible so that when you are "down on the ground" in your own study, you will have a better sense of where you are. Either way, welcome to the journey.

Each of the eighty chapters in this four-volume series begins with a key question to unlock, and ends with a summary of the answer from the Bible. At the beginning of each chapter there are signposts that point out discoveries you will make, truths you will learn, and insights that will help you to worship. Finally, in each chapter of the Old Testament volumes, you will find a "Spotlight on Christ" which will help you to see how the whole Bible points us forward to Jesus Christ.

Unlocking the Bible Story does not cover every chapter or even every book of the Bible, but it will take you through the whole of the Bible story, and show you how it fits together. It will also introduce you to the major themes of the Bible.

The Bible also uses some specialized words, like prophet, priest, atonement, and revelation. If we want to fully appreciate what God is saying to us in the Bible, we need to understand the words that He uses. Many areas of life have their own distinctive vocabulary. When I came to America five years ago, I had a very limited understanding of baseball. The basic idea was clear to me, but I quickly discovered that other people were seeing and enjoying things that I missed. The commentators talked about a "curve ball" and a "slider." Of course, I didn't need to know what these words meant to enjoy the game, but I soon realized that if I wanted to appreciate what was going on, I needed to learn some new words.

Unlocking the Bible Story will help you to understand the Bible's vocabulary. Each chapter introduces a key word in the Bible story, and as you grasp the Bible's major themes, you will begin to enjoy insights that otherwise you would have missed.

Unlocking the Bible Story will show you how the whole Bible points to Jesus Christ. He is the focal point of the whole story. If you take a diamond and move it in the light, each facet will reflect a different shade of color. The diamond sparkles as the light reflects on the stone at different angles. *Unlocking the Bible Story* will help you to worship as you see new facets of the glory of our Lord Jesus Christ.

THE BIBLE STORY:
ABRAHAM TO JESUS CHRIST

2000 B.C. ABRAHAM
           ISAAC
           JACOB

           FOUR HUNDRED YEARS OF SLAVERY
           IN EGYPT

1500   EXODUS FROM EGYPT (MOSES)
           ENTRANCE INTO CANAAN (JOSHUA)

           THREE HUNDRED YEARS OF CHAOS
           (THE JUDGES)

           SAUL
           DAVID
1000   SOLOMON

           FOUR HUNDRED YEARS OF DIVISION
           (NORTHERN AND
           SOUTHERN KINGDOMS)

           BABYLONIAN CAPTIVITY

500
           REBUILDING OF JERUSALEM
           (EZRA, NEHEMIAH)

           FOUR HUNDRED YEARS OF SILENCE

0   BIRTH OF JESUS CHRIST

Suffering

JOB 1

What does God

have to say

about the

suffering of

His people?

1 Suffering

JOB 1

DISCOVER
the story behind the story
of suffering.

LEARN
how you can defeat Satan's
purpose by your response
to pain.

WORSHIP
as you see what Jesus Christ
accomplished in His suffering.

GENESIS is the first book in the Bible, but Job is the oldest. The story comes from the time of Abraham or before, and the book of Job may well be one of the oldest books in the world. It is also one of the most important, because it deals with some of the deepest questions you will ever face in your life.

Job is the first of the Bible's wisdom books, that is books that deal with the skills we need for navigating our way through life. It also contains one of the most dramatic and compelling stories in the Bible.

When God chose to speak to us about suffering, He did not give us a book of philosophy. When we are in deep personal pain, we do not have a great deal of interest in theory or arguments. God speaks to us through a real-life experience of a man who suffered and records for us his thoughts and his struggles. As you enter Job's struggles, God will speak into your pain. Wherever you look in human history, pain is still pain, and God is still God.

THE GREATEST MAN IN THE EAST

Job was an outstanding man in every way. We are told that he was "blameless" and "upright" (1:1). This did not mean that he was perfect, but it did mean that if people were looking for anything to stick on him, they wouldn't find it. The same word is used in the New Testament for Christian leaders. They are to be "blameless" (Titus 1:6). No leaders are perfect but they must be above reproach. That was true of Job. He "feared God" and he "shunned evil" (Job 1:1). That means that he experienced the same temptations that all the rest of us do, but he had learned to push them off. He shunned evil, and the reason he was able to do this was because he feared God. Indeed, "he was the greatest man in the East" (v.3).

The second thing that we learn about Job is that he was wealthy. He had been highly successful and God had blessed him. In those days, wealth was measured in livestock. We are told that he had seven thousand sheep, three thousand camels, five hundred yoke of oxen, and five hundred donkeys (v. 3). His total net worth was pretty impressive.

We are also told that Job had seven sons and three daughters (v. 2), and it seems that they may have represented the one shadow on his horizon. The one thing that we are told about them is that their lives were an endless round of parties. "His sons used to take turns holding feasts in their homes" (v. 4). Their whole lifestyle seems to have been built around the pursuit of pleasure. If you had asked them what they were living for, they would have said, "We live for the weekend. We get our work done, and then we all have a blast."

Job did not like what they were doing. In fact after the parties were over, he used to offer a sacrifice for each of his children. He did this "thinking, 'Perhaps my children have sinned and cursed God in their hearts'" (v. 5).

If you had spoken to Job's sons or daughters, you would have thought them to be fine, upright people, but Job was worried that what they said and what they thought were two different things. He was worried about what was in their hearts, and it would not have surprised him if, when the wine had loosened some of their inhibitions, they had cursed God.

So here is a man who was wonderfully blessed, but had one nagging fear that haunted his mind. He felt that what was going on in his family was not pleasing to God.

CATASTROPHE

Then one day everything in Job's life changed. The day was like any other—until a terrified servant broke through the door of the house with desperate news. "The oxen were plowing and the donkeys were grazing nearby, and the Sabeans attacked and carried them off. They put the servants to the sword, and I am the only one who has escaped" (vv. 14–15).

Job did not have time to take this appalling news in, because while the servant was still speaking, another messenger came with the news that the sheep and other servants had been killed in what was probably something like a lightning storm.

"The fire of God fell from the sky and burned up the sheep and the servants, and I am the only one who has escaped to tell you!" (v. 16).

While he was still speaking, a third messenger arrived with news that three raiding parties of Chaldeans had swept down from the hills and taken off the camels. Then a fourth messenger arrived with the worst news of all. Job's sons and daughters had been eating and drinking at one of their parties, and suddenly the house was hit by a mighty wind that swept in from the desert. The house collapsed on them, and all of them were dead (v. 19).

In one day this man lost every familiar landmark of his life. His business was destroyed, his wealth was plundered, and his entire family tragically killed. It all happened in one day. By any standards, this is a catalog of unspeakable suffering.

GOD'S PEOPLE WILL SUFFER

Bad things happen to good people. Sometimes terrible things happen to wonderful people, and God allows it to be so. The Scripture tells us Job was "the greatest man among all the people of the East" (v. 3). So the story of Job clearly teaches us that the pursuit of a godly life will not put us beyond suffering.

Many Christians have an instinctive feeling that if we pursue a life of worship and service, it would be a reasonable expectation that God would keep us from significant suffering in our lives. But there is no such deal on the table. The book of Job makes that very clear. Christian faith does not inoculate us against suffering in a fallen world. That is why it is an absolute travesty of the gospel to suggest that if people come to Jesus, all their problems will be over. God does not immunize His people against suffering.

At the heart of the Bible story, we learn that the greatest and most godly person who ever lived suffered more than any other. He was rejected by His family. He wept at the graveside of one of His dearest friends. He was betrayed and suffered injustice, and then He was crucified. When He calls us to walk in His footsteps, that includes following Him into the mystery that He experienced, of the suffering God allows in the life of a godly man or woman.

When you suffer, you will probably ask the question "Why?" Jesus did. But you should not ask the question "Why is this happening to me?" That question betrays a mind-set that says, "It may be appropriate that this should happen to other people but not to me." Your faith in Christ does not and will not ever give you immunity from suffering. The apostle Peter wrote us, "Do not be surprised at the painful trial you are suffering, as though something strange were happening to you" (1 Peter 4:12). So the important question to ask is not "Why does suffering happen?" but "How can a man stand when all the navigating points of his life disappear?"

God's People Will Feel Pain

It is a wonderful thing that God has given us a whole book of the Bible that recounts the inner struggle of a believing man who faced terrible suffering.

The book of Job gives the lie to the superficial idea that if we "Take it to the Lord in prayer" this will somehow remove the pain. Job discovered that prayer does not act as an anesthetic. C. S. Lewis described this powerfully in his book *A Grief Observed*. In the deep pain that followed the death of his wife, Lewis felt that his attempts at prayer were like coming up against a great door that was then shut in your face, with the sound of bolting and double bolting inside, and then silence.

Lewis was discovering what Isaiah describes when he said that the Lord is "a God who hides himself" (Isaiah 45:15). God reveals Himself in Scripture and in Christ, but He also hides Himself, and we do not speak about God correctly unless we have grasped both these things. He has revealed Himself so we may know Him and love Him and trust Him; but He also hides Himself, so that there are times when we will say, "I just don't understand; I can't make any sense of His ways." There will be times when our heart will shout out *Why?* and there will be no answer.

Job's friends tried to comfort him. They said many things, some misguided, some true. But Job was not able to hear them. There were times in the past when he would have enjoyed a theological discussion with his friends, but now their words seem to float outside him and beyond him. He was simply overwhelmed by the pain.

Later in the story, the comfort of God broke through to him, but it was a long time coming, and Job never pretended that he was experiencing comfort when he was not. There is a relentless honesty about this man, and he refuses to say what he does not experience. "What I feared has come upon me; what I dreaded has happened to me. I have no peace, no quietness; I have no rest, but only turmoil" (Job 3:25–26).

God's people are not always so honest. Perhaps the reason for that is that we are afraid of "not having the answers." Job's testimony releases us from the pressure of feeling that we have to say things are well when they are not. There are times of pain and turmoil when peace seems to be beyond our grasp. And we must not be afraid of this; this was the experience of the greatest man in the east.

If the Christian life is presented as a life of constant victory in which the triumphs are always greater than the pain, and the certainties are always greater than the questions, then Christian people will not be able to make sense of their experience when the pain seems greater than the victory, and the questions seem greater than the answers.

I thank God for a book of the Bible that tells me the greatest man of his time struggled in deep darkness with unresolved questions, and battled with a level of pain that his closest friends could not begin to understand. And yet in all of this, he did not sin against God.

THE STORY BEHIND THE STORY

Here we come to one of the most fascinating scenes in the whole of the Bible. In Job 1 God pulls back a curtain so that we can get a glimpse of another story that is going on behind the pain that Job experienced. God wants us to know that there was more at stake in this story than Job ever knew or could begin to understand.

There is an old war movie that I have seen many times, but every time I see it, I discover something else going on in the plot. *Where Eagles Dare* tells the story of a group of special agents who are dropped behind enemy lines supposedly to rescue a captured military commander who has information that is crucial to the outcome of the war.

In actual fact, the man who has been captured is not a commander at all, but an actor who has no information whatever. The real reason for the mission is to flush out the identity of an enemy agent who has penetrated the secret service, and whose continued presence there would spell disaster for millions of people. The team thinks that they are risking everything to rescue one man from torture and death, but in fact they are involved in a far greater mission that has not yet been revealed to them. The outcome involves much more than the safety of one man; it involves the destiny of a whole nation.

The only person who really knows what is going on is the team leader, played by Richard Burton. His lieutenant, an American played by Clint Eastwood, has an implicit trust in his leader, but at times that trust is strained to the limit. His life is on the line a thousand times as he jumps from cable cars to escape the enemy, but it is not until the very last scene in the film that he discovers what the whole mission was really all about.

There is a story behind the story, and it is extremely difficult to make any sense of the film if you don't know the story behind the story, which is why I have enjoyed watching the film a number of times!

So what is the story behind the story of Job? What is really at stake as this man makes his journey through suffering? The book of Job tells us about a particular day when God summoned the angels to present themselves before Him, and we are told that Satan came with them.

The story behind the story is about vindicating the name of God.

The Bible is quite clear that in the beginning, God not only created the earth, but also the heavens. Alongside the visible creation, God also fashioned a creation that is invisible to us. The Bible indicates that evil originated in the heavenly creation before it ever infected the earthly creation. Lucifer (morning star) was an angel of God who wanted to take the place of God (Isaiah 14:12–15). His rebellion was unsuccessful and led to his being excluded from the presence of God and cast down to the earth. So right from the beginning of human history there was an enemy, bent on destroying the work of God. So in Genesis 3, we find this enemy coming to the first man and woman in a quest to involve human beings in his own rebellion against God.

This sets the stage for the great drama of human history in which God will redeem sinners. He will bring such a transformation within them that they will love good more than evil, truth more than lies, and God more than themselves. That is the big story behind our little lives.

In Job, God pulls back the curtain on the drama that was taking place in heaven. We're told that Satan, now an outcast of heaven, was summoned to stand before God.

"Have you considered my servant Job?" God asks the evil one. "There is no one on earth like him; he is blameless and upright, a man who fears God and shuns evil" (Job 1:8).

Satan uses the occasion to slander the name of God. "Does Job fear God for nothing?" (v. 9). In effect, Satan is telling God, "The only reason Job fears You is raw self-interest. You think that he loves You freely, but that's impossible! It cannot be done. Job is a man, and men love themselves!"

> "Have you not put a hedge around him and his household and
> everything he has? You have blessed the work of his hands, so
> that his flocks and herds are spread throughout the land." (v. 10)

Satan is saying, "Of course he will profess to be a lover of God as long as You give him everything that he wants; but take away his wealth, take away his work, take away his family, take away his health, and he will surely curse You to Your face."

Satan, who himself had rejected God's law and authority, was telling God, "Nobody could love You for who You are! Men may love the gifts of God, but sin is so deep that men will never come to love You for who You are." Satan was convinced that sin is an incurable disease, and that restoration from sin is impossible. No man could love God for His own sake.

So God says, "Let's see."

Job never knew the story behind the story. As far as he was concerned, this whole thing is about one man struggling to come to terms with a series of unexplained tragedies in his life. But something much more important is going on. The story behind the story is about vindicating the name of God.

The Bible never suggests that every experience of suffering is a direct result of the activity of Satan. Even in this story where Satan's activity was a direct factor in Job's suffering, his activity was within strict limits that were determined by God. But when suffering comes into your life, whatever its shape or cause, you have the opportunity to vindicate the name of God.

SAME PROBLEM: DIFFERENT RESPONSE

When tragedy came to this family, it produced two entirely different responses from Job and his wife. Job's wife said to him, "Are you still holding on to your integrity? Curse God and die!" (Job 2:9). That was exactly what the devil had figured she would say. Suffering did to Job's wife exactly what Job feared wine might do to his children; it lowered her inhibitions and exposed what she thought.

But Job's reaction was entirely different.

> *Job got up and tore his robe and shaved his head.* Then he fell
> to the ground in worship. (V. 20; EMPHASIS ADDED)

When Job worshiped, Satan was confounded. The worship of an ordinary man in the middle of his suffering vindicates the name of God. Job's worship must have reverberated among the angels of heaven. I like to think about Satan shrinking back in silence, dumbfounded by the power of the grace of God in the life of this ordinary man.

Your response to God in times of trouble will be one of the most revealing things about you. For Job's wife, integrity was a means to an end. As far as she was concerned, it was God's responsibility to fill her life with good things, keep the family healthy, and keep the business prospering. As long as that continued, she "loved" God. But when suffering came to this couple, their different responses were telling: Job loved God for who He is; his wife loved God for what He gave. One loved God unconditionally; the other loved God as a means to an end. One proved that the devil is sometimes right; the other gave evidence that the devil is finally wrong.

I will always remember the evening when about twenty members of our congregation met to share their stories of loss. I had become aware that a number of our people had walked through the dark valley of the death of a son or a daughter. Each of the families who came had the opportunity to tell their story. People spoke about what they had found most difficult, and also about what had helped them the most.

"I asked why and never got an answer!"

There were many tears and a strong sense of the fellowship that you discover when you recognize a reflection of your own experience in somebody else's story.

"I asked why and never got an answer!"

"I felt angry with God, and then I wondered if I should feel that way."

"The pain is still with me now."

But at the end of the evening one thing stood out to me more than any other. Here were twenty people who had experienced inexpressible pain. None of them could explain why it happened. Their suffering is a mystery to them, and the pain of it is with them still, *and yet every one of them loves God.*

How do you explain that? I know people whose suffering has been much less who say that they hate God! But here are people who have endured great suffering and yet truly love Him. Satan has no answer to that, so he falls like lightning, as the angels rejoice at the vindication of the name of God. It is possible for a man to love God freely, and to love Him not simply as a means to an end, but to love Him for who He is.

Job never knew the big story of what was at stake in his suffering. If he had a conversation with the angels after he died and went into the presence of God, they may well have said:

"Job, when we heard Satan slander the name of God we trembled, and we held our breath as we watched to see what you would do. God placed His name and His reputation on the line. And Job, when you worshiped, we can't tell you the shouts of joy and triumph that went up here as we watched the enemy shrink away in defeat and humiliation!"

In the New Testament, the apostle Peter writes to suffering believers and says that their trials "have come so that your faith…may be proved genuine and may result in praise, glory and honor when Jesus Christ is revealed" (1 Peter 1:7).

SPOTLIGHT ON CHRIST

I cannot think about this story without my mind running forward to the suffering of Christ. He was brought before a prejudiced judge and indicted on charges brought by false witnesses, but none of this made Him ask why. He was paraded through the streets; He was beaten, stripped, flogged, and crucified; but none of this made Him ask why.

But then as He hung on the cross, darkness covered the land and the comfort of God was withdrawn from His soul. He was entering into the heart of His suffering as He bore the sins of the world. Then He "cried out in a loud voice, 'Eloi, Eloi, lama sabachthani,' —which means, 'My God, my God, why have you forsaken me'?" (Matthew 27:46).

There was no answer to His question. Yet in the mystery of His unspeakable suffering, His final words were worship: "Father, into your hands I commit my spirit."

Then He breathed his last, and that splintered the gates of hell.

UNLOCKED

God does not give us an explanation of suffering, but He does tell us how we can stand in it. Our greatest need when suffering comes is not an explanation but the ability to withstand the pressure and to come through the struggle in a way that brings honor to God.

There may come a time in your life when you are facing the mystery of great suffering, and from deep inside, you will be asking, "What does God want of me?" The answer is, "God wants that you should love Him still," because when you do that, you bring glory to His name, and expose the enemy for the liar and slanderer he is.

The greatest evidence of a true work of God in a human soul is that when God allows a person to suffer, he or she loves Him still. That testimony may be more powerful than anything else that you do in the service of Christ.

PAUSE FOR PRAYER

Gracious Father,

Help those who are in great pain and distress to see Your greatness and to find strength in You. Help me to accept that there are many questions that I will never be able to answer this side of heaven, and to find peace in knowing that You know what is hidden from me.

Help me to love You for who You are and not just for what You give, so that my worship in times of trouble may bring glory to Your name. Through Jesus Christ our Lord. Amen.

2

Resurrection

JOB 19

How can I hold

on to my faith in

the darkest times?

2Resurrection

JOB 19

 ## DISCOVER
Job's secret of survival.

 ## LEARN
how to confess your faith in the darkest times.

 ## WORSHIP
as you see how you can count on the Redeemer and be certain of the resurrection.

ONE of the richest men in the world lost everything. God had given Job the joy of a large family, a thriving business, and great wealth. Then, in a single day, all the landmarks of his life were gone. His business was destroyed, his wealth plundered, and his whole family taken in a sudden tragedy.

The book of Job is the story of one man's struggle to come to terms with a catalog of suffering.

What more could happen? Plenty. Next Job's health broke down. His skin became covered in sores, and his whole body was racked with pain.

Then his wife decided to throw in the towel. Why don't you "curse God and die!" she told him (2:9).

Despite poor health and the suggestion by a bitter wife to curse God, Job remained resolute in his faith. He "tore his robes and shaved his head. Then he fell to the ground *in worship*" (1:20; italics added). It was one of the greatest moments in the whole of the Old Testament.

AFTER THE CRISIS

Those who have walked the path of deep suffering know that, after the moment of crisis, there is an ongoing process of living with a new and unwelcome situation. On the day of his tragic loss, Job had made a magnificent confession of faith, but now he had to find a way to get through another day when his mind was in turmoil and his body was in pain.

The crisis in Job's life plunged him into a desperate struggle to hold together his faith and his experience. The unanswered questions don't go away after the funeral—remember he had lost seven sons and three daughters. The mystery of suffering does not diminish with time. Faith may have triumphed yesterday, but there is still today, and then there will be tomorrow.

Job had kept the faith in his hour of crisis, but now he began to wonder how much longer he could keep this up! Sometimes he felt that it would be best if his own life ended immediately; at least then he could say, "I have fought the good fight and kept the faith." The problem was that God kept calling him to face another day, and he didn't know how much more of this he could take!

> "Oh, that I might have my request, that God would grant what I hope for, that God would be willing to crush me, to let loose his hand and cut me off! Then I would still have this consolation—my joy in unrelenting pain—that I had not denied the words of the Holy One." (6:8–10)

I've been told that there are three stages to seasickness. First you think that you are going to die, then you are sure you are going to die, then you are afraid that you might not die. That's where Job was! He was more afraid of the pain of living and denying the Holy One than he was of the prospect of dying.

Besides, there was nothing on Job's horizon that he felt he could look forward to. He might have looked forward to grandchildren, but his children were gone. He might have looked forward to some travel, but his wealth was plundered. Or he might have enjoyed some mellow years in the company of his wife, but she had given up the faith and, as we will see, walked out on him. So what was there left to look forward to?

With great candor and anguish, he cried out to God: "What strength do I have, that I should still hope? What prospects, that I should be patient? Do I have the strength of stone? Is my flesh bronze?" (6:11–12).

Job was getting to the point of saying, "I just can't go on like this." You can't read his words without sensing the great agony in this man's soul.

WHERE DO YOU TURN WHEN NOBODY UNDERSTANDS?

Job looked to his friends for help and support. We are told about three friends, Eliphaz, Zophar, and Bildad. You have to give them credit for being there, but they left a lot to be desired when it came to sensitivity! These friends were quite certain that all suffering is a punishment for sin, and that Job must have had some skeleton in the closet. They were convinced that Job was holding out on them and not telling the truth. Job told them straight; there was no hidden skeleton. But they didn't believe him.

For all their sincerity, Job's friends were of no help to him whatsoever. Eventually Job became frustrated with them and said, "How long will you torment me and crush me with words? Ten times now you have reproached me; shamelessly you attack me. If it is true that I have gone astray, my error remains my concern alone" (19:2–4). That's really a nice way of saying, "Why don't you all go away and mind your own business?"

Job didn't get much help from his wife either. We have already noticed that she was ready to throw in the towel as far as faith in God was concerned, and it appears that she gave up on Job as well. Job said "my breath is offensive to my wife" (v. 17), which seems like a good way of saying that his wife didn't want him anywhere near her, and the same seems to be true of the other members of Job's wider family. He said, "I am loathsome to my own brothers" (v. 17).

It appears that Job's wife came back to him at the end of the story, and his brothers and sisters joined him for a feast at his table, but in the middle of his suffering, he was utterly alone.

So it is difficult to imagine a more desperate situation. Here is a man who lost everything. His friends were no help to him, his wife didn't want to know him, and his own health was deteriorating to the point where he said, "I am nothing but skin and bones" (v. 20). People who went to visit Job would go away saying, "I don't think that he has long left you know."

So how are you going to get through when the wheels come off and there is no help at hand?

Job's Secret of Survival

Right in the middle of all this pain in his body and turmoil in his mind, Job made a confession of the faith on which he would stake his life. When there are a thousand things that you don't know, the most important thing you can do is affirm what you do know.

Many years ago someone said to me, "Never doubt in the darkness what God has taught you in the light." That is wise counsel. In the darkness of great suffering, hold on to what you know is true.

As I was thinking about this, a memory came back to me of a family vacation when I was about twelve years old. We were staying at a country cottage in the north of Scotland, and my brother and I were enjoying a game of soccer when I kicked the ball into a field.

My father said that he would get the ball, but the field was an extremely wet marshland, and as he walked toward the ball, it seemed as if the whole field was moving. For a few moments I was quite certain that he was going to go under and never appear again, and he might have, except for one thing. He was able to grab hold of something solid: the branch of a tree.

That is exactly how it was for Job. Everything around him was collapsing, and the only way to avoid being sucked down was to grab hold of something solid. That's what Job did when he identified and confessed the fundamental convictions on which he would stake his life. Here was Job's branch:

> "I know that my Redeemer lives." (v. 25)

That was Job's secret of survival. He knew that there was a living Redeemer, ready and able to deliver him.

We have discovered the word "redeemer" in volume 1 of *Unlocking the Bible Story*, in the book of Ruth. The kinsman-redeemer was someone who would get a relative out of a mess. The word was used most commonly in a financial crisis. If a family came on hard times, they might be forced to put their land on the market. Their best hope would be that somebody within their own family circle would have the means and the will to buy the land so that it would stay within the family. Then at least the suffering family could remain on the land and work for someone who had their best interests at heart.

He was staking his life on the Redeemer. That was all very well with land and money, but who in all the world could get Job out of the mess he was in when his whole body was breaking down and death was on the horizon. Who would get him out of that mess? The issue wasn't recovering his property; it was recovering his life!

Job's confession of faith was absolutely magnificent. He turned to his friends and said, "Now just listen to this: You have seen the tough situation that I am in, but of two things I'm sure: I have a Redeemer, and I know that my Redeemer lives."

If they had asked him who this redeemer was, he would not have been able to answer. All he knew was that God had somebody somewhere who would have the will and the means to do whatever was necessary to deliver him from this mess.

Job's physical condition was getting so bad that he was beginning to feel that he may well die before this Redeemer appeared on the scene. But that would make no difference. He was convinced that this Redeemer would come and even if he did not come until long after Job had died, he would still be able to deliver Job from ultimate loss.

Can you imagine the Son of God listening to these words? There would be at least another two thousand years of history before Jesus Christ would come into the world. But here was a man who was already looking for Him to come, and counting on it! He was staking his life on the Redeemer.

At the beginning of time, God had promised someone would come to get men and women out of the mess they are in, and Job held on to that promise of God. He believed that the pain, suffering, and loss of life in this fallen world would not be the end.

When the Redeemer came, He had to pay a price to redeem. Peter says, "It was not with perishable things such as silver or gold that you were redeemed" (1 Peter 1:18). It was not like the Old Testament days when you looked around for a wealthy uncle to buy your field to get you out of financial trouble. That was relatively easy, but the mess that we are in laid a much greater price tag on the Redeemer. Instead, Peter says, you were redeemed "with the precious blood of Christ" (1:19).

> The agony of the cross… ruptured the heart of God.

When God looked down on the suffering of His people in Egypt, God said, "I can't leave them there! I must go down and redeem them." That took overcoming Pharaoh's resistance and parting the waters of the Red Sea. But what is that to almighty God?

Then God looked at the world in its pain and suffering and death, and He said, "I can't leave them there. I must go down and redeem them." That took God giving up His Son. It took the agony of the Cross. It ruptured the heart of God. The Cross tells us that when the Redeemer came, He did something infinitely more difficult than anything else God had ever done in all the history of the world.

But the Redeemer has come, and He has paid the price. His blood was shed, and on the third day, He rose again. So even through your tears, you can say with absolute confidence, "I know that my Redeemer lives."

JOB'S CONFIDENCE

Right from the beginning of human history there were men and women who were looking for the Redeemer (Genesis 3:15; Job 19:25). After the fall, God warned the serpent that an offspring of the woman "will crush your [Satan's] head." Adam and Eve heard that promise of deliverance, and when they held their first son, they would have wondered if he was the Redeemer. But he wasn't, and Adam and Eve died before the Redeemer came. As time went on, there were more and more people who died believing that the Redeemer would come, but they did not live to see the great day.

Job was at the point where he felt that his body would give way before the Redeemer showed up. So he turned to his friends and said, "Now here is a second thing I want you to know. I am well aware that it is more than likely that I will die before the Redeemer comes. And if that happens, some of you might be tempted to think that my faith was in vain. So here is what I want to tell you. Even though worms destroy my body, I will see God. Death will not put me beyond the range of the Redeemer's power."

> *"After my skin has been destroyed, yet in my flesh I will see God."* (v. 26)

Now this is a remarkable statement of faith. Remember that Job is one of the oldest books in the whole Bible. God has chosen to reveal His truth progressively through history. Eventually, through the coming of Christ, "life and immorality [were brought] to light through the gospel" (2 Timothy 1:10). It was as if Christ came into a dark room and switched on a brilliant light.

[Job knew] that God had more in store after his funeral service was over.

But here, at least two thousand years before Christ turned on that gospel light, it is as if God had given Job a candle in a dark room. In its short flame, this man had enough light to know that God had more in store after his funeral service was over.

Job's wife didn't begin to grasp this. Her philosophy was very simple. "What you don't get now, you won't get ever!" As far as she was concerned, this life was everything, and death was a kind of black hole that led into a world of shadows where nothing was quite as it had been before. There are a lot of people today who would agree with her. As far as they are concerned, whatever lies on the other side of death cannot be half as attractive as suburban life here!

But Job knew there was more. "In my flesh I will see God." He only saw this dimly, but when Jesus Christ came into the world, the one true Light declared it: "I am the resurrection and the life. He who believes in me will live, even though he dies" (John 11:25; see also John 1:9; 3:19).

When you think about the Bible story, this is the only ending that would make sense. In the beginning, God created the man from the dust of the ground and breathed a living soul into him. The angels are spirit without bodies, and animals are physical beings without souls. But the unique glory of the human creation is that God has brought body and soul together, giving men and women a capacity for all the joys of physical and spiritual life.

Right from the beginning, Satan attacked this creation, seeking to destroy the soul by bringing temptation through the body. The purpose of God is to redeem men and women from every generation and culture. This is why the Son of God took human flesh. He assumed our flesh in order to redeem it.

If there was no resurrection of the body, the devil would have won a great victory. He would have forced God to abandon the original plan of creation, and change human beings into creatures without bodies, rather like the angels. If that was the case, the enemy could spend eternity savoring the pleasure of knowing that at least he had succeeded in overturning God's original purpose, and had successfully ruined some of the gifts that God had given to our first parents in the garden.

SPOTLIGHT ON CHRIST

That is the great significance of the resurrection of our Lord Jesus Christ. Why was it important that He should rise from the dead as opposed to returning to the Father in His Spirit and sending the Holy Spirit? In His resurrection, Christ became the prototype of a new humanity. His body was raised, adapted for everlasting life. The outcome of our faith will include the redemption of our bodies (Romans 8:23–24).

The day is coming when you will be done with sin forever. It will have no entrance to your soul or your body. Your whole being, body and soul, will be responsive to what is right, good, pure, and true. You will be filled with all the fullness of God. Temptation will be gone, confusion past, disability unknown, pain forgotten, and tear ducts superfluous.

There are two houses in the British Parliament: the House of Commons, where all the action is, and the House of Lords, where distinguished leaders of the past are able to carry on some fairly limited functions. Those in the House of Commons sometimes refer to the House of Lords as "the other place." Indeed, some very distinguished people walk the floor of the House of Lords, but it isn't really a very exciting place. I don't wish to be unkind, but as you see these folks sprawled out on the benches, it is not always easy to tell the ones who are asleep from the ones who may have become unconscious!

To some people, the House of Lords seems like a consolation prize for distinguished people who are past the rigors of a working life but may still have some useful contribution to make. When a politician gets to a certain age, people begin to talk about him "being ready for the House of Lords." And, of course, when your time comes to go there, it is the sort of thing that one should accept gracefully, but nobody really wants to go there!

If you think of heaven like that, you will never have a right view of your life in this world. We do not retire into the presence of God; we graduate there. I love the phrase that they use in the Salvation Army when a believer dies, "Promoted to glory!"

God has planned a life in heaven that will make the joys Adam and Eve knew in the garden pale into insignificance. The joys of body and soul in this life are so great that it is difficult for us to imagine this, and God tells us that what He has prepared is beyond what we can conceive and beyond what has entered our minds (1 Corinthians 2:9).

Job discovered that he was not in the land of the living on his way to the land of the dying. Rather, he was in the land of the dying on his way to the land of the living. In his ongoing pain and confusion over the tragedies of his life, he knew that he could count on the Redeemer, and that he could be certain of the resurrection.

UNLOCKED

In times of trouble, when we are surrounded by many unanswered questions, it is important to focus our attention on what we know for sure. Job gives us a wonderful model of this as he confesses his faith in the Redeemer and the Resurrection.

You can trust God to bring you through, and you can be certain that even death cannot put His people beyond His redeeming power. Never doubt in the darkness what God has taught you in the light. Faith grows as we fill our minds with the truth we know, and leave what we don't know in the hands of God. Perhaps you can follow the example of Job, and tell your friends what God has taught you. Confessing what you believe is a great way to keep the truth clear in your mind, and that will bring strength to your soul.

PAUSE FOR PRAYER

Almighty Father,

Thank You that Jesus Christ is the Redeemer, and that where there is a Redeemer, nothing can end in final defeat. Thank You for the Resurrection and for the knowledge that what we cannot understand now will one day be known.

Help me to stand strong in faith in times of trouble. Help me to find rest in the truth You have given. Thank You that Jesus Christ shines light into the deepest darkness. Help me to move forward in that light. In Jesus' name I pray. Amen.

3

Revelation

JOB 38

How can we

know God?

3Revelation

JOB 38

DISCOVER
why the Bible is different
from any other book.

LEARN
the first effects of a true
encounter with God.

WORSHIP
as you get a fresh glimpse of
the greatness and glory of the
living God.

R EVEAL and *revealed* are favorite words with journalists and headline writers. The whole purpose of a newspaper or other news media is to tell us things that we would not otherwise have known. Newspapers compete with each other for a major scoop. They want to be in the position of publishing a story that nobody else has, and when they do, they can claim that their story is a "revelation."

In the early 1970s, Bob Woodward and Carl Bernstein of the *Washington Post* kept pursuing a trail of information until they were able to bring the Watergate scandal to light. When the *Post* published their story, it was a *revelation*, a disclosing of something that would not otherwise be known.

Woodward and Bernstein were able to track down the players involved in the Watergate scandal, but who will track down God? God is invisible, and the only way we could ever be able to know Him would be if He revealed Himself. This revelation cannot be made by our investigation; it has to be given by God.

That is why the Bible story is so important. God has revealed Himself. He has disclosed what could not otherwise have been known to Abraham, Isaac, Jacob, Moses, and the Prophets—and this revelation is given to us in the Bible.

The Bible: God's Exclusive

If there is one word that people object to when it comes to religion, it is the word *exclusive*. Many people are deeply offended by the claim that "the Bible is the exclusive revelation of God," or that "God has revealed Himself exclusively in

Jesus Christ." But I have never met anybody who was offended by a newspaper telling us that their story is an exclusive.

When a paper runs an "exclusive," what they mean is that somebody has revealed information to them and to no one else.

Let's invent a newspaper, the *Cook County Chronicle*, which is trumpeting its own exclusive. The *Chronicle* has an exclusive interview with basketball superstar Michael Jordan. In the article, Jordan reveals previously unknown stories from the Chicago Bulls locker room. The *Cook County Chronicle* reports the story under the headline "My Secret Pain: Jordan Reveals Locker Room Agonies." The article begins: "In an *exclusive* interview with the *Cook County Chronicle*, Michael Jordan tells never before revealed secrets of the locker room."

Because the story is an exclusive, the only way you could know about these locker room agonies would be to get hold of a copy of the *Chronicle* and read this particular story. Other papers may copy the story, but the *Chronicle* has the "revelation." The accuracy of other versions of the story in competing newspapers will have to be measured against the paper to which the original revelation was given.

Some people might question why Michael Jordan would want to reveal things about himself to the *Cook County Chronicle*, but very few people would dispute his right to do so. If Michael Jordan wants to reveal the inner secrets of his world, then he is at absolute liberty to do so at any time and in any place that he chooses. Equally, if he chooses to draw a veil of privacy over his life, he is entitled to do that and reveal nothing at all.

Now the same is true when we come to God. God is under no pressure to reveal Himself. But if He chooses to reveal Himself to His creatures, He is at absolute liberty to do so in any way and at any time that He chooses.

God first made Himself known through the creation. The world is a theater of God's glory; it reflects the glory of God. But that revelation is limited. A wise person looking at the moon and the stars could comprehend that God exists and that His power is great, but they would not learn much more about God's character.

So God has given a fuller revelation of Himself in Scripture. The whole story of the Bible is about how God has come down to make Himself known to men and women. God wants to be known. That is why He walked with Adam and Eve in the Garden of Eden. Then God spoke to Abraham and revealed that He would bless people from every nation on earth through one man who would come into the line of Abraham's descendants.

God came down on Mount Sinai and revealed the terror of His presence and the holiness of His Law. He came down on the Day of Atonement and revealed that peace with God is found when the blood of a sacrifice is shed and God accepts the death of another in the place of the sinner. We could not have known any of this if God had not revealed it.

Then God revealed Himself through His greatest "exclusive"—*God became a man.* God had inspired, filled, or anointed many men and women throughout the Old Testament story. But there was only one occasion when God Himself actually took human flesh and became a man. The Son of God, who had always been at the right hand of the Father in heaven, came to earth. He revealed the way in which we could come to God and opened it for all who will turn to Him in repentance and faith.

That is the story of the Bible. It is not *a* revelation of God, but it is *the* revelation of God. It is God's exclusive, and there is no other revelation that we can put alongside it that has the same source or that tells us the same story.

TRUTH, SPIN, AND FANTASY

There are three different kinds of reporting in our news media. Some reports are factually accurate; some have a basis of truth but involve a significant degree of interpretation or spin; and some have very little connection with truth or reality at all. For example, when your newspaper arrives in the morning, you may look at the money section to find out what happened to your stocks or your mutual funds. Facts about the previous days' trading are revealed to you—if your eyes are good enough to read the tiny printed numbers! Either the Dow Jones went up or the Dow Jones went down, and assuming that there has not been a printing error in the paper, you accept the truth of these numbers. The information is factual.

But some newspaper reporting has a bias or spin to it. In some major cities where multiple newspapers exist, readers often choose a newspaper that reflects their own opinion. The political stance of most newspapers is well known. In Washington, D.C., for example, the *Washington Post* is admired for its willingness to take on the government, especially conservative government. Those who read its counterpoint, the *Washington Times*, do so because they know it has a conservative slant. You can tell a lot about a man by the newspaper that he reads.

Then there are supposed "revelations" that seem to have very little connection with truth whatsoever. You can't go to the grocery store without seeing tabloid newspapers at the checkout, often with the most bizarre headlines about celebrities, politicians, or aliens. You know the kind of thing: "The *Weekly Tickler* reveals astonishing new evidence that Oprah Winfrey was abducted by aliens when she was seven years old." The content of these newspapers seems to have nothing whatever to do with the truth. It is all about entertainment, and it appears that a significant number of people find such wild stories entertaining.

> Christians believe that (1) God has spoken, (2) God is true, and (3) God makes no mistakes.

When we talk about God's "revelation" in the Bible, we are talking about a revelation that is true. This is not like the fanciful imaginations of the *Weekly Tickler*. Nor is it the slanted reporting that comes from the pen of a journalist with an ax to grind or a personal point to make. In the Bible, God reveals Himself as He is and tells us the truth about ourselves and the world in which we live.

Christians believe that (1) God has spoken, (2) God is true, and (3) God makes no mistakes. These are the three pillars of what we believe about God's revelation in the Bible.

If God has spoken, and God is true, and God makes no mistakes, then what He has spoken must be true. God can be trusted. He cannot lie. He has spoken, and His word is truth.

THE MEASURE OF TRUTH

If God had not revealed Himself, then no word about Him could ever carry any authority. If God had not spoken, then all of our speculations about Him would be of equal value. None of us could actually know Him; we would all merely be guessing. And if that were the case, it would be arrogant for me to say that my guess was better than yours or anybody else's.

If God has not revealed Himself, then nothing we say about God could ever be universally true. It's all personal opinion.

But what if God has revealed Himself? What if God came down to the garden, spoke to Abraham, and became incarnate in Jesus Christ, just as the Bible says He did? If God has chosen to reveal Himself exclusively in Christ, and if that revelation is true, then it follows that this revelation must have authority for every person in every culture and every generation. It will be the rule by which all other claims to truth are measured.

When I spoke on this subject to our congregation, I asked them to hold their hands twelve inches apart. Everybody has some idea of twelve inches, but if we tried to put up a building using these guessed measurements, we would be in serious trouble. We need a rule by which to measure, so we buy rulers and tape measures. If we ask how we know that they are right, the answer is that there is a definitive measure of one foot in Greenwich in London. That is the measure; it is the rule by which anything that claims to be twelve inches can be tested.

The Bible is the measure of all claims to truth. This book stands in authority over me. I do not come to the Bible to judge it, analyze it, or evaluate its message. I am not at liberty to separate out what suits my taste and supports my lifestyle. The Bible examines me. It judges me, showing where I am wrong and need to change.

SNOWFLAKES AND CROCODILES

In Job 38, we have a marvelous example of God's revelation actually happening. Job had endured a period of great suffering in his life. He had struggled with all kinds of unanswered questions, and his friends had made matters worse by their narrow theories and their insensitive words.

But now as the end of the story neared, God revealed Himself. Almighty God spoke directly to Job. It must have been absolutely awesome.

Then the LORD answered Job out of the storm. (v. 1)

It seems that God spoke with an audible voice, and it is likely that this was a theophany, an appearance of God in visible form. Later Job would respond: "My ears had heard of you but now my eyes have seen you" (42:5).

God came down to this suffering man of faith who was in great darkness and spoke to him. What God gave to Job was not an explanation, but a revelation. The final chapters of Job will disappoint people who are looking for an explanation of suffering. George Bernard Shaw complained that instead of giving a proper explanation of Job's suffering, all God did was to brag about how He made snowflakes and crocodiles! But Job was satisfied with what God said to him. When God drew near and revealed Himself, Job felt that he could live without an explanation of his suffering.

God's revelation did not answer all Job's questions. It does not answer our questions, but it does tell us who God is. God revealed Himself as the one in whom we may put our trust, and when Job saw the glory of God, he found that he was able to live with the questions that God had not yet answered.

GOD'S UNANSWERED QUESTIONS

In Job 38–41, God asked Job nearly seventy questions, and Job was not able to answer one of them. It was as if the Lord was saying, "Job, you have wanted to enter the counsel of God. You have felt that you needed to know all things. But only God knows all things. So let's see if you are qualified to enter the counsel of God."

If Job was to enter the counsel of God, then he would need to have an interview for the position! So here we have the toughest interview for the highest position. You may have endured a demanding interview in which high-powered people asked hard questions, but you have never had an interview like this. It was the most devastating interview of all time.

> In the presence of God...[Job] could not think of a single question.

"Good morning, Job, please come in and take a seat. I understand that you want to know all things. Are you aware that in wanting to know this you aspire to the position of being God of the universe? You want to enter the counsel of God. Of course, if you are going to enter the counsel of God, you need to be qualified. It's a pretty exclusive position. So let me ask you this, Job, 'Where were you when I laid the earth's foundation?' (38:4).

"Tell me, 'Where were you 'while the morning stars sang together, and all the angels shouted for joy'?" (v. 7).

I love that touch about the angels. Have you ever thought about the joy of the angels when God created the moon and the stars and the galaxies? God called the morning stars into being, and all the angels said, "Oh yes!"

"Sorry you missed that one, Job," God was saying. "It was pretty spectacular!"

Then God continued: "Who shut up the sea behind doors?" (v. 8).

Next God asked Job about his experience with controlling the tides and the morning sun. "Have you ever tried talking to the waves and turning the tide, Job? Or what about telling the sun to rise?" (see vv. 11–12). If you wish to know all things, you need to learn how to do this.

Then God summarized:

> "Tell me, if you know all this." (v. 18)

Throughout his suffering, Job had wanted an opportunity to lay his case before

God, but when he had the opportunity, he didn't say a word. How could he? No one could answer these questions.

Job realized that he was way out of his depth. He used to think that he should be able to understand the whys of his life, but now he knew that this knowledge was way out of his league. So Job asked to be excused from the rest of the interview.

> "I am unworthy—how can I reply to you? I put my hand over
> my mouth." (40:4)

But God will not let this man go. "Brace yourself like a man; I will question you, and you shall answer me" (40:7). All through his suffering, Job has thought about what he would ask God. Perhaps you have thought that when you saw God, you would ask Him some pretty tough questions. But when Job was in the presence of God, it was altogether different from what he expected. He could not think of a single question to ask.

It is very difficult for us to grasp even the beginning of the glory of God. We talk about God and we sing about God, but often we have very little sense of His glory. Perhaps that is why the Lord continued the interview with Job for such a long time.

THE OUTCOME OF THE INTERVIEW
When the interview finally ended, Job must have been exhausted. But when God relented, Job was a changed man. He had an entirely new perspective on his life and his suffering.

> "I know that you can do all things; no plan of yours can be
> thwarted....Surely I spoke of things I did not understand,
> things too wonderful for me to know." (42:2–3)

The book of Job is dominated by the opinions of his friends Eliphaz, Bildad, and Zophar, with another man called Elihu throwing in his rather long-winded contribution. When Job's friends had finished all their counsel, Job was turned on himself in absolute misery and depression.

But at the end of the book, God took center stage. You might think that God's words to this broken man seem harsh. God's revelation seems crushing, but it has exactly the opposite effect. After his encounter with God, Job was no longer obsessed with himself, but filled with a vision of the glory of God who is sovereign over all things. The friends had focused Job's attention inward; God focused Job's attention upward. That's what the Word of God does. It takes you outside of yourself, and it brings you to God. Job said, "My ears had heard of you but now my eyes have seen you. Therefore I… repent in dust and ashes." (42:5–6)

When Job saw the glory of God, it changed the way he was thinking and the way he was feeling. His encounter with God did not end with him saying "now I understand" but "now I repent."

Job was a man of faith. At the beginning of the story, God described him as "the greatest man among all the people of the East." When tragedy struck, Job responded magnificently; he tore his robes, and he worshiped! But in the course of his suffering, and under the influence of his friends, he became increasingly consumed with himself and his unanswered questions.

Some people sin by thinking too highly of themselves, others sin by thinking too lowly of themselves, but all of us sin by thinking too much about ourselves. That's where Job was until the revelation of God broke through, and in a fresh encounter with the living God, this man of faith once again became a worshiper.

SPOTLIGHT ON CHRIST

Perhaps your experiences in life have raised unresolved questions, and gradually, like Job, you have become more and more preoccupied with yourself. You still attend church, but instead of worshiping God, you spend most of your time questioning Him. Your experiences of life have drawn you into a self-centered life with God at the outer edge.

God may not come to you in a theophany as He did for Job, but He has done something far greater in Jesus Christ. "In the past God spoke…in various ways, but [now] he has spoken to us by his Son" (Hebrews 1:1–2). When Christ came into the world, God did more than appear to man in a visible form, He actually became a man and entered into our suffering world. Christ "is the image of the invisible God," "the exact representation of his being" (Colossians 1:15; Hebrews 1:3). "No one has ever seen God," John tells us, "but God the One and Only, who is at the Father's side, has made him known" (John 1:18).

God's revelation in Christ is exclusive. There has been only one occasion when God became man. Nobody else has been or ever will be God in the flesh. This is why Jesus Christ can never be one figure in the line of religious leaders of history. He is God with us.

God's revelation in Christ is true. His words were not His own particular religious viewpoint or insight. He spoke the words that the Father gave Him (John 14:24) and insisted that God's Word is truth (John 17:17).

God has not left us guessing about who He is or what He might be like. In Christ, God has revealed Himself. He has made Himself known. Christ came to do for us what the theophany did for Job. He has come to bring us to God and to repentance. He came so that we should no longer live for ourselves but for the glory of God our creator.

UNLOCKED

If we are to know anything about God, we are utterly dependent on God making Himself known. He is beyond the range of human investigation and research. The good news is that God has made Himself known. He reveals something of His power and glory in the creation, but He has revealed Himself more fully in His Word, which points us to Jesus Christ, who is God with us.

God has spoken. He is there and He is not silent. He has revealed Himself because He wants to be known.

PAUSE FOR PRAYER

The following suggested prayer is from Psalm 139:23–24:

Search me, O God, and know my heart; test me and know my anxious thoughts. See if there is any offensive way in me, and lead me in the way everlasting.

4

Wisdom

PROVERBS 8–9

How can I put

my life together

with success?

4 Wisdom

PROVERBS 8–9

DISCOVER

what wisdom is and where we can find it.

LEARN

the subtle power of sexual temptation.

WORSHIP

Christ, who is the wisdom of God.

DURING a recent visit to northern England, our family had the opportunity of visiting Durham Cathedral. I had never been there before, and it was absolutely magnificent. The craftsmanship is exquisite. Parts of the cathedral are over one thousand years old, and the main structure took two hundred years to build. There must have been men who spent their whole lives working on one level of the building and then died knowing that even their grandchildren would not live to see it completed!

The following day, we drove south and went past some really depressing high-rise apartments that were thrown up in the 1960s. After just forty years their dilapidated exteriors signaled that they were near the end of their useful life.

The contrast was stunning! One building had been brilliantly put together and was still inspiring to look at after one thousand years. The other had been thrown together, and within a short time was a complete mess.

It takes skill to put up a quality building, but it takes greater skill to live a successful life. The word that the Bible uses to describe that skill is *wisdom*. In the Hebrew language *wisdom* can mean *knowledge, shrewdness, training, good judgment, right values,* or *skill*. When God's people were in the desert, the Lord gave them instructions about making the ark and the tabernacle. God filled a man called Bezalel with the Holy Spirit and with "skill, ability and knowledge in all kinds of crafts—to make artistic designs for work in gold, silver and bronze, to cut and set stones, to work in wood, and to engage in all kinds of craftsmanship" (Exodus 31:3–5).

When people looked at his work in wood, stone, or precious metal, they would say, "Wow, this man is a *skilled* professional," and the word that they used when they said that was the Hebrew word for wisdom. Wisdom is all about the skills we need for life, or as Stuart Briscoe notes, wisdom is about life skills.

When God speaks about wisdom, He is telling us the skills we need to put our lives together. Your life could either be something magnificent that would lead people to say, "That was put together with great skill" or else, it could be thrown together in a way that would lead people to say, "That's a mess."

You may recall that when King Solomon was given the opportunity to ask for one gift from God, he requested wisdom (1 Kings 3:5–12), and the book of Proverbs records for us some of the wisdom God gave him. It is full of practical counsel for navigating the course of life.

Proverbs tells us its purpose right at the start:

> The proverbs of Solomon son of David, king of Israel: for attaining wisdom and discipline; for understanding words of insight. (1:1–2)

Solomon began the book of Proverbs by emphasizing the supreme importance and value of wisdom. It is "more precious than rubies" (3:15). Whatever you do, he says, "get wisdom" (4:5).

There is a big difference between wisdom and knowledge. It is possible to have many academic degrees and yet have very little idea of how to put your life together. You could be a genius when it comes to technology, and yet be almost bankrupt when it comes to life skills. Our generation has seen an unprecedented explosion of knowledge, but not of wisdom.

LOOKING THROUGH THE WINDOW

Imagine Solomon in his study, pen in hand, writing down the words of these proverbs. His mind is full of this great subject of wisdom, and he has all kinds of practical wisdom or life skills that he wants to get down on paper. He has finished the opening section of the book setting out the priceless value of wisdom.

As he is writing, he looks out the window.

> At the window of my house I looked out through the lattice. I saw among the simple, I noticed among the young men, a youth who lacked judgment. (PROVERBS 7:6–7)

There on the street, right outside his window, Solomon saw a fellow who looked like a perfect example of absolute stupidity. Solomon watched for a moment, and then he tells us what he saw.

> He was going down the street near her corner, walking along
> in the direction of her house at twilight, as the day was fading,
> as the dark of night set in. (PROVERBS 7:8–9)

This fellow was just drifting through the streets. He didn't have anything particular to do, he was just drifting—in the direction of a certain woman.

Then, a woman came out to meet him (v. 10). Remember Solomon was simply recording what he saw. The woman was making a play for this man. She took hold of him and kissed him and said, "I have fellowship offerings at home" (v. 14). This lady was obviously very affectionate, and she *sounded* pretty spiritual as well!

She must have made this aimless man feel rather good about himself, because she told him that she had come out to meet him. "I looked for you and have found you!" (v. 15). That was like saying, "You are the person I have been looking for all my life. I have never felt about anybody, the way I feel about you!" The man was flattered and enchanted. He hadn't felt like this before, or at least, if he had it hadn't been for a long time.

Solomon was still watching them from his window, when suddenly it seemed as if the man made a decision and went with her. Solomon says,

> All at once he followed her like an ox going to the slaughter. (7:22)

That's a powerful description. He was driven by impulse. His actions were guided by feelings that became overwhelmingly powerful.

It did not occur to him to ask the simple question "If I do this, where will it lead?" Solomon tells us the answer to that question. "Her house is a highway to the grave, leading down to the chambers of death" (v. 27).

After seeing this, I think Solomon must have put down his pen and put his head in his hands. Here he was writing about God's wisdom for life, and he only needed to look out of his window to see that even among the people of God, some folk were heading for disaster!

The story deals with the deep issues of the soul that give rise to our choices and our behavior. This is searching stuff. Solomon reminds us that if we drift without a purpose, and allow ourselves to be driven by impulse, and disregard the consequences of our choices, then it is very likely that our lives will end up in an absolute mess.

THE ROOTS OF FOLLY

Solomon pointed to several danger signs on the road to folly that we ignore at our peril. First, folly often begins when we are drifting. King David was hanging around the palace when his troops went off to war. Instead of being with them or tending to the kingdom affairs, he wandered to a window and spied a beautiful woman bathing. He was drifting, with no particular purpose in mind. Instead of turning away, he looked some more. The result was adultery with Bathsheba and the eventual murder of her husband.

Perhaps the truth is that your life has no particular direction right now, and you are hoping that something might happen that will make your life interesting. When you're drifting, you're in danger.

The second danger sign is operating on impulse. Have you noticed how when people often try to explain a decision they have made, they say, "Well, I just felt…" There is nothing wrong with that, so long as the feeling is aligned with sound reason. But the problem with operating on impulse is that our feelings vary like the wind. They can be driven by faith, fear, anger, lust, greed, pride, or love. People who are driven by impulse are like a furrow plowed by an animal with Mad Cow Disease! It ends up all over the place; it's a mess!

Christians are often in danger of this. It is very easy for us to be driven by impulse, and to give our choices a spiritual gloss by calling it "the Lord's leading." I will never forget, when I was assisting my pastor in Scotland, hearing a lady give a glowing testimony of how the Lord had led her to become a member of the church. It was only a couple of months later that she came to see the pastor again to explain that the Lord was leading her to go somewhere else! The truth was that she was living at the level of impulse, and every time she encountered a problem, she moved on. She had deceived herself by calling all her feelings "the Lord's leading."

The third danger sign is not considering the consequences of a decision. Solomon saw the young man make a quick decision without thinking through its implications. Wisdom asks where a choice will lead. A new job opportunity opens up; it will be a great move, but how will it affect the person's spouse or children? A boy asks a girl for a date. The girl is a Christian, but the boy is not. If she dates him, where will it lead? Or suppose there is a long-term problem that you have been avoiding for some time. What will things look like in six months or ten years if you turn a blind eye and refuse to confront it?

It is impossible to live for the moment, because we are alive for more than the moment. You live today with the decisions you made yesterday, and the decisions you make today, you will live with tomorrow.

One way to learn the path of wisdom is to look at the path of folly and to head in the opposite direction. That would mean (1) stop drifting and get committed to a clear purpose; (2) stop making decisions on impulse and start making choices that are guided by the Word of God; and (3) stop living for the moment and start to live in the light of eternity.

LIFE SKILLS 101

The fear of the LORD is the beginning of wisdom. (9:10)

The very first step in putting your life together in an appropriate manner is that you let God be God in your life. He leads; you follow. This is where life skills begin.

Jesus told a story about a man who made a pile of money in his business. From a small beginning, his whole enterprise continued to expand. He had a target figure in mind that would give him financial security, and eventually he achieved it. His friends and colleagues would have regarded him as a great success. They would have made marvelous speeches about the way he had put the business together, his extraordinary capacity for hard work, and the power of his vision. But Jesus described him as a fool, because the day he thought everything he had worked for was about to begin, was the day it all came to an end. That night he died (Luke 12:20).

He had climbed his ladder, but when he got to the top, he found that it was against the wrong wall. That is the height of folly. Jesus said, "This is how it will be with anyone who stores up things for himself but is not rich toward God" (Luke 12:21).

The Gospels also tell us a story about a man whose life had been an absolute mess. A convicted thief, he now hung on a cross, dying a slow death. During his suffering, he could think of nothing better to do than to shout abuse at Jesus. On the other side was another thief. Though he had made several wrong choices in his life, he rebuked the first thief, saying, "Don't you fear God?" (Luke 23:40).

The fear of the Lord is the beginning of wisdom. The second criminal was displaying wisdom, and that led him to trust in Christ.

When you let God take His place as Lord in your life, you are at the starting point of putting your life together with skill. When you know that your life is a sacred trust from God and that you are accountable for your stewardship of it, then you will not live for the moment, or drift with the tide, or go with the flow of impulse.

LIFE SKILLS MODELED IN PRACTICE

In Proverbs 8, wisdom speaks with a voice. Literary types call this *personification*, as wisdom becomes a person.

> *Does not wisdom call out? Does not understanding raise her voice?* (v. 1)

Wisdom comes to the crossroads of life. She enters the gates of the city, where difficult judgments have to be made, and looks for an audience. This person, who is wisdom in flesh and blood, wants to appeal to people who are drifting through life, driven by impulse, and who have disregarded the consequences of their actions. She invites them to come and to listen and to follow.

Later in the chapter, wisdom makes some incredible claims:

> *"I was there when he set the heavens in place, when he marked out the horizon on the face of the deep, when he established the clouds above and fixed securely the fountains of the deep, when he gave the sea its boundary so the waters would not overstep his command, and when he marked out the foundations of the earth. Then* I *was the craftsman at his side."* (vv. 27–30, EMPHASIS ADDED)

This person says, "I was the craftsman! It was my skill that brought the creation together." God said, "Let there be lights in the sky," and through the agency of the craftsman,—through wisdom—the sun and moon were created and the stars were suspended in space. God said, "Let the waters teem with living creatures, and let birds fly across the sky," and by the agency of the craftsman—through God's wisdom—it was all brought together. Wisdom puts things together with great skill, and it is this wisdom we need to put together a successful life.

SPOTLIGHT ON CHRIST

One thousand years later, the wisdom that was only a voice to Solomon became flesh and blood. The craftsman of creation became a carpenter. The wisdom of God, the skill that put creation together, came to us in human flesh. "Through him all things were made; without him nothing was made that has been made" (John 1:3).

Think of how Jesus lived His life. There was no drifting. His purpose to do the will of the Father was absolutely clear. He was not driven by impulse, but submitted His feelings to the purpose of God. Facing the horrendous prospect of the cross, He said to the Father, "Not my will but yours be done." Rather than living for the moment, which the devil would have liked Him to do, Jesus chose a path of obedience, and that choice has brought the blessing of God to all His people.

It is uplifting to stand in England's Durham Cathedral and marvel at the skill that brought that magnificent building together. But go under the night sky and marvel with awe at the skill of the hands that brought all that together! If Christ has the skill to make the cosmos out of nothing, think what He could do with your life if it was placed wholly into His hands! And that is what Christ, the skilled craftsman of God, invites you to do.

That will mean that you let Him teach you the way of wisdom. The New Testament speaks about Christ as the "wisdom from God" (1 Corinthians 1:30). "All the treasures of wisdom and knowledge" are hidden in Him (Colossians 2:3).

Christ told a story about two men who were trying to put their lives together. Jesus compared it to building a house. He told listeners that to put their lives on a solid foundation, they must hear "these words of mine and [put] them into practice" (Matthew 7:24).

THE SPIRIT OF WISDOM

It is all very well to talk about putting the teaching of Jesus into practice, but that is easier said than done. The Christian life is much more than a valiant effort to put life together on principles taught by Jesus. The Holy Spirit is described as "the Spirit of wisdom" (Isaiah 11:2; Ephesians 1:17). When you come to Christ, He will give you the power of the Holy Spirit to move you in the direction of wisdom.

There was a young pastor in the New Testament called Timothy. He had been given significant responsibility for an important church early in life, and he was beginning to feel overwhelmed. He tended to listen too much to his feelings and his moods, and that made him nervous and cautious. So Paul wrote to encourage him. "God did not give us a spirit of timidity, but a spirit of power" (2 Timothy 1:7). "Timothy, you don't need to be driven by impulse," Paul was saying. "The Spirit of God lives within you!"

That's how you can rise above living at the level of impulse! That's how the man Solomon saw in the street could have lived above the temptation he experienced—by the power of the Spirit of God. You can come to God every day and ask Him to fill you with His Spirit, so that your choices will not be made at the level of prevailing feelings, but according to the wisdom of God as you find it in Jesus.

WISDOM LOOKS FOR COMPANY

Solomon gives us a wonderful picture of wisdom sending out an invitation. Wisdom has built a house and is inviting people to come in and share a meal (9:1–2). The extraordinary thing is the guest list.

When the wisest person in the world prepares a meal, who would you expect her to invite for company? Surely it would be those who have made something of their lives, whose choices have been sound and who have the ability to talk about profound things. But wisdom invites "those who lack judgment." She says,

> *"Let all who are simple come in here!"* (v. 4)

That's precisely the way Solomon described the naive man he saw from his window (7:7). He too could have received wisdom.

Christ invites all who know they have made stupid mistakes and foolish choices. He says, "I want you to come in My company at the feast. I want you to sit and eat and drink with Me." The only qualification for the guests at wisdom's feast is their need for wisdom! Christ invites us to come to Him with all our mistakes and all our regrets. Through His Word He will teach you what to do, and by His Spirit He will give you the power to do it.

UNLOCKED

Fearing God is the first step toward a life that is successfully put together. Without that foundation, our success is at the level of a man building a house with cards. He may be thrilled with his achievement, but in its very nature it is short lived. We are God's creatures, and we are made for His glory. A godless life is an exercise in futility.

When we fear God, we will see our need of Christ and respond to His invitation to come to Him. Christ is the wisdom of God, and by His Spirit, he will lead His people to put their lives together with skill.

A life that is put together well will be marked by a clear sense of purpose that centers round bringing glory to God. It will be marked by decisions made in the light of God's Word rather than on impulse, and choices considered not only in the light of their immediate impact but also in the light of their long-term consequences. The result of this wisdom, over years, will be a life which, like Durham Cathedral, has the mark of greatness about it. Such a life will cause those who see it to give praise and thanks to God.

PAUSE FOR PRAYER

For our prayer for wisdom, here are words adapted from the hymn "Teach Me Your Way," by B. Mansell Ramsey (1849–1923).

> Teach me your way O Lord, teach me your way,
> Your gracious aid afford, teach me your way,
> Help me to walk aright
> More by faith less by sight
> Lead me in heaven's light
> Teach me your way.

I pray this in the name of Jesus, my Savior. Amen.

5

Holiness

ISAIAH 6

What is

God like?

5 Holiness

ISAIAH 6

1000 B.C.

971–931   SOLOMON

931   KINGDOM DIVIDES

900

800

792–740   UZZIAH

750–731   JOTHAM
740   ISAIAH'S VISION
735–715   AHAZ
729–686   HEZEKIAH

ISAIAH

700

696–647   MANASSEH
(COREGENT)

606–536   BABYLONIAN
CAPTIVITY
600

586   FALL OF JERUSALEM

500

DISCOVER
what happens when God's presence comes near.

LEARN
why your greatest strength may be a point of weakness.

WORSHIP
as you take in a fresh glimpse of the awesome glory of God.

SEPTEMBER 11, 2001, is a date marked forever in American history. With thousands of civilian lives lost, it has eclipsed December 7, 1941, that "day of infamy" when Japanese fighter pilots attacked Pearl Harbor, launching America into World War II. On September 11, a deadly terrorist attack struck America.

On a cloudless morning in New York City, two hijacked aircraft plowed into the twin towers of the World Trade Center. A third aircraft rammed into the Pentagon in Washington, D.C. A fourth, believed to be heading for the U.S. Capitol or the White House, crashed into a remote area of western Pennsylvania as passengers wrestled the terrorists for the controls.

Within hours of the tragedy, the media asked Christian leaders for comment. What was God doing? Was this a judgment on America? Was it the beginning of the end of the world? Where was God in all this suffering?

Across the country, pastors, myself included, were abandoning carefully planned sermons for the following Sunday and searching the Scriptures as we tried to discern how best to apply the Word of God to the most extraordinary event (to date) in the new millennium. It was an awesome responsibility.

And that got me thinking: What would it be like if God spoke to me directly so that I would know exactly what God Himself was saying to the nation, and be given the precise words that I should use to communicate that message?

That was the experience of the prophets. As we saw in volume 1 of *Unlocking the Bible Story* (chapter 18), the prophets stood in the counsel of God and received the Word of God by a direct revelation so that they could communicate exactly what God was saying to His people in the precise words that God had given. They were able to say, "This is what the Lord says."

Pastors today seek the guidance of the Holy Spirit in applying the words that God has already given to the great issues of our time. We seek to discern the appropriate application of God's truth. But the prophets received direct revelation from God. He told them clearly and unmistakably what He was doing in the great events of world history. So the prophets make compelling reading. They give us the meaning of the great events of the Bible story up to the coming of Christ, and help us to understand how God works in the world today.

The prophets spoke the Word of God throughout the events that are recorded in the historical books that we studied in volume 1. There we discovered what happened to God's people. Now, through the prophets, we will discover what God was doing through all these events. It is a fascinating story.

The first of the writing prophets were probably Joel and Obadiah, somewhere around 850 years before Christ. The last was Malachi in the time of Nehemiah when the temple was rebuilt, about 430 B.C. So for more than four hundred years God spoke through these prophets.

GROWING CASUAL TOWARD GOD

Isaiah's ministry was in the southern kingdom and spanned the reigns of four kings: Uzziah, Jotham, Ahaz, and Hezekiah (Isaiah 1:1). So his ministry stretched over sixty years. But it was a vision from God given in the year King Uzziah died, that would shape Isaiah's whole life and ministry.

King Uzziah ruled in Jerusalem for fifty-two years. That was longer than David or Solomon or any other previous ruler in the southern kingdom. During these years, the nation enjoyed a remarkable period of prosperity. We might have called it the longest running bull market in history. There was a huge increase in construction, a remarkable growth in farming, and a significant strengthening of their defenses. All of this had generated a feeling of confidence among the people, and as that confidence grew, they became increasingly casual toward God.

The opening chapters of Isaiah make it quite clear that there were plenty of people coming to the temple. They offered the sacrifices and observed the feasts and festivals. Yet God refers to their actions as "this trampling of my courts" (1:11–12). They did all the religious things, but the time in the temple seemed to have little impact in their lives; God rebuked them for "bringing meaningless offerings" (v. 13). The temple that was once filled with God's glory was now something of a national treasure, a symbol of traditional values. Indeed, for all their profession of faith in God, there seems to have been little difference between these people and the pagan nations around them.

Their situation speaks powerfully to the church today. America is also a prospering nation where many people acknowledge God but behave in a way that is hardly different from the surrounding culture.

One evangelical church in the Midwest was honest enough to do a survey of patterns of behavior among their congregation. The survey showed that in a period six months prior to the survey, 33 percent said they had lied and 18 percent said they had stolen. Meanwhile, a survey at one of the Promise Keepers men's conferences, attended largely by men committed to the Christian faith, revealed that 50 percent of the men who attended the event had viewed pornography within the past week.[1] These figures may not be representative, but they remind us that our greatest danger is to be worshipers of God, whose lives are scarcely distinguishable from the world around us.

> Many people have lost sight of the awesome holiness of God.

Like Israel in the time of Isaiah, we have people who participate in services of worship and yet lie to their parents, claim false expenses from their employer, abort their babies, cheat on their wives, and throw themselves into materialism that is indistinguishable from the world.

The important thing to grasp is that this is not new. It always happens when people lose their vision of God.

A. W. Tozer put it this way in his great book *The Knowledge of the Holy.*

> What comes into our minds when we think about God is the most important thing about us....The gravest question before the church is always God Himself, and the most portentous fact about any man is not what he at any given time may say or do, but what he in his deep heart conceives God to be like....Were we able to extract from any man a complete answer to the question, "What comes to your mind when you think about God?" we might predict with certainty the spiritual future of that man.

Were we able to know exactly what our most influential religious leaders think of God today, we might be able with some precision to foretell where the church will stand tomorrow…Always the most revealing thing about the church is her idea of God.[2]

What you think about God is the clearest indicator of where your spiritual future will be. If a man thinks of God only as loving and forgiving, we should not expect him to be too diligent in the pursuit of a moral life. If a woman thinks of God primarily as one who affirms everybody, then it should not surprise us if she feels affirmed even while she is still in her sins. The great issue in Isaiah's time, and ours, is that many people have lost sight of the awesome holiness of God.

"I SAW THE LORD"

When God's people had lost sight of His glory, God chose to reveal Himself to one man, and commissioned him to go and tell the people who God is. Isaiah was given that incredible privilege and awesome responsibility.

> *In the year that King Uzziah died, I saw the Lord.* (6:1)

It seems that this glimpse of God was in the form of a vision, rather like the vision of Christ given to John in the New Testament. Isaiah had already been preaching for some years, but now on this particular occasion, God came to him in a way that would shape a lifetime of ministry.

When Isaiah says that he "saw the Lord," one wonders what he actually saw. What does God look like? Isaiah writes:

> *[He was] high and exalted, and the train of his robe filled the temple.* (v. 1)

We wait for more, but that is all that Isaiah can say.

You find the same kind of description whenever there is a revelation of God in the Bible. God's brilliance is overwhelming. When Moses and Aaron saw the God of Israel, Moses said, "Under his feet was something like a pavement made of sapphire, clear as the sky itself" (Exodus 24:10). Moses could not look directly at the brightness of His glory; he could only describe the brightness of what lay beneath God's feet.

It is the same in the book of Revelation when John sees the glory of the risen Christ. He says, "His face was like the sun shining in all its brilliance" (1:16). You can't look directly at the sun shining in all its brilliance, of course. The apostle is telling us he could not look into the face of the risen Christ because of the brightness of His glory.

It is exactly the same here. Isaiah was saying, "The invisible God revealed Himself to me, but I could not look at His face. All I can tell you is that He was high and lifted up, and the train of His robe filled the temple." The temple was a vast building that had taken years to construct. It was the pride of the nation, but the whole place could scarcely contain the end of God's robe!

Then Isaiah heard angelic creatures called seraphs calling out to one another.

> "Holy, holy, holy is the LORD Almighty." (v. 3)

If we want to give emphasis to a statement, we can <u>underline</u> it, put it in *italics*, or use a **bold** typeface. In the Hebrew language, if someone wanted to give something special emphasis he would say it twice. When Jesus wanted to emphasize a point, He said, "Truly, truly, I say to you" (John 3:3, 5 NASB). That was a customary way of saying, "This is something of special significance, so listen carefully!"

There is only one truth in the whole of the Bible that is <u>triple underlined</u>, and that is the holiness of God. "Holy, holy, holy." There is never a time when the Bible says that God is wrath, wrath, wrath, or love, love, love, or power, power, power. So we must conclude that the holiness of God is so foundational to who God is, that if we do not grasp His holiness, we do not know Him as He is.

If we ask "What is holiness?" it is rather like asking "What is fire?" The best way to understand fire is by observing its effect. If you watch the effect that fire has on what it touches, you will have some understanding of the awesome thing that it is. The best way to understand the holiness of God is by observing its effect on what it touches.

THE ANGELS WHO COULDN'T BEAR TO LOOK

When the presence of God came down, He was surrounded by seraphim, who were calling to each other, announcing the presence of God. You would think that angels, who inhabit heaven, would be comfortable in the immediate presence of God, but Isaiah saw that they were covering their faces.

Why would they do that? These angels hadn't sinned as we have. They have nothing to be ashamed of. Their whole lives are spent in obedience to God. The angels cover their faces because they are creatures, overawed in the presence of their Creator. If you were to live the most perfect life in history, and then entered

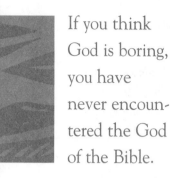

If you think God is boring, you have never encountered the God of the Bible. the presence of God, you would still shrink back in awe and wonder as a creature before the glory of your Creator. That's how it was for the angels when the invisible God came down.

Many people today have the idea that God is nothing more than a spiritual side of their own being, and that being at peace with God amounts to little more than being at peace with yourself. But the God of the Bible is "wholly other." Even to the angels, He is something else.

CAUGHT IN AN EARTHQUAKE

When God came down,

> *the doorposts and thresholds shook and the temple was filled with smoke.* (v. 4)

This must have been absolutely terrifying to Isaiah. The earth shook when God's presence came near. As the English Christmas carol "In the Bleak Midwinter" affirms: "Our God heaven cannot hold him, nor earth sustain; heaven and earth shall flee away when he comes to reign."

David Wells has coined a phrase to describe the challenge of our times when he talks about the "weightlessness of God."

> It is one of the defining marks of Our Time that God is now weightless...He rests upon the world so inconsequentially as not to be noticeable.

Wells describes the God many people believe in today as "less interesting than television, His commands less authoritative than their appetites for affluence and influence, His judgments no more awe-inspiring than the evening news, and His truth less compelling than the advertisers sweet fog or flattery and lies."[3]

That is why the people who worshiped in the temple were not very different from those who did not. Their experience of worship sent them home feeling good but it brought no lasting moral change in their lives. At one time, the cloud of God's presence had filled the temple, but in Isaiah's day, there were thousands of people crowding into the temple, enjoying their favorite music, hearing a few uplifting thoughts, but never experiencing the awesome presence of God. It would never have occurred to them that if God came among them the very foundations of the building would shake.

Ultimately this kind of worship becomes boring. A God who is there simply to satisfy our felt needs is not a God who is worthy of the devotion of our lives. He is not the God of Abraham, Isaac, and Jacob, or the God and Father of our Lord Jesus Christ. If you think God is boring, you have never encountered the God of the Bible.

There is a great irony about the worshipers of Isaiah's day. They were the people of God, but they did not know God. They had no experience of the God they claimed to be worshiping. So God came down and revealed Himself to one man so that this man could bring the truth of God to his generation.

COMING APART AT THE SEAMS

The most significant effect of God's holiness was not on the angels or on the foundations of the temple, but on Isaiah the prophet himself. When Isaiah saw the Lord, he said,

> "Woe to me!...I am ruined!" (6:5)

The word *ruined* literally means coming apart at the seams. If someone is very competent or successful, we sometimes say, "He or she has got it all together." Isaiah says the opposite. When he saw God, it all fell apart.

Isaiah was one of the most respected people of his day. He had already been engaged for some time in a prophetic ministry of speaking the Word of God. Throughout chapter 5, he had been saying "woe" to all kinds of people but now in the presence of God, he can only say "woe" to himself! The holiness of God makes even the best people feel their own sinfulness.

Isaiah felt that sin had infected the area of his greatest gift. "I am a man of unclean lips" (v. 5). As a preacher and a prophet, Isaiah's lips were the tools of his ministry. This was the area of his spiritual gift. But in the presence of God, he felt that even his greatest gift had to be cleansed, lest it be subverted for another purpose. Sometimes our greatest strength will become the point at which we are most vulnerable to the sin of pride.

Then Isaiah said, "I live among a people of unclean lips." Things that he would have become used to, now seeed dirty to him and he had a new sensitivity to how far the whole community is from the purity of God.

Tozer wrote, "Unless the weight of [this] burden is felt, the gospel can mean nothing to a man, and until he sees a vision of God high and lifted up, there will be no woe, no burden."[4] A God who loves and forgives will be compelling only to those who have stood in His presence and have felt their need to be forgiven. We will never discover our need until we have seen the holiness of God.

A HOT COAL

The knowledge of the Holy One will bring a man to feel that he has come apart at the seams, and that his whole life has been unraveled, but God will never leave a man there. Isaiah would have been ruined in the presence of God except for one thing.

Isaiah had seen the glory of God, and the seraphim had announced the immanent presence of the holiness of God. Then smoke filled the temple. So after a momentary glimpse of the glory of God, Isaiah was surrounded by darkness. He was conscious of the presence of God, but God was hidden from his view. Then the foundations of the temple began to shake. It must have been absolutely terrifying!

Then as Isaiah peered into the smoke, it seemed as if one of the angels was coming toward him from the direction of the altar where the fire that consumed the sacrifices was always burning.

> One of the seraphs flew to me with a live coal in his hand,
> which he had taken with tongs from the altar. With it he
> touched my mouth and said, "See, this has touched your lips;
> your guilt is taken away and your sin atoned for." (vv. 6–7)

The angel had picked up a burning coal from the altar and flew toward Isaiah. He pressed the hot coal onto Isaiah's lips. It seared the prophet's flesh.

The altar was the place where the sacrifice of atonement was made. Now the effect of that atonement was being applied to Isaiah's particular need. Isaiah had made his confession, "I am a man of unclean lips" and now the angel of God said, "See, this has touched your lips; your guilt is taken away" (v. 7). That which is touched by holy fire will never be the same again.

Having seen God's holiness, Isaiah was conscious of his own sins as never before. God's grace had touched his own life at the point of his deepest need, and that was the foundation of a life of ministry. Having discovered the grace of God in this deep and personal way, Isaiah wanted to serve.

> I heard the voice of the Lord saying, "Whom shall I send? And
> who will go for us?"
>
> And I said, "Here am I. Send me!" (v. 8)

And God sent Isaiah. It was as if God said, "You go, Isaiah, because you've understood who God is, and you know what sin is, and you have grasped what grace is."

Filled with a new wonder at God's grace in his own life, and sensing the privilege of serving this God, Isaiah went out into a culture that had lost touch with the reality of who God is, to make the living God known.

SPOTLIGHT ON CHRIST

Isaiah's encounter with the holy God points us toward the coming of Jesus Christ. The Old Testament tells us that Isaiah saw the glory of God. But the New Testament adds that Isaiah saw the glory of Christ. "Isaiah said this because he saw Jesus' glory and spoke about him" (John 12:41). Significantly, we are told later by John that the glory of the Father and the glory of the Son are the same glory (John 17:5).

Throughout the Bible story, the Father is made known by the Son. The theophanies were appearances of the second person of the Trinity, who is the image of the invisible God. He came down to give His people glimpses of the knowledge of God in preparation for the time when He would take human flesh and, by coming among us, make the Father known.

The holiness of God that was revealed to Isaiah points us toward another day when the holiness of God would be revealed. The day came when the Holy One Himself, whose glory Isaiah had seen, was placed on the altar of the cross and became the sacrifice for our sins.

The holiness of God the Son was revealed when He bore the sins of the world. Just as Isaiah sat there in complete darkness as smoke filled the temple, so when Christ was on the cross, darkness covered the whole earth. And just as the foundations of the temple shook when the presence of God came down, so when Christ died on the cross, the earth shook and the rocks split (Matthew 27:45, 51). When the Son of God bore the sins of the world and the Father poured out His judgment on the Son, the earth itself trembled.

In His death, Christ made a sacrifice so that people who are unraveled by the holiness of God may be touched and healed by the grace of God. Just as the angel brought a live coal from the altar in the temple, God is ready to touch our lives with the effects of the death of Jesus. From the altar of Calvary, God comes to us in grace and says, "Your guilt is taken away and your sin is atoned for."

UNLOCKED

God is holy, holy, holy. His holiness is so foundational to His character that if we do not grasp it, we do not know the God of the Bible. Without the holiness of God, the gospel message would not make sense. Sin is terrible because it is an offense against a holy God. An atonement is needed because without it sinners would be ruined in the presence of God's holiness. Grace is amazing because it is God's love flowing to us out of His judgment. The good news of the gospel is that Jesus, God's Son, satisfied the judgment of a holy God, becoming a sacrifice that atoned for all our sins.

A proper vision of the holiness of God is essential. Without it, our worship descends to entertainment, our sins become mistakes, and our lives will drift on with little evidence of significant growth.

As we begin the twenty-first century, the church desperately needs to rediscover the awesome holiness of the God whose immediate presence made buildings shake and caused the greatest man of his time to feel his sins. Then, like Isaiah, we will begin to appreciate the wonder of what God has done for us in Jesus Christ, and we will feel that our greatest privilege in life is to serve this awesome, glorious, holy God.

PAUSE FOR PRAYER

Think about what it must have been like for Isaiah when the seraph brought the coal from the altar. The area of his life in which he felt most in need of God's cleansing was touched by the symbolic coals taken from the place where the sacrifice was offered.

Think about the area of your life that most needs to be cleansed. The Spirit of God brings the grace that flows from Jesus' sacrifice right over to where you are, and touches you so that your sin is atoned for and your guilt taken away.

Gracious Lord,

In the light of Your holiness I feel deeply aware of my own sin. I know that apart from Your grace I would be ruined. So thank You for the grace that comes from Jesus Christ to all who believe.

Touch my sin with Your cleansing power, and let what is touched be changed forever. Then let me live as Your servant, and for Your glory.

Through Jesus Christ my Lord I come. Amen.

NOTES

1. As cited in Laurie Hall, *An Affair of the Mind* (Colorado Springs: Focus on the Family, 1996), 236.

2. A.W. Tozer, *Knowledge of the Holy* (New York: Harper and Row, 1961), 9.

3. David Wells, *God in the Wasteland* (Grand Rapids: Eerdmans, 1994), 88.

4. Tozer, *Knowledge of the Holy*, 11.

6

Comfort

ISAIAH 40

How can

I live with

problems that

won't go away?

*6*Comfort

ISAIAH 40

DISCOVER

the comfort of the sovereignty
of God.

LEARN

how God strengthens the
brokenhearted.

WORSHIP

as you see how no disaster can
thwart God's purpose for your life.

IMAGINE the chief executive officer of a Fortune 500 company who cannot read a financial sheet, motivate his employees, or attract new business. As a CEO, he has little charisma and only slight knowledge of the company history. He knows the company has some kind of mission statement, but he can't remember it and doesn't know if it's really important.

But he has lots of money and his grandfather was the founder of the company.

It's not difficult to predict the future of the company. Unfortunately, that's pretty much how it was with several of the kings in the southern kingdom. They ruled from Jerusalem, home to King David and later his son Solomon. But over time, they knew less and less about those two kings and their vision for God's kingdom. Some were indifferent, if not downright hostile, to God.

Consider King Ahaz. No doubt Ahaz professed faith in God, but when you looked at the things he promoted, it was difficult to believe that he knew anything about God at all.

The king did nothing to uphold the ancient commandment of God that human life is sacred. In fact, he actually promoted an abominable practice in which children were sacrificed in a fire (2 Kings 16:3). This taking of the lives of infants was so offensive to God that it made His judgment on the nation inevitable.

Ahaz was also responsible for a sinister attempt to reshape religion to fit the prevailing trends of the day. The power of Assyria was growing, so Ahaz made a visit there. He admired their religion and took measurements of their altar so that he could construct a replica back in the temple in Jerusalem.

It was an extraordinary attempt to absorb God's people into the surrounding culture, and it must have deeply offended all who loved the Lord and wanted to live by His Word.

The Bible records a sad epitaph about this king. Ahaz "reigned in Jerusalem sixteen years.…He did not do what was right in the eyes of the LORD" (2 Kings 16:2). When his time came to an end, I have no doubt that there was a great sense of relief among God's people. They had endured sixteen years of political leadership that had taken them in the wrong direction. They longed to see the name of God honored in their nation, and as the time for change drew near, there was a growing sense of anticipation.

When the day came for the coronation of the new king, there must have been great expectations in the hearts of many good people. The new king's name was Hezekiah, and he met those high expectations. The first we learn of him in 2 Kings is that "he did what was right in the eyes of the LORD, just as his father David had done.…Hezekiah trusted in the LORD, the God of Israel. There was no one like him among all the kings of Judah, either before him or after him" (18:3, 5).

So at last godly leadership had returned to Judah. But as we follow the story, we find that the best leader was faced with some of the worst problems. It is right to pray for godly leaders in the nation, but leaders do not control the future, and even the best leaders can only respond to circumstances as they arise. The future is shaped by the hand of God.

A GODLY KING AND AN OVERPOWERING ENEMY

When Hezekiah came to the throne in Jerusalem, he was faced with the power of an overwhelming enemy. Assyria had become a world superpower, and under the leadership of Sennacherib was poised to expand her borders.

King Sennacherib had invaded the northern area of Israel, and the people of the ten tribes were scattered. So by the time of Hezekiah, the growing empire of Assyria extended right up to the borders of this tiny southern area of Judah. It could hardly have come as a surprise to Hezekiah that a few months after the fall of the northern kingdom of Israel, Sennacherib was back, camped a few miles outside Jerusalem (18:13).

Hezekiah tried to negotiate, and in the end, he managed to buy Sennacherib off by giving him the silver and gold from the temple (vv. 14–16). The king had to order the gold plating to be taken from the doors and the doorposts of the temple. It must have been terrible to watch.

But payments for peace are rarely successful, and it was not long before Sennacherib was back at the gates of Jerusalem again, intimidating Hezekiah's tiny army with propaganda that pressed home the impossibility of their situation.

Then God intervened. It seems that some kind of plague hit the army, and they withdrew. (You can read about it in 2 Kings 19:35–36.) Eventually two of Sennacherib's sons slew him (v. 37). Almighty God had delivered.

A FATAL MISTAKE

Some years later God spared Hezekiah's life when the king became terminally ill. Hezekiah cried out to God in prayer, and again God intervened, restoring the king to health (20:1–6).

When the king of Babylon heard about Hezekiah's illness, he sent messengers with letters and gifts. By the time they arrived, Hezekiah had recovered from his illness, and the economy seems to have recovered from the plundering it took at the hands of Sennacherib. According to Isaiah, "Hezekiah received the messengers and showed them all that was in his storehouses—the silver, the gold, the spices and the fine oil—his armory and everything found among his treasures. There was nothing in his palace or in all his kingdom that Hezekiah did not show them" (20:13).

That was a fatal mistake. It was like lighting a slow burning fuse. Isaiah told the king what would happen. The power of Assyria that had been such a problem would decline, and the power of Babylon that nobody took very seriously would rise. Hezekiah had just shown all his treasures to his future enemy.

Isaiah prophesied the outcome: "The time will surely come when everything in your palace, and all that your fathers have stored up until this day, will be carried off to Babylon. Nothing will be left, says the LORD" (20:17; Isaiah 39:6).

That is exactly what happened. Within three generations, Babylon became a superpower, and under the leadership of Nebuchadnezzar, the Babylonian army marched on Jerusalem, killing many, reducing the city to a heap of rubble, and deporting the most able people.

By the end of Hezekiah's reign, Isaiah was an old man. The prophet had kept preaching through nineteen years of the reign of Jotham and the twenty dreadful years of Ahaz, and now Hezekiah was well into his reign that lasted forty-three years.

Things had changed since the days of King Uzziah, when the prophet began his ministry. Then confidence was sky high, and the people of God thought that all things were possible. That confidence had led many of the people to be increasingly casual toward God. Now the old confidence had gone, and God's people had to live with the prospect of increasingly difficult days ahead.

WHAT TO DO WHEN YOU CAN'T FIX IT

Isaiah 40 is God's Word to people who have just received devastating news. God's people in Judah had all kinds of hopes and dreams for the future, but Isaiah's prophecy of Babylon's rise (39:5–7) made it clear that the future would bring hardship and suffering.

Suffering can strike any of us, including those close to God. (Remember Job in chapter 1?) That was the experience of two friends of mine, Barbara and Brian Edwards. Barbara suffered from severe rheumatoid arthritis. She began to experience severe pain early in their marriage, and eventually was confined to a wheelchair. As her vertebrae began to crush her spinal cord, she faced surgery that involved fusing two pairs of vertebrae to relieve pressure and then bolting her head and neck together with a pair of titanium rods. Barbara faced this with extraordinary courage. She is now free from pain in the presence of the Lord.

> We thrive on solutions…But what about the things we cannot fix?

In Brian's book, *Horizons of Hope*,[1] he described the roller-coaster of their battle with disability throughout their thirty-five years of marriage, as well as the stories of mutual friends who love the Lord and face a long-term journey through suffering. Andrew and Helen Bryant's fourth child, Charlotte, was born with a rare skin disorder that required them to cover their daughter's body with grease every two hours, day and night. Pastor Claude Trigger had his entire voice box removed, and now he has to communicate through an electronic device attached to his throat.

Brian, Andrew, and Claude were all colleagues of mine in the pastoral ministry in England. Challenges like these do not get easier, and they do not diminish with time.

These are often the hardest situations for us to face. We thrive on solutions. "Tell us the problem and we will fix it!" But what about the things we cannot fix: the serious illness, the crippling disability, or the irreplaceable loss?

People may pray for a miracle, but what if God has called you to live with a burden that will not be lifted? There's a hollow sound when people say "I hope things will be better soon," because deep in your heart you feel that it may well get worse.

What does God have to say to those who have to live with an ongoing burden that can reduce life to a daily struggle to survive? How do we find strength when the future does not hold hope for something better, but dread of something worse? That's the issue Isaiah addresses. This is the Word of God to people who face difficult circumstances in which there is no reasonable prospect of change.

GOD IS IN CONTROL

> *Comfort, comfort my people, says your God. Speak tenderly to Jerusalem.* (40:1–2)

When God told Isaiah to go and comfort His people, Isaiah's response was predictable: "What shall I [say]?" (v. 6). God's first answer is that Isaiah is to tell the people that God is in control.

Isaiah 40 is one of the greatest passages in the Bible on the sovereignty of God. It reminds us that God reigns over all the events of history. Under the inspiration of the Holy Spirit, Isaiah mobilizes the power of language to communicate this truth to these discouraged people.

> *He sits enthroned above the circle of the earth, and its people are like grasshoppers....He brings princes to naught and reduces the rulers of this world to nothing. No sooner are they planted, no sooner are they sown, no sooner do they take root in the ground, than he blows on them and they wither.* (vv. 22–24)

God is as much in control through our disasters as He is in our triumphs. God was in control when Sennacherib's armies came to the gate of Jerusalem and when they suddenly withdrew in retreat. God was in control when Assyria's power weakened and when Babylon's power rose. God was as much in control when Jerusalem was destroyed and the exiles were taken off to Babylon as He was when Nehemiah led the exiles back and Jerusalem was rebuilt.

On the darkest day in human history, when God's own Son was taken and nailed to a cross, God was in control. And on the greatest day in human history, when Christ rose from the dead, God was in control.

God is in control through the darkest day of your life. The sovereignty of God does not make God the author of evil, but it does mean that no evil, however great, can finally overturn the purpose of God. Your faith can feed on the sovereignty of God.

THE MYSTERIOUS WAYS OF A SOVEREIGN GOD

Around the turn of the century, there was a pastor in London, by the name of J. Stuart Holden. He had purchased two tickets for the maiden voyage of a new ship that many people were talking about at the time. About a week before the ship was due to sail, Holden's wife took ill, and to their great disappointment, they were unable to make the trip. So here they were with two unused tickets for the maiden voyage of the *Titanic*.

Of course, later they saw the hand of God in this. Holden had the tickets framed, and underneath, he had the words inscribed "a testimony to the love of God." Some months later, a visitor was in their home, and his attention was drawn to the tickets and the inscription. "Mr. Holden," he said, "that is a very moving picture, but I think you have the wrong inscription."

The visitor went on to explain. "I have a friend who did sail on the *Titanic*. He was an evangelist from Glasgow by the name of Harper, and he had been booked to speak at some meetings in the States." Harper led several people to Christ in the water before he died.

"Now," said the visitor, "tell me, Mr. Holden, when you say 'a testimony to the love of God,' did God love you more than he loved Mr. Harper?"

Holden had no answer, except to ask, "What should I have written?"

"You should have written 'a testimony to the sovereignty of God.' God called you to glorify Him in your life. God called Harper to glorify Him in his death."[2]

Here were two wonderful servants of God, Harper and Holden. The love of God towards them both was exactly the same, but in the mystery of His sovereign will, one was taken, and the other left.

Isaiah reminds us that none of us will be able to understand the sovereignty of God. "Who has understood the mind of the LORD, or instructed him as his counselor?" (v. 13). I do not understand the mind of God, but I know of no greater comfort than to hold on to this great truth: God makes no mistakes.

GOD WILL FULFILL HIS PURPOSES

When things go terribly wrong, we sometimes feel that God's plans for us must have been overturned. Most of us have certain ideas of what we would like to do for God. We have certain hopes and dreams. Then something unexpected happens, and we are faced with an entirely new situation. The people of Isaiah's day must have wondered what hope there could possibly be for the future if Jerusalem was destroyed.

Remember that the whole story of the Bible is about how God would bring salvation through someone from the line of Abraham. God had raised up a great nation of twelve tribes all descended from Abraham, but now ten of these tribes had been scattered. It was as if a strong rope of twelve strands had been frayed, so that only two strands were left to hold a great weight. Just two vulnerable tribes of the once great nation of Israel remained free, and now God said that they were going to be overrun and scattered!

So what hope could there possibly be for the promises and purposes of God? There are times when God's work seems so vulnerable, and then perhaps another key worker is taken away or some other setback occurs, and we wonder how on earth God's purposes could ever be fulfilled. God gave Isaiah a wonderful promise for the people in their darkest hour.

God will never become weary of you.

> *The glory of the LORD will be revealed, and all mankind together will see it. (v. 5)*

The Sennacheribs and Nebuchadnezzars who blasphemed the name of God seemed to be unassailable. But God said, "All men are like grass" (v. 6) and "the breath of the LORD blows" on them (v. 7). God would blow away the wicked like the wind blows away the chaff (see Psalm 1:4).

Then the Lord added, "But the word of our God stands forever" (v. 8). Long after Sennacherib and Nebuchadnezzar were gone, the promise of God to bring blessing to the world would still stand. And God would not become weary of His people.

> *The LORD is the everlasting God, the Creator of the ends of the earth. He will not grow tired or weary. (v. 28)*

Have you ever watched a young child with too many toys? He plays with one for a while and then discards it. He gets tired of it; he gets weary of it and wants to play with something else. Isaiah says, "Whatever you do, don't ever imagine that God is like that. He will not tire of you. He will not lose interest in you or put you aside. God will never become weary of you!"

You may find that God allows circumstances that will change the whole direction of your life so that you wonder what He is doing. It may look as if the problems you face would make it impossible for the purposes of God to be achieved in your life. Don't be so sure!

When Jesus Christ came into the world, His disciples had great hopes and dreams about what the future might hold, and then the unthinkable happened. Christ was crucified.

GOD WILL REMAIN IN CONTROL

It must have seemed to the disciples that all hope of God's purposes being fulfilled was gone. And yet God was in control even when evil was unleashed in its most horrendous and violent form—the death of God's Son. There is a deep mystery in this, but God's greatest purpose was fulfilled in the world's darkest hour.

It is helpful to think about this when it seems that our lives have been thrown into chaos or confusion. What has taken us by surprise and brought deep disappointment was always known to God, and has its place in His purpose.

God told Isaiah to comfort His people. God's people find comfort in knowing that He is in control and that He will fulfill His purposes. But those who face great burdens still have to find a way to get through today and tomorrow.

GOD WILL SUSTAIN HIS PEOPLE

Isaiah reminds the people of how God will sustain them.

> He gives strength to the weary and increases the power of
> the weak. Even youths grow tired and weary, and young men
> stumble and fall; but those who hope in the LORD will renew
> their strength. (vv. 29–31)

Notice how God recognizes that unrelenting pressures can wear us down. Even at our strongest, we do not have unlimited resources. Even youths grow tired and weary. The word Isaiah uses for "young men" is related to another word that means "chosen men." So Isaiah is talking about men who are the pick of the bunch, the kind of athletes who would catch the selector's eye.

Even the Olympic athlete, at the very peak of condition, has limited resources of strength, and when that strength is drained, he will stumble and fall. But those who hope in God will renew their strength. Those who know that God is in control, and believe that God will fulfill His purposes will find their strength renewed. They will be given the ability to press on and persevere.

In *Horizons of Hope*, Brian Edwards describes the painful journey he shared with his wife as she battled her way through the last months of her illness. He writes, "For months on end there seemed to be no light at the end of the tunnel, until gradually it dawned on me that perhaps I was expected to find light in the tunnel."[3]

God leads His people through some pretty dark valleys, but He promises to sustain us in them. "Let him who walks in the dark, who has no light, trust in the name of the LORD and rely on his God" (Isaiah 50:10).

UNLOCKED

God sometimes leads His people through dark valleys, where it will not be possible for them to see what He is doing. When God's people faced their darkest time, God sent Isaiah to tell them that God is in control.

This is the foundation of our faith. God also promises that He will fulfill all of His purposes. There are times and circumstances that make us feel that this would be impossible, but it is the promise of God. God will sustain us through the darkest times.

PAUSE FOR PRAYER

You may like to read Romans 8:28–39 before praying this prayer.

Sovereign Lord,

Sustain me in my darkness, and help me to find my strength in You.

Help me to know that You are in control and to find comfort in knowing that Your purpose will be fulfilled. Thank You that nothing can ever separate me from Your love shown in Jesus Christ my Lord. In the name of Jesus I pray. Amen.

NOTES

1. Brian Edwards, *Horizons of Hope* (Day One Publications, 2000).

2. I recall this story vividly from a sermon preached by Leith Samuel, a respected pastor and Christian leader in England, who is now with the Lord. In my office I have a framed facsimile copy of Holden's ticket to the *Titanic*. For obvious reasons, it is one of the few tickets that remains. Friends who were helped by the story presented it to me after they spotted a plaque for sale during a visit to the *Titanic* exhibition at Chicago's Museum of Science and Industry. The plaque displays a ticket bearing the handwritten name of J.S. Holden.

3. Edwards, *Horizons of Hope*, 44.

7

Servant

ISAIAH 42, 49, 53

How can God's

will get done?

7Servant

ISAIAH 42, 49, 53

DISCOVER
the power of compassion.

LEARN
God's pattern for a ministry that will
bring blessing to the world.

WORSHIP
as you see how Christ fulfills the
role of God's Servant.

I WILL never forget my first view of Rishikesh, India. The opulence of the temples contrasted sharply to the desperate poverty of so many people. Sadhus in their saffron robes sat next to their ashrams, some of them in altered states of mind, others looking as if they did not have a hope in the world. The streets were lined with idols shaped in the image of a lion, a monkey, or a snake.

The place was crowded with people from east and west who had come as pilgrims to this Hindu holy place on the Ganges River. This was where the Beatles had come in the sixties, looking for spiritual meaning. The place seemed to be bereft of the presence of God.

As I walked farther into the city, I wondered what it would take for the will of God to be done there.

The same question comes to mind in other less exotic places: the inner city, the local prison, or the affluent suburb. Isaiah probably asked the same question when he looked at the realities of his own time.

God had called His people to be a model community in the world. They were to live by His laws and bear the name of God in the world. But they had become divided and then had turned to other gods, and now they were coming under the discipline of God themselves. Isaiah had prophesied that Jerusalem would become a desolate wasteland. The place where God had put His name would become a smoldering ruin. So what hope would there be of God's blessing coming to the nations? If God's light among the nations became darkness, then the darkness would be very great indeed.

God had told Isaiah to comfort His people by telling them that God is in control: that God would sustain His people through the dark times, and that His purpose would be fulfilled. God's people must have wondered how this could possibly happen. What would it take to get the will of God done?

MEET "THE SERVANT"

It is at this point in the story that we are introduced to someone who is simply called "the servant."

> *"Here is my servant." (42:1)*

A servant is a person who gets his master's will done. If you are a servant, your job description is very simple. Whatever your master tells you, do it! The servant is at the beck and call of his or her master, and the role of the servant is to get what the master wants done.

Now God introduces His Servant. He is saying, "Let Me tell you about the person who will get My will done in the world." God is telling us about how His ancient promise to Abraham to bless His own people and then bring blessing to the nations of the world will be fulfilled.

As we read through the book of Isaiah, it becomes increasingly obvious that this Servant is of great importance. He is the executor of the will of God, and He delivers the promises of God.

When we come to the New Testament, the Servant is clearly identified with our Lord Jesus Christ. But before we see how Jesus fulfills the role of the Servant, it is important to remember that Isaiah was speaking to God's people about how God's will would be done seven hundred years before Christ came into the world.

God's words about the Servant give us a pattern for the kind of ministry that will get His will done in dark places and the kind of person God will use to bring His blessing to the nations.

MAKING THE MAXIMUM IMPACT

> *"Here is my servant, whom I uphold, my chosen one in whom I delight; I will put my Spirit on him and he will bring justice to the nations." (42:1)*

God's Servant has some very remarkable privileges. The Servant would be chosen, loved, anointed, and sustained in His ministry. The Servant's calling would be to bring justice to the nations. This means much more than getting right decisions in a court of law. The Servant's task would be to put things in order and make them as they ought to be.

By any standards, this would be an extraordinary ministry, and when God tells us about the magnificent results of the Servant's ministry, we are bound to ask how this kind of transformation could possibly be achieved.

How do you think a servant of God should change the world? If you were casting a vision for a ministry that would restore a right order of things in the world, where would you begin? Perhaps you would call a national press conference, or initiate an education program, or even take to the road in a white suit with a series of religious revival meetings.

But the Servant Isaiah was describing would do none of these things. Instead, we are told,

> "He will not shout or cry out, or raise his voice in the streets." (42:2)

God said, "The person I am going to use to get My will done is not going to have anything of the showman about Him. He will not promote Himself. He will not be the kind of person who tries to dominate everybody else. He will not shout. In fact, the outstanding thing about Him will be the quietness of His ministry. He will get on with doing the will of God without drawing attention to Himself."

The Power of Compassion

The will of God does not get done in this world through the genius of spectacular programs or by the glamour of mega-personalities. The Servant's style is altogether different.

> "A bruised reed he will not break, and a smoldering wick he
> will not snuff out." (v. 3)

Few people try to mend broken reeds. The instinctive thing to do with a broken reed is to break it off. When a reed bends, it usually gets trampled on. And if a candle is almost burned out on your dinner table, you snuff it out and get another one. But God says that His Servant will not be like that. He will not break bruised reeds and He will not snuff out smoldering candles. He will show compassion.

The church I served in London is like many evangelical churches in England: Its building is a rather plain rectangle with white walls. We have not had a strong tradition of artistic imagination; it's probably an overreaction to all the cathedrals. On one occasion, Bible teacher Warren Wiersbe told me that going to an Evangelical Free church in England gave him the feeling of sitting on the inside of a milk carton!

So we decided to do something about it, and a number of the ladies formed a group to make banners. They did a superb job, producing stunning banners that depicted various scenes from the Bible. My favorite one is taken from this verse. It shows a number of reeds, and one in particular where the stalk is split. But there is a hand holding it. Without the hand, the stalk would snap under the pressure of its own weight.

Our world is full of bruised reeds. Perhaps you can identify with that description. You have been hit by something and it has bruised you and almost broken you. You are hardly able to stand up under a crushing weight that seems too great to bear. Take heart. The Servant will support you.

Or perhaps you can relate to the picture of a smoldering wick. There was a time when you were aflame with passion for the Lord Jesus Christ, but now it is as if you are running out of fuel. Your inner resources of patience, hope, and love seem to be burning low and the light within you is flickering. Having thrown yourself into ministry, you find that you need to receive before you can give. The church is called to ministry for God, but we all stand in desperate need of ministry from God.

Broken, bruised, and burned-out people will never be drawn to the loudmouthed showman. People who feel that their lives are flickering will not be helped by high impact promotions. The servant who gets God's will done will have a quiet ministry that touches the lives of wounded people with great compassion.

This kind of ministry can seem extremely slow and can be very discouraging. Those who are looking for quick results and glowing reports will not find this kind of ministry easy or attractive. But God's servant will stick at his or her ministry with great faithfulness.

> "In faithfulness he will bring forth justice; he will not falter or
> be discouraged." (vv. 3–4)

God has given us a powerful picture of the Servant He will use to get His will done in the world. That Servant—any servant useful to God—has a heart of compassion for the broken and the bruised. He or she does not get discouraged, but is sustained by the staying power of the Spirit. The servant does not need to see his or her own name in lights. If you want to be useful in the hand of God, cultivate humility, cultivate compassion, and cultivate faithfulness.

THE SCALE OF THE CHALLENGE

The people to whom God sends His Servant are not only bruised and broken, but also blinded and bound. So the Servant would face an overwhelming challenge. He was to

> "open eyes that are blind, to free captives from prison and to
> release from the dungeon those who sit in darkness." (v. 7)

Sin blinds us to God's glory and binds us by its power. It follows that if the blessing of God is to flow to the nations, there must be healing from sin's blindness, and freedom from sin's power.

The scale of the challenge that God's servants face today points us to the resources needed for ministry. If people had the capacity of spiritual sight, it would be relatively simple to flood the world with the good news of the gospel. People would immediately see their need of the gospel and come to Christ. But the problem God's servants face is that even when they have described the glory of God and the good news of the gospel, their hearers lack the capacity to appreciate this truth and respond to it. They are blind.

And even if they had the capacity to see clearly, they are incapable of responding positively to God because they are bound. If sin were simply a choice, it would be relatively easy to give people guidance toward better choices. But sin is a power.

Effective ministry is never less than proclamation, but it is more than proclamation. God's servants are utterly dependent on God creating the capacity of spiritual sight and of spiritual life that will make it possible for a person to see God's glory and respond to God's law when it is proclaimed. Apart from that ministry, the servant's hearers are like blind people in an art gallery, or prisoners who have a map but sit behind bars.

God says, "My Servant will deliver you from blindness to truth and He will release you from the binding power of sin."

WHO FITS THE PROFILE?

As God gave more information about His servant, His people would have become increasingly curious. Who might fulfill this role? Certainly Isaiah must have wondered who could possibly fit the profile.

When God first spoke about "the servant," it must have seemed to Isaiah that He was talking about Israel.

> *"O Israel, my servant, Jacob, whom I have chosen, you descendants of Abraham my friend, I took you from the ends of the earth….I said, 'You are my servant.'"* (41:8–9 EMPHASIS ADDED)

God had called Israel to fill this ministry. He had said, "I will be your God and you shall be My people," and God's people were called to fulfill the role of God's servant among the nations. They had been given the light of God's truth, and they had been given the law and the sacrifices. God's people were to be the channel through which His name would be known and His blessing would flow to the nations of the world.

NOT ISRAEL…

But God's people could not live up to their calling. The servant was to bring sight to the blind and to release those who were bound, but God said, "Who is blind but my servant, and deaf like the messenger I send?" (42:19). Then He added:

> *"You have seen many things, but have paid no attention; your ears are open, but you hear nothing."…This is a people plundered and looted, all of them trapped in pits or hidden away in prisons.* (vv. 20, 22)

The servants who were supposed to bring sight and freedom to others turned out to be blind and bound themselves! The servant who was called to give ministry now turns out to be the very person who needs to receive ministry!

The prospects for God's blessing coming to the nations seemed to be bleak at this point. Israel was chosen as God's servant, but was not in a position to fulfill the role. Before Israel can bring light to the nations, she needed to receive ministry from someone who will bring light to her.

At one point, it seems as if God might be calling Isaiah to be that person.

In Isaiah chapter 49, God speaks about the servant again, but this time, the Lord was not speaking about the nation, but about an individual who would minister to the nation. God was saying, "I called Israel to reflect My glory, so that the world may see, but it has not happened, so Isaiah, I am calling you to fulfill this ministry instead. "He said *to me*, 'You are my servant'" (v. 3; italics added).

NOT ISAIAH...

But Isaiah knew that the job was way beyond him.

> I said, "I have labored to no purpose; I have spent my strength
> in vain and for nothing." (49:4)

He was saying, "There is no way that my little ministry with its puny results can begin to fulfill the role of the Servant!" That was true. The people were remarkably unresponsive to Isaiah's ministry.

Then God told Isaiah that the Servant would be called to a ministry that would go far beyond Israel.

> "It is too small a thing for you to be my servant to restore the
> tribes of Jacob and bring back those of Israel I have kept. I will
> also make you a light for the Gentiles, that you may bring my
> salvation to the ends of the earth." (49:6)

This is not mission difficult; this is mission impossible! There is no prophet in all of the Bible who achieved this or even came close.

SPOTLIGHT ON CHRIST

After God had revealed the character, calling, and commission of the Servant, He gave Isaiah a vision of the person who would fulfill this role. What Isaiah saw was so staggering to him, that he hardly knew how to report it. It seemed to him that nobody would believe what he had seen.

> Who has believed our message and to whom has the arm of the
> LORD been revealed? (53:1)

"If I tell you what I saw," Isaiah was saying, "you will never believe it." But Isaiah tells them anyway (vv. 2–3). Imagine Isaiah describing this Servant to those who asked.

"I saw the Servant! I saw Him! The One who would get the will of God done."

"What did He look like, Isaiah?"

"That's what I can't get over. I saw Him despised. I saw Him rejected and hounded out of town. I saw violence being poured out on Him in such a way that I could hardly bear to look at Him. He was so disfigured. I saw people around Him hiding their heads in their hands because they didn't want to look at Him. Others who did watch said, 'He's just getting what He deserves.'"

THE SUFFERING SERVANT

Isaiah must have winced as he saw the vision of what would happen to the Servant on whom all hope of God's blessing depended. Isaiah tells us that He was pierced, He was crushed, He was punished, and He was wounded.

As Isaiah contemplated what happened to the Servant, it must have seemed the greatest disaster. Then God told Isaiah something that must have made him gasp. "It was the LORD's will to crush him and…[make] his life a guilt offering" (53:10).

The suffering—and death—to be inflicted on the humble and compassionate Servant of the Lord was actually the will of God! Then the Lord said something else that would have been staggering to Isaiah.

The will of the LORD will prosper in his hand. (v. 10)

This is how the will of God would be done. This is how God's blessing would flow to the world. The humble, compassionate Servant who has been anointed and commissioned by God to bring the blessing of God to all nations will accomplish His mission through His suffering and death.

Christ fulfilled what Isaiah saw.

He was pierced for our transgressions, he was crushed for our iniquities; the punishment that brought us peace was upon him, and by his wounds we are healed. (v. 5)

God also gave Isaiah a profound insight into why the Cross was necessary.

We all, like sheep, have gone astray, each of us has turned to his own way; and the LORD has laid on him the iniquity of us all. (v. 6)

All the sin, failure, pride, and selfishness that belongs to those who wish to be God's servants are laid upon the One who is God's Servant. What no nation or prophet could ever accomplish, Christ achieved.

Christ is specifically identified in the New Testament as the gentle, compassionate Servant who would not break a bruised reed or snuff out a smoldering wick. Matthew tells us that His ministry fulfilled the words God had spoken through the prophet Isaiah (12:17–21).

The character of the risen Christ has not changed. He is compassionate to the bruised, broken, and faltering who will come to Him in faith. He opens our blind eyes to know God and He cuts us free from the power of sin that binds us. His ministry is not restricted to certain groups of people but is for people from every nation.

GETTING OUT THE GOOD NEWS

Later in the New Testament, there is a story about a deeply religious African leader who had come to Jerusalem to worship. While he was traveling home, he was reading from the Old Testament. The passage he was reading described the suffering servant of Isaiah 53.

A man named Philip joined him on the journey, and the African "asked Philip, 'Tell me, please, who is the prophet talking about, himself or someone else?' Then Philip began with that very passage of Scripture and told him the good news about Jesus" (Acts 8:34–35). I have no doubt that Philip told him everything Isaiah said about the Servant.

"Listen," Philip may have said, "the Scripture says that the person who gets God's will done will have a ministry of compassion to bruised reeds and smoldering wicks. Let me tell you about Jesus. He touched the lepers and forgave sinners. He had compassion on people because He knew they were sheep without a shepherd.

"Isaiah said that the Servant would restore Israel, and Jesus affirmed that He had come first to the lost sheep of Israel, but added that He had also come for the nations. He said, 'I have other sheep, which are not of this fold' [John 10:16 NASB].

"But then let me tell you what happened. They brought forward false witnesses and tried Him on false charges. He was crucified in the very city you have just come from. What He suffered was unspeakable. He was pierced, crushed, punished, and wounded, and then they took Him down and laid Him in the grave.

"But do you see where Isaiah says, 'After He has suffered, He will see the light of life'? That is exactly what happened on the third day. He rose again! The Servant, prophesied by Isaiah, has come, and His name is Jesus. The will of God will prosper in His hand. It will be through Him that God's blessing will come to all who will receive Him, whatever their background or nationality. He is the one through whom the ancient promise to Abraham is now fulfilled."

Those who come to Christ have a great privilege and an awesome responsibility. Christ said to His disciples, "As the Father has sent me, I am sending you" (John 20:21). Those who know Jesus are to go out into the world as His servants. We are to go into a proud world and show the humility of Christ. We are to go into a hard world and show the compassion of Christ. We are to proclaim the truth of what

God has done in Jesus Christ, so that people who do not know may come to see who He is, and people who are bound may come to enjoy the freedom He gives.

And we are not to limit our horizons to one town or city. Christ has commissioned His people to go to the nations. He has told us to go whatever the cost. Safety is never promised. Christ said, "I am sending you out like lambs among wolves" (Luke 10:3). On another occasion He said, "If the world hates you, keep in mind that it hated me first" (John 15:18).

But Christ promises that as we go and minister in His name, the will of God will be done, the blessing of God will come to many people, and Christ will see of the fruit of the travail of His soul and be satisfied.

UNLOCKED

God's purposes do not depend on programs or personalities, but His will is accomplished through the quiet, humble, and faithful ministry of His servants who show compassion in a broken and hurting world.

The heart of the human problem lies in the fact that we are blind to God's glory and bound by sin's power. So God's servants depend on Him to create the capacity of spiritual sight and the ability to fulfill His law. They look to God to do this as they declare His glory and call people to repentance and faith.

Jesus Christ is the Servant who gets the will of God done. Incredibly, God's purpose was achieved through Jesus' awful suffering and death. Without Him the purposes of God could never have been fulfilled.

God sends His servants to all the nations of the earth, so that people from every tribe and language may see God's glory, discover the freedom that He offers through Jesus Christ, and then become His servants themselves.

PAUSE FOR PRAYER

Almighty Father,

Thank You that Your Son, Jesus Christ, took the form of a servant, was made in human likeness, and humbled Himself even to death on a cross. Thank You that He became the one Isaiah spoke about.

Thank You that He is highly exalted and that You have given Him the name above every name that at the name of Jesus every knee should bow.

I acknowledge Him as Savior and Lord of my life and count it my privilege to be a servant of Christ.

Use me as Your servant. Fill me with the compassion of Christ. Give me a wider vision for Your kingdom among the nations of the world. Thank You that on the last day there will be people from every tribe and nation who will glorify the name of Christ and enjoy Your blessing forever.

Through Jesus Christ my Lord I pray. Amen.

8

Calling

ISAIAH 55

What does Jesus

Christ offer, and

how can it

be yours?

*8*Calling

ISAIAH 55

DISCOVER
the amazing auction in which what
is offered goes to the lowest bidder!

LEARN
how Christ can satisfy the deep
thirsts of your soul.

WORSHIP
because God offers His greatest
gifts to all who will receive.

IN the town where my wife, Karen, and I used to live in north London, market day was every Thursday and Saturday. Right in the center of the town there is an open area called the Market Square. Its cobblestones have been there for hundreds of years. Every Thursday and Saturday, the crews would arrive at around six in the morning and set up the scaffolding and the canopies for the stalls. There were probably about fifty traders who had a license to trade, and some of them were real characters.

There were stalls with fruit and vegetables, a luggage rack, clothing stalls, and a man who strangely seemed to do nothing but sell parts for vacuum cleaners. The place was always milling with people looking for a bargain. Then, at the end of the day, the crews took the whole thing down, and after it was swept, the old cobbled Market Square would be completely deserted.

One of the enjoyable things about markets is the noise and banter of the traders. When the market is going, the whole place is a cacophony of noise. The traders' stalls were probably no more than six feet apart, and as you wandered between them, the traders would try to attract your attention.

"Lovely mushrooms—pound for a pound."

"New towels—feel the softness."

"New luggage—unbeatable prices."

It was almost a relief to go past the man selling parts for vacuum cleaners. He just sat there lost in a book he was reading.

In Isaiah 55, God uses the picture of a marketplace to explain an incredible offer. Try to imagine yourself walking by the stalls, with many voices calling you. Back there in the third row on the left, you see a stall. The trader is quiet compared to most but ready to make a special offer.

> "Come, all you who are thirsty, come to the waters; and you who have no money, come, buy and eat! Come, buy wine and milk without money and without cost." (55:1)

This trader is offering something of great value. He calls out:

> "Listen, listen to me, and eat what is good, and your soul will delight in the richest of fare....Hear me, that your soul may live." (vv. 2–3)

Who is this trader? And why do many rush past an offer that seems so good?

THE TRADER REVEALED

The identity of the street trader is revealed by the words of one who spoke centuries later: "If anyone is thirsty, let him come to me and drink" (John 7:37). Jesus took the words of Isaiah 55 and applied them to Himself. The street trader is the Son of God!

So it is Christ who is calling to attract the attention of anybody who will listen. He is one voice among many, and He is inviting people to come over to His stall where He offers to satisfy the deepest thirst.

In Isaiah 55, the spotlight is already on the coming Christ, so in this chapter we will turn on that spotlight early. Actually, Isaiah 55 is a floodlight, casting lots of light on Jesus Christ, the Trader with an incredible offer.

SPOTLIGHT ON CHRIST

Jesus' invitation goes out, but not everybody who hears the invitation responds to it. Some people hear, and others don't. This is one of the great mysteries of the Bible.

One reason for this is that some people in the marketplace are preoccupied at other stalls. They are within earshot of the sound of the invitation, but their attention is so taken up with what they are doing that they do not hear. The invitation is going out, but it is not heard because it is drowned out by other voices and other interests. The street trader is competing for an audience with many other voices. Christ calls out to them as they rummage through the products displayed in other stalls.

COMPETITION IN THE MARKETPLACE

Recognizing that rival products exist, the Trader asks, "Why spend money on what is not bread, and your labor on what does not satisfy?" (v. 2).

In today's market, some people are preoccupied at the stall that is marked "Sport." Others are looking for what will satisfy on the stall that is marked "Marriage." Others are rummaging around in the stall that is marked "Career" or "Popularity" or "Family."

Many of those stalls involve good things, but Christ is saying to us, "Come over here; I have something to offer that you will not find anywhere else."

DEAFNESS

Other people don't respond to the invitation because they don't hear it. They are unable to hear the voice of God.

When a meal is ready in our home, either Karen or I will usually shout, "Dinner's ready!" so that our boys know that it's time to come. Sometimes there is no response, and so one of us goes downstairs to investigate. Sometimes the problem is very simple: headphones!

In a sense, it's not the boys' fault that they don't hear. There was a blockage over their ears that prevented them from hearing the call. Some people do not hear Christ's invitation because there is a spiritual blockage in their lives. If we knowingly hold on to something that God forbids, it can prevent us from hearing the voice of God.

PREJUDICE

Others are not listening to the call of Christ because of prejudice. I am rather like this myself with sales calls from telephone companies. We've had so many of them that in the end I have lost interest in hearing. I'm prejudiced, and I just can't be bothered. The phone company offer actually may be better than the phone service we have, but I'm not listening. If a telephone company calls with another deal, I want to say, "No thanks. I've made up my mind, and I'm not open to reconsider. I have spent more than enough time considering my choices of telephone company, thank you. Good-bye."

I don't say all that, of course, but I'd like to. That's how some people feel about Christ. "I made up my mind long ago." But Christ is still calling out in the marketplace to all who will listen. He has something to offer that is not available on any other stall and He wants us to have it.

A ONE-OF-A-KIND OFFER

A good trader will do an excellent job of displaying his product. When you go into a store, it's frustrating if you find that the sales assistant knows less than you do about the product that he is selling! A good trader will tell you what a product will do and why it is of value. So what exactly is Christ's offer?

"Come, all you who are thirsty, come to the waters" (v. 1). The Trader offers to meet the fundamental thirsts of the human soul. Christ is saying, "I will satisfy the deep thirsts that God has created within you."

When Adam and Eve were in the garden, every thirst within them was fully satisfied. But when sin entered the world, they found that things went strangely wrong. Their marriage, that had been so wonderful, now seemed to change as they blamed one another for their problems. Their work that had given them such joy now became mixed with frustration. Their bodies that had been so healthy now began to age, and they began to experience pain. They began to wonder what was wrong with them. They became thirsty.

Have you ever wondered why there are deep thirsts within your soul? Adam and Eve knew the answer. In the garden they had walked with God, but that changed when they were thrown out of the garden. Now they were separated from God, and they were thirsty. We experience the same thirsts and so we find ourselves in the marketplace of the world trying to find fulfillment, satisfaction, and life. That is why Jesus announced one day, "If anyone is thirsty, let him come to me and drink" (John 7:37). Christ was calling out to us: "Come over here! I can satisfy the deep thirsts that are within your soul."

Indeed, that is why Jesus came into the world. He said, "I have come that [you] may have life...to the full" (John 10:10). He came to restore what was lost in the garden to all who would receive. At the end of the Bible story, John described a vision of heaven where a shepherd "will lead them to springs of living water" (Revelation 7:17). One of the joys of life in heaven is that we will always be satisfied, and yet Christ will continually lead His people into new discoveries of delight.

That's the product; now let's talk about price!

THE PRICE IS RIGHT!

"Come, buy…without money and without cost." (v. 1)

This is staggering. Selling is usually about the trader arguing the customer up to his price, but here we have Christ doing the opposite. He is arguing the price down!

Perhaps you enjoy going to an auction sale. It can be fun watching the price go up, especially if you're not bidding. The auction starts with many bidders, but people begin to drop out as the price gets too high, and then it becomes a battle of the big spenders. Sometimes I wonder if there isn't more than a hint of pride that creeps in as the fat wallets slug it out to the finish.

Christ is conducting an auction in reverse. Everything is turned on its head, because Christ has chosen to sell to the *lowest bidder*. So come with me in your imagination to this auction sale! Christ is standing in the stall, and He says, "I am pleased to be able to offer to you today total forgiveness and reconciliation with God. This offer includes bringing you out of your old way of life and onto a new path of holiness. It includes satisfying the deep thirsts of your soul, and it includes the ultimate value of everlasting life. All of this is available today to the *lowest* bidder."

AN AUCTION LIKE NO OTHER

So let's attend an auction where bids are being made for a great item: reconciliation with God and eternal life.

A man in a pin-striped suit steps forward with the first bid.

"Well, I've led a good life and run an honest business. I have been faithful to my wife and have been a good father to my children. I have been sensitive to the needs of the poor, and I have served on the boards of three charitable organizations. I offer all those good works so I may live forever with God."

A murmur rises from the rest of the bidders. That's a pretty impressive offer.

"It's with the man in the pin-striped suit," says the auctioneer.

Then a lady in a blue coat lifts her hand.

"I haven't done as much as the man in the pin-striped suit," she says, 'but I have attended church faithfully, and I have had wonderful experiences with God. I think that I have become a spiritual person, and I'd like to have what you are offering today."

"It's with the lady in the blue coat," says the seller. "Can anyone make me a better offer?"

A girl in blue jeans raises her hand.

"I haven't attended church like the lady in the blue coat, but I am sincere in wanting to do what is right, and I have tried to live a life that is pleasing to God."

"Well," says the auctioneer, "that's not very much, but *it's going to the lowest bidder,* so you have it. Am I hearing any other bids?"

A man in a red sweater, with a bit of a red face to go with it, gets up slowly.

"I've not lived up to my own expectations," he says. "I have let people down, and I've done some terrible things, but at least I have been sorry. I didn't intend to do what I did, so let me offer the fact that I am truly repentant."

"Well, that's even less than the girl with blue jeans," says the seller. "It's with the man in the red sweater. Does anyone want to make a lower offer?"

A kid with red hair and freckles raises his hand.

"I am not sure if I am truly sorry, and I'll tell you why. There are some things that I said I was sorry for, and then I go right ahead and do them again! But at least I can say that I believe."

"Well," says the seller, "that really isn't much. The Bible says that even the devils believe and they tremble. But it's going to the lowest bidder, so your meager bid has it right now. Is anyone going to make me a lower offer?"

This is not a battle of pride; it is a battle of blushes. Many people have opted out of the bidding, not because the cost is too high, but because the offers are embarrassingly low. Most people are just watching to see if anyone would dare to offer less than the boy with freckles. How could anyone offer so little to God?

Finally someone steps forward, and says, "I don't have anything to offer. My repentance isn't what it should be; my faith isn't what it should be; my works aren't what they should be. Nothing is as it should be! I have nothing to offer." And the auctioneer brings down His hammer. "It's yours," He says. "It's yours."

WHAT DO WE BRING?
Maybe you're saying, "OK, but don't we have to bring something to God? Don't we have to be sorry? Don't we have to believe?"

Yes. But we do not receive salvation because we offer these things. Salvation is a gift. Many people become confused at this point. They think of salvation as a trade in which God offers forgiveness and life, and we bring repentance and faith, and somehow we get together and make the trade. But that's not the gospel.

The blind man did not come to Christ because he had sight; he came to Christ to receive sight. You do not come to Christ with a changed life; you come to Christ for a changed life. You do not come to Christ because you are brokenhearted about your sin; you come to Christ in order to be brokenhearted over your sin, and that will only happen when you see your sin in the light of the Cross.

In the words of the old hymn "Rock of Ages,"

> *Nothing in my hand I bring,*
> *Simply to Thy cross I cling.*

Your salvation does not rest on your good works, your spiritual experience, your repentance, or even your faith. You come to Christ to receive. If God were to ask you on the last day why He should let you into heaven, the answer is not "Because of my good works…my repentance" or even "…my faith." Our salvation does not rest on anything we have done. It rests on Jesus Christ alone.

If we are resting on our repentance and faith, we will never have assurance, because our faith and our repentance are never what they might be. Our salvation depends entirely on Christ. Faith is the open hand that receives what He offers, and repentance is the response of a heart that has received.

OFFERING THE LOWEST BID

Many people have difficulty in offering worship to God the Father and God the Son because they have never received what Christ offers. When they hear others talking about "loving Christ," they find it hard to relate to that, and the reason is that they have not received anything. They are merely following a moral code and offering that to God. In fact, all that they have ever done is to offer things to God. Their hands are full. They have never come to Christ to receive.

The only offer Christ will receive is nothing. The only price for which He will release salvation is zero. God has made it so that every one of us can make the lowest offer. Only pride stands in your way. The man in the pin-striped suit and the lady in the blue coat may have this blessing also, but they must stop trying to buy it. They must lay aside their works and come to Christ empty-handed.

One reason we find this so difficult is that we don't like debt. This came home to me a few months ago, when a friend offered to fix a problem in our home. He must have spent a couple of hours working on it, and I was grateful. I had some money to slip in his pocket, but he wouldn't take it.

"I'm happy to do it," he said.

"Yes, I know, but I'd like to give you something for it. It's better that way."

So we had this rather stupid argument.

Why did I want to pay him? Because we are equals, and I didn't want to be unreasonably in his debt. If I got some help and he got some money, then we were level in the deal. And somewhere deep in our hearts that's often how we think when it comes to Christ. "He offers something that I need. Let me offer something that He wants." That gives me some credibility, some self-respect. And Christ says, "On that basis, no deal."

The only basis on which we can receive what Christ offers is with the empty hand that reaches out to Him and offers nothing in exchange, and that leaves us incalculably in His debt for the rest of our lives and for all eternity. That's what the Christian life is like. We look up into the face of Christ saying, "I cannot begin to express the debt that I owe to You for what You have freely given to me. So I will worship, love, and obey You for the rest of my days; not so that I may receive, but because I have received."

MAKING THE PURCHASE
"Come, buy." (55:1)

Why does Christ talk about buying when there is no payment being made by us? I think that there are two reasons.

First, salvation comes at a price, even though that price is not paid by us. Think about the Trader at the market stall. He is offering something at no cost to the buyer, but He had to obtain what He offers.

How did Christ obtain the blessing that He freely offers to all who will receive? He bought it. What Christ offers was obtained at the price of shedding His own blood for sinners.

But Christ speaks about buying for a second reason; buying indicates a definite transaction. When Christ says, "Buy," He is telling us that there must be a definite transaction in which what was obtained by Christ actually becomes yours. Buying is a transaction in which what Christ has in His stall is placed into your hands and becomes your possession, and unless this transaction takes place, what Christ offers remains on the stall. It remains His, and it isn't yours.

LOOKING ISN'T BUYING

Some people enjoy "just looking" in shops, and there is absolutely nothing wrong with that. That's where some people are spiritually. They are wandering around in the marketplace and have heard the invitation of Christ. They have come over to His stall and started asking questions about the Bible and salvation. They are like the shopper who picks up some clothes and holds them up to feel the texture of the material.

I have found that some shops are "seeker friendly" and others are "seeker hostile." You go into some, and the assistant offers to help. You say, "No, I'm just looking," and that's fine with him. But it's not always like that. I went into a jewelry store recently because I wanted to get some ideas of price range for a gift. I quickly regretted it when an over-zealous salesperson approached me.

"Can I be of help to you?"

"No, I really just want to look around today, thank you."

"Do you have a particular occasion in mind?"

"Well, I might have."

"And when might that occasion be, may I ask?"

Sometimes I think that the only cure for these folks would be to draw up a chair, ask them to sit down, and then take an hour to tell them your entire life story in excruciating detail. But I didn't have the time for that.

"I'm just looking," I said with a note of finality. "Is that all right with you?"

Looking is great, but looking isn't buying. The greatest commitment of your life is worthy of the deepest investigation, so look into the claims of Christ carefully. But don't confuse looking with buying. If what Christ offers is to become yours, you must close the deal.

TRYING ISN'T BUYING

And trying isn't buying either. I'm thankful for that, because if we had bought every dress my wife has tried on over the last twenty years, we would be truly bankrupt! But trying isn't buying. You could be in a store from nine till five, Monday to Friday and never buy. And you can come to church, read the Bible, join a study group and still never close the deal with Christ. You can hear fine sales pitches from your pastor, and enjoy them, and still never buy. You can be moved to feel that you should buy and never buy.

And knowing isn't buying. We were looking at washing machines a few months ago. We did our research and found a brilliant sales assistant. He was like an encyclopedia of washing machines.

"This one," he said with a rather nasal voice, "rotates with twenty-three minutes of agitation; and this one has the cork-screw spindle, but it does not have the automatic temperature gauge."

We began talking with him, and eventually he told us that he didn't own a washing machine himself because he lived on his own, had plenty of socks, and he went to the laundry once every month. He knew all about the products but had never bought one himself. We didn't buy the washing machine either.

Maybe that is where you are spiritually. You have learned many things about Jesus, but what He offers has not yet become yours. Knowing isn't buying.

We have been in the market for trees. We lost three in a storm, and our backyard looked like a desert. I am ashamed of how little I know about trees, so we took the opportunity to try and learn a few things. We went to garden centers and made a pain of ourselves asking endless questions, gathering information, comparing prices, and pondering alternatives. Then one day I said to Karen, "Today's the day. We've got to buy. We have done the research; now let's make a decision." We did. And three trees were moved from the nursery to our yard. They became ours.

That's the picture. There is a definite transaction, with no returns and no going back. It is like making a purchase, entering a marriage, or signing a covenant. And when you buy, what Christ offers becomes yours.

Christ says, "Come, buy, without money, without price." Are you ready to buy?

UNLOCKED

Jesus Christ offers to meet the deepest thirsts of your soul. He offers to bring you into a relationship with God in which your sins are forgiven and you begin to experience His power to live in a way that pleases Him. This life will continue beyond death for eternity.

You cannot buy this gift, but you can receive it. In order to receive, you must lay aside any idea that there is something that you can offer to God. You must ask Him to give what you do not have. That is the only basis on which the gift can be received.

Receiving the gift is a definite transaction in which what Christ offers actually becomes yours. Faith is like a hand being opened to receive what Christ offers. Even Christ cannot place His gift of salvation in a closed hand, but He stands ready to give to all who will receive. If you have come to the point of wanting to receive what Christ offers, you can use the words of the following prayer to God.

PAUSE FOR PRAYER

Almighty God,

My soul is thirsty for You. I feel my need to be forgiven for my sins, and I want to know Your presence in my life.

I believe that Jesus Christ is able to meet the deepest thirsts of my soul. I believe that He died on the cross so that my sins can be forgiven and that He rose again in power. I believe that His power can come into my life and make me a new person, and I believe that He offers that gift to me now.

Gracious Lord, I ask that You will forgive my sins and that Your Holy Spirit will enter my life. Make me one of Your people, and help me to live for Your glory.

By faith I take what You offer, through Jesus Christ my Lord. Amen.

If you have prayed the above prayer, you have accepted the greatest offer of all time— forgiveness of sins and eternal life with God in heaven. Congratulations! For information in growing as a new believer in Jesus Christ, please contact the publisher at the address shown at the end of this book. They will send you free books on the Christian life (and they'll let me know too, so I can rejoice as well and pray for you personally).

Heart

JEREMIAH 31

What is the

key to real and

lasting change?

9 Heart

JEREMIAH 31

 ## DISCOVER
why discipline, education, and
religion cannot produce a godly life.

 ## LEARN
how sin defaces the heart and
how God cleans it up.

 ## WORSHIP
because God gives what
He commands.

800 B.C.

792–740	Uzziah
750–731	Jotham
740	Isaiah's Vision
735–715	Ahaz
729–686	Hezekiah
722	End of North Kingdom

700

696–647	Manasseh (coregent)
640–609	Josiah
608–598	Jehoiakim
606–536	Babylonian Captivity

600

598–597	Jehoiachin
597–586	Zedekiah
586	Fall of Jerusalem
536	First Return to Jerusalem

500

ISAIAH

JEREMIAH

JOHN'S credit card debt had spiraled out of control. His wife had insisted on him seeing a counselor, and so, reluctantly, he agreed to go. The counselor made an assessment of his income and his expenses. It wasn't going to be easy. Eventually the counselor came up with a plan. It would involve a radical change in John's lifestyle, and it would take ten years to solve the problem.

John winced as he looked at the figures. "I know what I need to do," he said. "The problem is that I don't want to do it."

John's predicament gives us an insight into why change is so difficult. Knowing what to do is easy, finding the heart to do it is much more difficult.

Early on in the Bible story, God had told His people what they were to do. There was never any difficulty in understanding the commandments. The problem was finding the heart to obey them. At one point God spoke to His people through the prophet Jeremiah about this matter of the heart, and told them how real, deep, lasting change would be possible in their lives.

HIGH HOPES AND BIG DISAPPOINTMENTS

God's Word first came to Jeremiah the prophet in the thirteenth year of the reign of Josiah. This would have been around six hundred years before the birth of Christ. Josiah was a good king. It must have been a great relief to many people when he came to the throne. Before that time, Israel had suffered under the rule of Manasseh, the worst of the kings of Judah. He promoted the worship of other gods and burned his own children in the fire. There is a tradition that Manasseh executed the prophet Isaiah by sawing him in two. He reigned for fifty-five years, and there was so little interest in God's truth during his reign, that the book of God's Law became lost in the temple.

When Josiah came to the throne, the book of God's Law was found. The king asked for the Scripture to be read to him, and when he heard the law of God for the first time, he tore his clothes. That was an ancient way of expressing repentance or regret. He was saying in effect, "We're not doing this! The way we are living is nothing like the way God has told us to live. We are supposed to be the people of God, but we have not even known what the Law of God says!"

So Josiah launched a personal campaign to turn things around in the nation. The king went around the country and personally supervised the dismantling of all pagan sites of worship. He reinstated the feast of the Passover and called on the people to return to the living and true God (2 Kings 22–23).

Jeremiah's ministry began during this moral reformation, and it was through this prophet that God spoke to the people.

> "Judah did not return to me with all her heart, but only in
> pretense," declares the LORD. (3:10)

God was saying, "Jeremiah, you've seen this great campaign for moral reformation led by the king. There have been a certain number of changes. The pagan shrines are gone, and the Passover is now being observed. But here is the problem: While there has been some change of behavior, it has not touched the hearts of the people."

Jeremiah lived through the greatest attempt to restore godly values to the land. But for all the good things that Josiah did, the hearts of the people were not changed.

It is very interesting that when Jehoiakim succeeded his father, King Josiah, the new king went in exactly the opposite direction. You can read about him in Jeremiah 36. God told Jeremiah to write the Word of God on a scroll, and it was read to Jehoiakim as he was sitting by a fire in the winter room of his palace. Jehoiakim asked his secretary to read a few columns of the scroll and then he took his penknife and cut them off and threw them in the fire. Then he said, "Read me some more of what God says." The secretary read some more, and then the king took his penknife, and cut off the pages, and threw them in the fire, until the whole scroll was burned.

What a contrast. Josiah heard the Word of God and tore his clothes in repentance.

His son, Jehoiakim, heard the Word of God and tore the Scriptures, tossing the scraps into the fire.

Jeremiah prophesied through the reigns of both these kings. He saw some outward change among many people during the time of Josiah, but it didn't touch the heart, and when the next king came to the throne, there was a reaction, and things went back exactly as they had been before. Jeremiah must have wondered, "If Josiah's massive moral crusade can't change the people, what will?"

A PROMISE FOR A DISCOURAGED PROPHET

It was at this time that God gave a wonderful promise to the discouraged prophet. "Jeremiah, let me tell you what I am going to do. You have seen Josiah's noble attempt to change the nation. You have experienced the disappointment of it. You have seen how little is achieved by attempts to impose the truth on people. It simply cannot be done. So let me tell you, Jeremiah, what I am going to do."

> *"This is the covenant I will make with the house of Israel....I will put my law in their minds and write it on their hearts." (31:33)*

God told Jeremiah He would make a new covenant, and the heart of the new covenant would be a change in the heart. In effect, God was saying, "This new covenant will not require a king saying, 'You shall.' It will succeed through an inner transformation in which, by My Spirit, I will bring people to the place of saying, 'We will.'

Perhaps you have been searching for this for a long time. I have lost count of how many people have said to me something like this: "Pastor, you need to understand that I was taken along to church as a child and I hated it. I didn't understand what was being said, and when I did, it made me feel bad. It was boring and I could not see how it was possibly relevant to life. The whole thing was a matter of duty imposed on me, and so as soon as I had the opportunity, I broke free."

If that was your experience, you have probably rejected a system of religious rules and duties but perhaps there is also something within you that still wonders whether you can know and love God from the heart. That is exactly what God is talking about here.

THE PROBLEM WITH THE HEART

The book of Jeremiah contains one of the clearest statements about the fundamental problem of the human heart in the whole of the Bible.

The heart is deceitful above all things and beyond cure. Who
can understand it? (17:9)

The heart is devious and sometimes quite baffling. You cannot predict the direction in which the heart will lean. Jeremiah also wrote that "Judah's sin is engraved with an iron tool, inscribed with a flint point, on the tablets of their hearts and on the horns of their altars" (17:1).

When sin gets written into our hearts, it becomes engraved on our character.

Think about the walls of the living room in your home. Suppose that thieves break into your home, and they ransack the place. Suppose that they toss out the contents of your drawers in your bedroom, and suppose that they spray graffiti on your walls. That is the picture that God gives to Jeremiah.

Sin is written in two places. First it is written or recorded "on the horns of [the] altars" (17:1; see also Leviticus 4:18–20). That is the place where God's presence is. If I sin, my sin brings guilt in the presence of God and I need to be forgiven. But sin is also written on our hearts. It is as if graffiti has been inscribed over this hidden and private place at the very center of our lives. An enemy has come in and written all the wrong things there!

When sin gets written into our hearts, it becomes engraved on our character. It creates the power of habit within us and sets up all kinds of battles once it has gained an entrance to the private world of the heart.

This happens in different degrees. For some people, over a period of time, the heart has become a place where ugly, foul, and obscene things are deeply engraved. It's not easy to live with a heart like that. For others, the defacing effects of sin have been less severe, but the Bible is clear in telling that in some degree, sin is scrawled over every human heart.

When King David was recovering from a massive moral failure in his life, he asked God for two things. First, he came to God recognizing that his sin was written in God's presence, and he said, "Cleanse me with hyssop, and I shall be clean; wash me, and I will be whiter than snow" (Psalm 51:7). But he did not stop there. He knew that he needed more than forgiveness, and so he prayed, "Create in me a pure heart, O God" (v. 10).

David knew that what happened was a reflection of his own heart. He asked God to deal with his heart, because he knew that unless there was a change, his heart would lead him down that same sinful path again. So he prayed, "Lord, deal with the heart that led me to do this!"

Our actions are not a matter of random chance; they are the fruit of the prevailing dispositions of our hearts. Things don't just happen. Our actions are the fruit grown in the secret garden of the heart.

CLEANING UP THE GRAFFITI

When God speaks about the heart, He is talking about the prevailing disposition of the soul, the mainspring that gives rise to our actions. There is a disposition that governs your thinking, your feeling, and your choices. We sometimes talk about "the way we are wired." That gets at it. There is a disposition within us that leads us to choose in certain directions. So when we talk about the heart, we are talking about the absolute foundation of a person's whole being.

God said that He would write His law on the hearts of the people. This would be quite a transformation considering that the graffiti of sin was scrawled all over their hearts. It would be like decorating a room that had been vandalized and violated.

How can we get from the external "thou shalt" to the internal "I will"?

This is the fundamental change that every one of us needs. If you are going to live the kind of life that God calls you to lead, then His law will need to be worked into the very core of your being so that it is not a set of external rules, but a set of inward desires. The Old Testament story shows that you cannot live a righteous life simply because God says, "You shall." If you are to become what God wants you to be, there must be an inner transformation that brings you to the point of saying freely, "I will."

God is looking for more than behavior modification. It is not simply that we stop stealing, lying, and coveting. God wants to clean up the graffiti in the heart.

It is important to realize that this was not a new idea that God introduced in the New Testament. Some people have this idea that in the Old Testament, God was interested in rules, regulations, and duties, but in the New Testament, He saw that wasn't working, and so introduced a new religion of the heart. But there is one God and there is one story, and right from the beginning, God makes it clear that the only way we can become what He calls us to be is through a change in the heart.

> *Love the LORD your God with all your heart and with all your*
> *soul and with all your strength. These commandments that I*
> *give you today are to be upon your hearts.* (DEUTERONOMY
> 6:5–6; EMPHASIS ADDED)

This has always been the purpose of God. The question is, How can we get the Law of God into our hearts? How can we get from the external "thou shalt" to the internal "I will"?

The Old Testament story shows us three routes that will not take us there. It is important to understand this because there are many people who are still persevering on routes that won't take them where they need to go.

FEAR WON'T CHANGE YOUR HEART

When God gave the Law at Mount Sinai, the people were absolutely terrified. They looked at the mountain and saw smoke and lightning, and they heard the sound of trumpets as the presence of God came down. It was so awesome that even Moses was terrified. God's people were given a glimpse of the terrors of God Almighty, but it did absolutely nothing to change their hearts. Within a few weeks, they were dancing around the golden calf!

Some parents think that strictness, discipline, and an abundance of punishment will deliver the kind of character they want to see in their children. Discipline has its place, it will usually modify behavior, but it will not change the heart. The fear of hell will not change the heart. It is important for pastors to preach the whole of God's truth. That includes judgment and hell, and God may use that to make a person think deeply. But the preaching of judgment and hell will not change the heart. It is powerless to do so.

PROSPERITY WON'T CHANGE YOUR HEART

There are people who think that the answer to the human condition is primarily social and economic. The argument is that if people do not have enough money, or if they live in appalling conditions, and if they have no horizons of hope, they will turn to evil, and the way to change this is through programs of economic aid and social reform.

There is some truth in this. If a person is taken out of poverty and given hope, his patterns of behavior will probably change. But his heart will not. God brought His people out of the desert and into a land flowing with milk and honey. They were blessed with freedom, opportunity, and every material blessing you could imagine, but it did not change their hearts. You cannot erase the graffiti of sin on the human heart by changing a person's circumstances.

RELIGION WON'T CHANGE YOUR HEART

I can understand why some people might think that coming to church, saying prayers, or reading the Bible might change their hearts, but again, the Old Testament story makes it clear that although these things may lead to some changes in behavior, they will not change the heart.

In the history of the world there have never been a people more religious than the nation of Israel. And yet one of the most conscientious Jews who ever lived said, "In my mind I know that God's laws are good, but I find that my heart pulls me another way, so that while I want to pursue the Law of God, I find that I am moving in a different direction." That's the apostle Paul in Romans 7:22–23 (author paraphrase). He threw the whole energy of his soul into the pursuit of a godly life but found that it was like pushing a stone up a hill. The Law was powerless to change him. It was overwhelmed by the prevailing disposition of his soul.

Parents often struggle over this with their children. They raise them in the discipline of an ordered home; they shower them with material things and bring them to church to give them a good dose of the religious program. Then they are alarmed to find that there is still a prevailing disposition in the soul that takes their children in a wrong direction. And when they see this, they say, "What can we do?"

Perhaps you see that same struggle in yourself. After a great trauma, an accident, or a near death experience that was absolutely terrifying, you feel that you need to change and take a different path. But when you try, you find that you are up against the prevailing disposition of your soul. Or perhaps you started coming to church and studying the Bible, hoping that it would change you. But then you found to your astonishment that the prevailing dispositions of your soul toward selfishness, pride, lust, and greed are every bit as strong as they were before.

A CHANGE OF HEART

So the great question is, How can we get the law of God into our hearts? If we can find the answer to that question, we will have discovered the secret of real and lasting change. God answers that question in Jeremiah 31.

Notice that God says, "I *will put* my law...on their hearts" (31:33; italics added). The story of the Old Testament demonstrates that no matter how heard you try, there is no way that you can align your heart with the law of God. So God says, "I will do what you are incapable of doing. I will write My law on your heart." God made the same promise to the prophet Ezekiel. "I will give you a new heart and put a new spirit in you" (36:26).

The technical word for this is *regeneration*. It is God changing the prevailing disposition of the heart. And when God does it, you find something deep within you that wants to know Him in a way that you didn't want to know Him before. You have a new hunger and thirst for the Word of God. You feel drawn to Christ and become responsive to God.

The best illustration I know of this new life in the soul is the way in which human life begins. The living seed comes, and in a secret, mysterious, and wonderful way, new life is conceived. It is instantaneous. It happens in a moment! Hidden within the woman's body there is a new life, and here is the amazing thing: At that moment, she may not even be aware of it!

Lasting change is something that God does. The next day she goes to work, and it seems that everything is exactly as it was before. But some weeks later, she begins to feel that something has changed inside her. She does not feel quite as she felt before, and she thinks, *I wonder if I could be pregnant?*

That is how new life begins, and it is a wonderful picture of how new life begins in the heart. It is a direct work of the Spirit of God to implant the seed of the life of God in your soul. And that has either happened or it has not happened. There's nothing in between.

This may have happened to you and you don't even know it yet. But, like every pregnancy, it will eventually show! Repentance and faith in the Lord Jesus Christ are the first visible evidence of new life that comes from God. But it all begins with God changing the heart! This is what He promised to Jeremiah: "I will write My Law on their hearts." He will bring this inner change to the fundamental disposition of the soul.

It's natural for us to want a program or a plan to change our own hearts. "Pastor, make it simple! Give me five steps to lasting change and I'll try three of them!" But lasting change is something that God does. And God says that He will do for you what you cannot do for yourself. This is why David prayed, "Create in me a clean heart." He realized that the only way to change would be for God to change him. This is precisely what God promises to do in the new covenant.

Perhaps you can look back and see how God has done this in your life, and it's wonderful to you. There was a time when you were unresponsive to God. You came to church, but it did not mean much to you; the whole thing was on the outside. But then things began to change inside you. All you knew was that you had a new hunger for God, a sense of need, a desire to be clean. You couldn't explain it! You didn't know it at the time, but the life of God was implanted within you by the power of the Holy Spirit.

Has this happened to you? Is there, at the core of your being, a deep hunger and thirst after God? That desire is something that God has placed within you. He is fulfilling His promise and changing your heart.

SPOTLIGHT ON CHRIST

Nobody ever spoke more powerfully about the state of the human heart than our Lord Jesus Christ. He said,

> *"Out of men's hearts, come evil thoughts, sexual immorality, theft, murder, adultery, greed, malice, deceit, lewdness, envy, slander, arrogance and folly. All these evils come from inside and make a man 'unclean.'"* (MARK 7:21–23)

On one occasion, a deeply religious man called Nicodemus came to talk with Jesus. Jesus knew that his fundamental problem was that he needed a new heart. His life was an uphill struggle of attempting to please God. Jesus said, "You must be born again" (John 3:7).

Nicodemus pointed out that it would be difficult for a middle-aged man to return to his mother's womb, but Jesus explained that He was not talking about a physical birth but a spiritual one. Just as flesh gives birth to flesh, it is the Holy Spirit who gives birth to spirit. The Holy Spirit could do what God had promised through Jeremiah, and give Nicodemus a new heart.

Nicodemus needed a work of the Holy Spirit within him that would redirect the prevailing disposition of his soul. The result, a repentant and believing heart, would lead him to be a lifelong follower of Jesus.

When you are in the presence of Christ, what is at the heart of you will become the whole of you. In other words, if God has implanted that new life in your heart, then the deepest desire of your heart will be satisfied. In God's presence, you will become the person you always wanted to be. And until then, there will be a process of wonderful growth in that direction.

If the prevailing disposition of your heart is toward sin, it is still true that in eternity, what is at the heart of you will become the whole of you. One of the most terrifying statements in the Bible is when God says, "Let him who does wrong continue to do wrong; let him who is vile continue to be vile" (Revelation 22:11). In eternity, you will have the desire of your heart. What is the prevailing disposition of your soul?

UNLOCKED

The problem of the human heart is that it is written over with the graffiti of sin. Our great need is that the Law of God should be written in our heart so that it is not just an external command, but an internal desire. But it is not possible for us to make this change in our hearts. Only God can write His Law within our hearts. This is the work of the Holy Spirit, which is sometimes referred to as *regeneration*.

If you want your heart changed, you need to cast yourself upon God. You may be able to change your circumstances and even your behavior, but you cannot change the prevailing disposition of your heart. Only God can do that.

PAUSE FOR PRAYER

Almighty Father,

I confess that without Your Spirit, I would not love You or hunger after You. So thank You for putting within me a true desire to live for Your glory. Deepen that hunger within me. Strengthen my desire to follow You in a life of faith and obedience. Nourish the life that You have implanted within me.

Thank You that along with the commands of Your law You have given me a desire to obey and, by the power of Your Holy Spirit, the ability to pursue that desire.

In Jesus' name I pray. Amen.

Tears

LAMENTATIONS

How should

I deal with

discouragement

in God's

service?

10 Tears

LAMENTATIONS

DISCOVER
why God values your tears.

LEARN
how God's plan continued when His city was destroyed and His people were scattered.

WORSHIP
the God who will one day wipe away all tears from our eyes.

722   END OF NORTH
        KINGDOM

700 B.C.

640–609 JOSIAH

— JEREMIAH —

606–536 BABYLONIAN
         CAPTIVITY

608–598 JEHOIAKIM

600

598–597 JEHOIACHIM
597–586 ZEDEKIAH

586   FALL OF JERUSALEM

536   FIRST RETURN
         TO JERUSALEM

500

THIS is God's world, but it is not as He made it. It has been spoiled by an intruder, and that is why God will not allow this world to remain as it is forever. God will create a new heaven and a new earth, and when He does, the old order of things will pass away. Cancer will pass away. War will pass away. Terrorist outrages will pass away. Pain will pass away. Death will pass away. God promises that He will make everything new (Revelation 21:5).

In the meantime, the people of God are called to serve in this fallen world as it is. That means that we will shed tears. But it will not be like this forever. One day, in heaven, God will wipe away our every tear (Revelation 21:4).

Our tears can be traced back to sin in the Garden of Eden. When Adam and Eve sinned, there were two things that God could have done. He could have locked them *out of* the garden forever and left them to experience the full horrors of sin. He could have abandoned them to evil. But God did not do that because God is love, and the true lover will never abandon the loved.

Alternatively, God could have locked them *in* the garden. He could have banished the evil one to some remote corner of the universe, given him no access whatever to human beings, so that every external source of evil was removed from them. The problem with that, of course, was that Adam and Eve had a desire for the knowledge of evil, and keeping them from the possibility of evil would have been like imprisoning them. God did not do that because God is love, and true love never forces itself on a loved one.

What kind of relationship could there be between man and God if the only reason man was in God's presence was that he had no opportunity to explore the knowledge of evil outside the garden? It would be like a child suffering through adult company when he really wanted to go outside and play. Heaven would not be heaven if it were like a prison where people lived wanting to sin but were denied the opportunity! The great purpose of God is that eternity will be filled with the joy of those who have no desire for sin.

So how will this happen? How will God bring people who have a desire for evil to love Him freely so that their greatest joy will be to enjoy God and live in harmony with Him for all eternity? That is the great story of the Bible, and it involves a people, a place, and a purpose.

GOD'S DISCREET REVELATION

God has made Himself known discreetly, so that those who seek Him may find Him, and at the same time, those who do not want to know Him should be able to remain without Him forever. God revealed Himself to one man, Abraham, and said, "I will bless you…and [through you] all peoples on earth will be blessed" (Genesis 12:2–3).

We have followed the story of how God brought the nation of Israel from this one man. They were to be the channel of God's blessing to the world. God's purpose was that this community of people, rightly related to God, would model a life of worship and obedience to God's law so that the nations would be able to watch and then desire life under the authority and blessing of God.

Then God had designated a particular place where God would meet with His people. While God's people were in the desert, it was a movable place. God met with His people in the tabernacle, where the ark of the covenant was housed, and where the sacrifices were made. But when they came into the land, God said that there was to be a particular place where He would make His presence known (Deuteronomy 12:5). That place was the city of Jerusalem. King David made this city his capital, and when the ark, the symbol of God's presence, was brought to Jerusalem, there was great joy.

THE MOST BLESSED CITY ON EARTH

A few years later, David's son Solomon built a temple there, and when he did, the cloud of God's glory filled the whole place. This was the high-water mark of the Old Testament story. God's people were united, the place where God would meet with them was established, and God's purpose was beginning to be realized as kings and queens from surrounding nations came to Jerusalem to hear the wisdom of Solomon. Israel was the envy of the world. Jerusalem was the most blessed city on earth.

But all that changed very quickly. After the death of Solomon, the kingdom divided, and the quality of leadership among God's people was desperate. One king after another led the nation down the wrong track. The worship of other gods multiplied, and the whole basis of a moral life was lost.

God's people ended up being little different from the surrounding nations who never knew the Lord. Instead of true worship where God's presence was known among His people, there was hollow ritual. Instead of obedience among God's people, religious life was motivated by raw self-interest. Instead of God's blessing, there was increasing evidence of the clouds of God's judgment beginning to gather.

Instead of true worship where God's presence was known... there was hollow ritual.

Time after time, God sent His prophets to call His people back to paths of obedience, but there was little response. So finally, God drew a line in the sand, and judgment began. At this most desperate time, Jeremiah had the unenviable task of being God's mouthpiece.

As we saw in chapter 9, Jeremiah's ministry began during the reign of Josiah, the young king who led a personal crusade to clean up life around Jerusalem. He threw out the idols and personally supervised the destruction of pagan altars. No doubt many people would have thought this was a good thing, and it was so far as it went, but Jeremiah realized that unless there was a change in the hearts of the people, it would be short lived. And so it was.

When Josiah's son Jehoiakim came to the throne, he asked for the Word of God to be read, and then cut it up with a scribe's knife and threw it into the fire. It was during the reign of Jehoiakim that God's judgment on His people began. Nebuchadnezzar, the king of Babylon, laid a siege to Jerusalem. That was the way a city was conquered in those days. An army camped outside and waited until the people ran out of food and water, and then the Babylonian force went in and took over. That's what the Babylonian army did, and eventually they rounded up the most talented people in the city of Jerusalem, including a young man called Daniel, whose story we will come to later.

THE KING WITH THE CHIN

When the best leaders are taken out of a community, people of lesser ability are promoted to take their place, and after the siege, Jehoiakim's son Jehoiachin (also known as Jeconiah) came to the throne at the age of eighteen. I have a caricature of him in my mind with a huge protruding chin, and probably a very large beard to cover its eccentricity! No one knows, of course, the size of this king's chin, but it's a great way to remember Jehoiachin's name. King Jehoiachin was eighteen years old when he came to power, and it is hardly surprising that Nebuchadnezzar seized the opportunity of sending another expeditionary force. Jehoiachin's reign lasted only three months.

This time the Babylonians took about 10,000 of the most able people from Jerusalem. This group included a colorful character called Ezekiel, whose story we will come to later. He was taken off to join Daniel and the rest in Babylon, and young King Jehoiachin was taken with them. At the age of eighteen, Jehoiachin didn't have a son to succeed him as king in Jerusalem, and so his uncle Zedekiah took the position. They were running out of members of the royal family!

THE DARKEST HOUR BEFORE THE DAWN

Zedekiah had to decide how to handle a difficult situation. Should he try to form an alliance with some other countries to stand up to Nebuchadnezzar, or should he accept that Nebuchadnezzar's power was within the plan of God and submit to it? Jeremiah was in no doubt about the answer. Jerusalem would fall; it was time to surrender to the king of Babylon (Jeremiah 38:17). But Zedekiah didn't like that message, so he ignored the Word of God.

King Zedekiah decided, with a bit of encouragement from Egypt, that he would rebel against Nebuchadnezzar. He did, and sure enough, the armies of Babylon came and laid another siege against the city. What happened was just about as bad as it gets.

> Nebuzaradan commander of the imperial guard, who served the king of Babylon, came to Jerusalem. He set fire to the temple of the LORD, the royal palace and all the houses of Jerusalem. Every important building he burned down. The whole Babylonian army under the commander of the imperial guard broke down all the walls around Jerusalem. Nebuzaradan the commander of the guard carried into exile some of the poorest people and those who remained in the city, along with the rest

of the craftsmen and those who had gone over to the king of Babylon. But Nebuzaradan left behind the rest of the poorest people of the land to work the vineyards and fields. (52 :12–16)

Then, in an unspeakable act of cruelty, all of Zedekiah's sons were killed before his eyes. Then, Zedekiah's eyes were put out, and he was taken to Babylon where he died a short time later (2 Kings 25:7).

This was the lowest point and the darkest hour in the whole story of the Old Testament. The temple, where God's presence had been known, was destroyed. All the king's sons had been killed. The city where God had put His name was destroyed. The people in the north had been scattered, and now the people in the south were taken into exile in Babylon. What hope could there be now for the purpose of God?

Lamentations ...is a lament, a book written in tears.

It was at this lowest point that the book of Lamentations was written. Jeremiah was walking through the rubble, with the smoke still rising from the ashes of the once beautiful temple where God's presence had been known. The walls that had once been a strong defense against the enemies of God's people were completely destroyed. There was hardly one stone on top of another.

When Jeremiah saw this, it broke his heart. That is why the book is called *Lamentations*. It is a lament, a book written in tears. It is the cry of a heart that had been broken by the torn-down state of the work of God in the world.

THE TEARS OF ONE WHO CARES

Try to picture Jeremiah walking through the rubble, with dust and smoke still rising from the ashes. "How deserted lies the city, once so full of people!" he began (Lamentations 1:1). The city that once was a thriving community under the blessing of God, now seems like a ghost town. Jeremiah looked down the roads that once were crowded with happy people making their way up to Jerusalem to worship God and saw no one. "The roads to Zion mourn, for no one comes to her appointed feasts," he wrote (1:4). The roads were deserted, because there was no city for guests to visit.

All the splendor has departed from the Daughter of Zion. (1:6)

He thought about the temple, the royal palace, exquisite craftsmanship, now all reduced to rubble. Now there was no place for the sacrifices to be made. There was no place for worship, no meeting place between God and man.

*My eyes fail from weeping, I am in torment within, my heart is
poured out on the ground because my people are destroyed. (2:11)*

Now Jeremiah's tears began to flow. Notice, though, that Jeremiah was not shedding
tears over personal pain or loss. God has important things to say to us about that issue
(we have looked at some of them in the book of Job), but that is not the issue here.
The book of Lamentations is about a godly man whose heart is broken over the state
of the work of God in the world. He is weeping over Jerusalem.

If you set out in ministry with the idea that strong faith mixed with hard work and
prayer will lead to unbroken success and blessing in the work of God, you will be
in for some big disappointments. That's a key truth, and it is so important that God
has given us a whole book of the Bible to teach it to us. God's work often advances
through tears.

Jeremiah became known as "the weeping prophet." I don't want to make too big a
thing about shedding tears, because some people are naturally more moist than others. But however you express emotion, freely or with greater reserve, you can't live
a life of service to God without sometimes experiencing a broken heart. If you have
never experienced that, it may be either that your heart is insensitive, or that you
have never given yourself fully to the work of God.

A heart that cares will break over squandered opportunities, over sin in the church,
over souls that might have been saved but were not, over the suffering of those who
are persecuted, and over the hardness of an unbelieving world. But these are good
tears, because they are the tears of a person who cares.

The tears of
God's people
are of great
value to God.

The apostle Paul shared the same experience. "For I wrote you
out of great distress and anguish of heart and with many tears,
not to grieve you but to let you know the depth of my love
for you" (2 Corinthians 2:4). On another occasion, he
told the church in Galatia that ministry was like giving birth!
"I am again in the pains of childbirth until Christ is formed
in you" (Galatians 4:19).

Perhaps you have thrown yourself into some venture for Christ. You wanted to see
His blessing and His purpose advance in the world, but you have come up against
overwhelming difficulties that you find impossible to explain. It breaks your heart
and causes you to cry out to God. You are weeping over "Jerusalem."

It doesn't help for someone to say, "Cheer up; you know it will work out in the end." That can sometimes be offensive, because it does not recognize the reality or the value of your pain. What you need to know is that God values your tears.

David once asked the Lord to collect his tears in a bottle (Psalm 56:8 NKJV). That is a beautiful picture. The tears of God's people are of great value to God, because they are the tears of people who care. When your heart is breaking over the work of God, you are giving one of the most precious offerings of worship in the sight of God. God's work advances through many tears.

GOD'S PURPOSE WILL FINALLY PREVAIL

If the people God had chosen to bless were scattered, and the place God had chosen to put His name was destroyed, what hope could there possibly be of God fulfilling His promise and bringing blessing to the world? If the last king's sons were all killed, what future could there be for the royal line of David?

The answer lay in the man with the chin, the eighteen-year-old king who only lasted three months before he surrendered and was taken off into exile in Babylon. Jeremiah tells us that Jehoiachin was released. "Jehoiachin put aside his prison clothes and for the rest of his life ate regularly at the king's table" (Jeremiah 52:33). His life was preserved, and so the royal line was continued. And when Matthew lists the royal line of David into which Jesus Christ was born, Jehoiachin (or Jeconiah) has an honored place (1:11). The king who lasted three months and did nothing but surrender to the enemy became a link in the chain that leads us to Christ!

Of course, Jeremiah did not know that when he was walking through the ruined city of Jerusalem and writing the book of Lamentations. If we had asked him how God's promise of a Savior who would be born into the line of David could happen given that all King Zedekiah's sons were dead, I don't suppose he would have had the faintest idea. But he believed that God is faithful to His promise, and he staked his trust and hope on the faithfulness of God:

> Yet this I call to mind and therefore I have hope: Because of the
> LORD's great love we are not consumed, for his compassions
> never fail. They are new every morning; great is your faithful-
> ness. (3:21–23)

Looking back over the centuries, it is a wonderful thing to see that even in the darkest hour, God is faithful.

SPOTLIGHT ON CHRIST

After seventy years, a small group of people returned to the ruined site of Jerusalem and rebuilt the city. Then, about five hundred years later, Jesus Christ came to the city, and like Jeremiah, He wept over it.

> *"O Jerusalem, Jerusalem, you who kill the prophets and stone those sent to you, how often I have longed to gather your children together, as a hen gathers her chicks under her wings, but you were not willing!"* (LUKE 13:34)

Later He came back to the city, and "as he approached Jerusalem and saw the city, he wept over it and said, 'If you, even you, had only known on this day what would bring you peace—but now it is hidden from your eyes'" (Luke 19:41–42).

The city where God had placed His name did not want to receive His Son. God came to His own city and was herded out of it and nailed to a cross. But in His death and resurrection, Christ accomplished the purpose of God, and He is the channel by which the blessing of God will come to all the nations of the earth.

People with a sensitive heart will still weep over Jerusalem today. But at the end of the Bible, God gave the apostle John a vision of how the story will end. John tells us that he saw "the Holy City, the new Jerusalem" (Revelation 21:2). That's Jerusalem as God intended it to be. The place for God's people, where God has put His name and where His purposes will be fulfilled.

That New Jerusalem will come "down out of heaven from God, prepared as a bride beautifully dressed for her husband" (Revelation 21:2). And John reports that a loud voice from God's throne will announce:

> *"Now the dwelling of God is with men, and he will live with them. They will be his people, and God himself will be with them and be their God. He will wipe every tear from their eyes. There will be no more death or mourning or crying or pain, for the old order of things has passed away. He who was seated on the throne said, 'I am making everything new!'"* (REVELATION 21:3–5)

There is nothing greater in all the world than to be one of God's people, fulfilling God's purpose and headed for God's place. God's work may advance through many tears, but God's purpose will always finally prevail. Weeping goes on for the night, but joy comes in the morning (see Psalm 30:5). God's people know the day is coming when "God will wipe away every tear from their eyes" (Revelation 7:17). Can you imagine God doing that for you?

Whatever the circumstances you face in ministry, whether God calls you to serve Him at a high-water mark in the story of His people or at the darkest hour before the dawn, "Let nothing move you. Always give yourselves fully to the work of the Lord, because you know that your labor in the Lord is not in vain" (1 Corinthians 15:58).

UNLOCKED

Knowing how to handle discouragement is a key to sustaining a lifetime of ministry. Unrealistic expectations usually lead to deep disappointment, and the Bible story reminds us that there are no instant formulas for success in God's work. Ministry often advances through tears, and learning that principle will help us when we face discouragement.

Remember that God values the tears of a person who cares about His kingdom. A broken heart can often be a sign of spiritual health. Our deepest ministry may come out of a broken heart.

We can thank God that Lamentations is not the last book in the Bible. God was working His purpose out even at a time when Jeremiah would have been unable to see how any good could ever come out of the ashes of the ruined city of Jerusalem. God is faithful. The day will come when all His people will be gathered and made perfect in His presence, and His purpose for all eternity will begin.

PAUSE FOR PRAYER

Gracious Father,

Thank You that You value the tears of a person who cares about Your kingdom. Give me a passion to see Your name honored and Your purpose fulfilled in the world. When my heart is broken, help me to offer my tears to You as worship, the expression of a heart that cares.

Strengthen those who face particular discouragement in Your work at this time and give them a glimpse of Your faithfulness. Help them to trust in the amazing power by which all of Your purposes will be fulfilled. Thank You that the day is coming when You will wipe every tear from the eyes of Your people.

Through Jesus Christ my Lord I pray. Amen.

Glory

EZEKIEL 1, 10

In what sense is

God's presence

always with us?

*11*Glory

EZEKIEL 1, 10

DISCOVER
the amazing story of God's flying platform.

LEARN
how God deals with persistent sin among His people.

WORSHIP
Christ who is the glory with us.

722	END OF NORTH KINGDOM
700 B.C.	
606–536	BABYLONIAN CAPTIVITY
605	FIRST DEPORTATION
600	
597–586	ZEDEKIAH
586	FALL OF JERUSALEM
516	REBUILT TEMPLE COMPLETED
500	

EZEKIEL

MOST adults look forward to their thirtieth birthday. They're far beyond a "just starting" twenty-one, but certainly not entering the middle age of forty. A career often is taking off; a family may be growing (or starting). But for the prophet Ezekiel, the thirtieth birthday may have been the hardest day of his life.

Ezekiel had spent his whole life preparing for a ministry in the temple of God, but at age twenty-five, in the middle of his training, war broke out and he was carted off as a hostage to the Kebar River, which must have seemed like the other end of the earth. Now, five years later, he reached his thirtieth birthday, and all that he could think of was what might have been.

A priest's thirtieth birthday was the day on which his ministry in the temple would begin, and if Ezekiel had been back home, it would have been a great day of celebration. But what can a new priest do if he is seven hundred miles away from the temple?

The whole situation must have seemed like a disaster. Ezekiel was a man with crushed hopes and shattered dreams. If only he had lived at another time. If only he had not been taken from his home by the Babylonians. If only! But now circumstances seemed to have blocked his path to ministry, and he found himself among a group of confused and discouraged people in a backwater near Babylon.

Perhaps you can relate to Ezekiel. Maybe you had high hopes and big dreams, but in your wildest imagination you didn't ever think you'd be in the situation you find yourself in now. And you wonder, "What on earth is God doing in my life?"

That was where Ezekiel was. But then something wonderful happened:

> *In the thirtieth year, in the fourth month on the fifth day, while*
> *I was among the exiles by the Kebar River, the heavens were*
> *opened and I saw visions of God. (1:1)*

God met this displaced and disappointed man. And he discovered something far greater than lighting candles or offering sacrifices in the temple. God showed this man His glory, and when Ezekiel saw the glory of God, he was able to find his way forward.

When we face times of confusion and circumstances that are hard to understand, or when we find ourselves in a place we never thought we would be, our greatest need is to get a glimpse of the glory of God. Then, like Ezekiel, we will find direction for our lives.

THE GLORY APPEARS

Ezekiel saw "an immense cloud with flashing lightning and surrounded by brilliant light" (1:4). It must have been like gazing through smoke into a blazing fire. As Ezekiel looked into this cloud, he could see four living creatures. We find out later that they are cherubim (10:1, 9–10), and they are described here in symbolic language.

Each of them had four faces and four wings (1:6). Their faces represent the pinnacles of God's creation, the face of a lion (speaking of nobility), an ox (speaking of strength), an eagle (speaking either of speed or more likely compassion), and the face of a man (representing the highest point of God's creation). These angels had four wings. They were positioned in a kind of square, with their wings connecting at the corners, and above them was an "expanse, sparkling like ice" (1:22), like a platform of some sort. Above the platform rested the throne of God (vv. 10–12, 26).

Then Ezekiel saw some wheels. Even people who have never read the Bible have probably heard the song "Ezekiel Saw Da Wheels." The wheels that he saw were sparkling, and each wheel was intersected by another wheel. If you can imagine a wheel facing north to south, being intersected by another wheel going east to west, then you have the picture. These wheels could move in any one of four directions, which would be extremely useful if you were parking your car and found yourself two feet from the sidewalk. You could just switch to lateral mode, and slide in!

These wheels gave mobility to this giant platform upon which the throne of God was situated. Bible scholar Don Carson compared their movements to that of a cursor on a computer screen. Up and down, left to right, but never diagonally. This is telling us that the glory of God's presence is not fixed to any one location. There are no restrictions on God. You cannot tie Him down. He is free to move in any direction.

Then Ezekiel saw that the cherubim who were supporting the platform could also rise or fall (Ezekiel 1:19), so that the whole platform could take off like a helicopter. This, no doubt, is why people who get excited about UFOs are drawn to the book of Ezekiel. But of course, this has nothing whatever to do with UFOs. This is a vision of the majesty and glory of God.

Then, we discover something that often appears in Ezekiel, Daniel, and the book of Revelation, and that is a mixed metaphor. We are told that the wheels were "full of eyes" (Ezekiel 1:18). This is simply a way of saying that nothing is hidden from the throne of God. Just as there is no place that God cannot go, so there is nothing that God cannot see.

As Ezekiel peered at this incredible vision, he just kept looking up and up, like a small boy at the foot of the Washington Monument. Above the creatures, there was a "sparkling expanse," or platform. Above the platform, he saw "what looked like a throne of sapphire," and high above the throne he saw "a figure like that of a man" (v. 26). He looked like fire, and brilliant light surrounded him.

"When I saw it, I fell facedown."

The higher Ezekiel looked, the more difficult it was to find words to express what he saw. The best description he can give is to say, "This was the appearance of the likeness of the glory of the LORD. When I saw it, I fell facedown" (v. 28).

Pastor and author Stuart Briscoe has said that Ezekiel's putting what he saw into words would have been like a man hearing Beethoven's Fifth Symphony and then being given a tin whistle, and asked to convey to people who had never heard an orchestra what it sounded like. How could anyone do that? Ezekiel was struggling for words. All that he could really say was that when he saw the glory of the Lord, he fell facedown.

The glory of God appeared. There is no place God cannot go, and nothing that He cannot see. He is high and exalted, enthroned above the angels on the throne of the universe.

SCANDAL IN THE TEMPLE

Some time later, some of the leaders of the exiled community by the Kebar River came to Ezekiel's house (Ezekiel 8:1). While they were there, the Spirit of God came on the prophet and he saw another vision. This time he saw the temple in Jerusalem, and looking from the north gate, he saw a massive idol. When he looked in the other direction, toward the center of the temple area, he saw the same glory of the Lord that he had seen in his earlier vision (8:2–4).

It was as if God was squaring off with the idol. The Lord was getting ready to destroy the false worship that had taken over His own temple. There were many false prophets who were telling the people that Jerusalem could never fall because the temple of God was there (Jeremiah 7:4–8). But now God was showing Ezekiel not only that Jerusalem would fall, but that Jerusalem would fall because God had determined to destroy His own temple!

Then the Lord brought Ezekiel, in this vision, to a hole in the wall in the temple court. Ezekiel found a secret door, and God invited him to look inside. When he did, Ezekiel found images of all kinds of detestable animals and idols scrawled on the walls of the temple of God (8:7–10). They may have been astrological signs, going back to the time of Manasseh (2 Kings 21:5).

God was making it clear that, even in the temple, obscene things were going on in secret, and people were saying, "The LORD does not see us" (Ezekiel 8:12). That's what happens when people lose their vision of God. If they had seen Ezekiel's vision of the wheel full of eyes, they would never have dreamt of saying, "The LORD does not see us." God sees everything!

So now it was very clear to Ezekiel. The days of the temple were numbered. Judgment was coming to the household of God. God was coming to destroy His temple.

THE GLORY DEPARTS
Some time later, Ezekiel saw the vision of the glory of God again. He saw the cherubim (four creatures), the platform, the wheels, and the throne of God. But when he saw what happened next, he must have been completely horrified.

> The glory of the LORD rose from above the cherubim and moved to the threshold of the temple. (10:4)

The wheeled vehicle was moving from the center of the sanctuary toward the door. God was getting on the moving platform to leave His own temple!

There was one simple message behind all this rather strange imagery. God's presence was on the move. God had summoned His wheeled platform and was about to leave the city where He had put His name. God was heading off!

The great question, of course, was where was God's platform heading? As the vision unfolded, Ezekiel discovered the answer. First

> The glory of the LORD departed from over the threshold of the temple and stopped above the cherubim. (10:18)

But soon,

> The cherubim, with the wheels beside them, spread their wings, and the glory of the God of Israel was above them. The glory of the LORD went up from within the city and stopped over the mountain east of it. (11:22–23)

This must have been an awful thing for Ezekiel to see. He probably thought back to the days of Solomon when the glory of God filled the temple. Jerusalem was the place where God had placed His name. People had said Zion could never fall, for God was within her. But now Ezekiel sees in his vision the glory of the Lord moving from the temple to the edge of the city, and now, outside of the edge of the city, to a mountain in the east.

[God] had not abandoned His people or His promises.

But suddenly it must have dawned on Ezekiel. God had already given him a vision of this same flying platform, by the Kebar River! God was abandoning Jerusalem, but He had not abandoned His people or His promises. The focus of His redeeming work was moving away from Jerusalem, and was now focused on this strange backwater, the Kebar River, where ten thousand of God's people would be preserved and eventually in the goodness of God, they would be brought back.

That's why God said, "For a little while I have been a sanctuary for them in the countries where they have gone" (11:16). But then He also said, "I will gather you from the nations and bring you back" (11:17). And God promised that when they were brought back, they would have a changed heart and a new spirit (vv. 19–20).

This must have been wonderful news for Ezekiel. The man who thought that his door to ministry was closed at age thirty because he was seven hundred miles from the temple, now discovered that he was in the very center of the will of God! God's presence was leaving the temple, and His glory would now be made known among an obscure group of displaced people beside the Kebar River. Ezekiel was at the center of the action after all!

THE GLORY RETURNS

Twenty years after Ezekiel's first vision of the glory of the Lord, the prophet was still ministering to the exiles by the Kebar River. Ezekiel was fifty years old when God spoke to him again (Ezekiel 40).

God gave Ezekiel a vision of a massive temple. Its dimensions were not in yards, but in miles. It was one gigantic place of worship. The scale of this temple is emphasized over and over, as the huge measurements of every wall and gate are given in painstaking detail. There is some debate as to whether this is referring to a literal temple to be built in Jerusalem at the end times or whether it is referring to the worship of all God's people in the New Jerusalem in Revelation 21–22. Certainly, the descriptions are very similar.

The significant thing for Ezekiel was that in the vision he saw "the glory of the God of Israel coming from the east" (43:2). The east, of course, was the direction in which the glory of God had headed twenty years earlier when the Lord had abandoned His temple and focused His redeeming work on the community of His people by the Kebar River. Ezekiel wrote, "The vision I saw was like the vision I had seen when [God] came to destroy the city and like the visions I had seen by the Kebar River, and I fell facedown" (43:3).

What he saw next must have brought joy to his heart.

> The glory of the LORD entered the temple through the gate facing east…and the glory of the LORD filled the temple. (43:4–5)

Have you got the picture? Ezekiel was a desperately discouraged person who must have wondered what God was doing in his life. But he saw the glory of God and realized that there was no place God could not go, and nothing that God could not see.

Then God showed Ezekiel that the focus of His redeeming work for the next seventy years would not be on the temple in Jerusalem; it would be with the people in the east, by the Kebar River. God would not abandon the city of Jerusalem where He had placed His name forever. There would come a time when God's presence would return to the great city, and His glory would fill a new temple. But this new temple would not be like the old one that had been destroyed. It would be massive, beyond any scale of imagination. It would be so large that it would become a center of worship for people of every tribe and nation who would turn from their idols and seek the true and living God.

THIS COULD BE YOUR STORY

Ezekiel saw the glory of God when he was thirty years old. He was a gifted man in the prime of life, yet he found himself relegated to an obscure backwater in Babylon. His prospects seemed bleak, his personal hopes for the future shattered. There must have been times when he sat down by the Kebar River hundreds of miles from home and said to himself, *This isn't how it was supposed to be!*

Maybe you have felt like that. Something happened in your life that shattered your dream, and you say to yourself, *This isn't how it was supposed to be! I never imagined I would be in this situation.* Or maybe God has taken you from a place where you were happy and blessed and put you somewhere else. It is not easy when God puts you in a place you would rather not be.

Think about Ezekiel's flying platform. It reminds you that God's glory and His blessing are not limited to one place. If God moves you on to another place, then His presence will go with you. He says, "I will never leave you nor forsake you." He sees you and knows all about you. Remember, there is no place on earth where His presence cannot go. Ezekiel discovered that it was better to be in Babylon with the presence of God, than to be in Jerusalem without it!

THIS IS THE CHURCH'S STORY

The story of the church is a story of the movements of God. There have been times when God's presence has come to His people. We call those movements *revivals.* And there have been times when God's presence has left. Christ spoke through John the apostle to the church in Ephesus, telling them He would remove His presence from them if they did not repent.

A church without Christ's presence is like the temple without God's glory, nothing more than an empty shell. It is not difficult to find places that were once great centers of gospel preaching with thriving churches, where there is very little evidence of spiritual life today.

The church needs the presence of God like the human body needs blood. Without the blood, the body cannot sustain life. Without the Spirit of God, the church becomes like a corpse. A local church may have many strengths and assets, but take away the presence of God, and none of them will amount to anything much for long.

Though Ezekiel's glimpse of the flying platform of God's presence was only a vision, I find it helpful to think of God's presence also hovering over the ministry of the church where I serve. God's presence empowers the local church. That is why we must be careful not to grieve the Spirit of God. God's Spirit is a sensitive guest among His people.

THIS IS THE BIBLE STORY

If you understand the story of Ezekiel, you will be able to understand the story of the whole Bible. Remember, the Bible story began in a garden—which was God's place. The man and the woman enjoyed the presence and the blessing of God there. He not only hovered over them, He came down and walked with them.

But then they turned away from Him and chose to experience evil. And when they did, they were thrown out of God's place, just as God's people were thrown out of the city of Jerusalem. Indeed the place itself was destroyed. The Garden of Eden is nowhere to be found today. But although they were thrown out of God's place, God did not abandon them. He came to this strange, alien, and sometimes hostile place in which we live so that those who would seek Him might find Him and know His presence.

And God will bring His people back, not to the Garden of Eden, but to a new creation, greater and more glorious than anything we have ever seen before. The Bible story points forward to the time when the great exile of human history will be over and God's people will be brought to God's place, to enjoy His presence forever.

SPOTLIGHT ON CHRIST

Six hundred years after Ezekiel's visions, Jerusalem had been rebuilt and a new temple had taken the place of the old one. Into this setting was born Jesus Christ, "the radiance of God's glory and the exact representation of his being" (Hebrews 1:3). The glory of God came down among us. The apostle John wrote, "We have seen his glory, the glory of the One and Only, who came from the Father, full of grace and truth" (John 1:14).

God came off the platform! The eternal creator, the Lord of glory, came down from the throne, took human flesh, and was born in a small town outside Jerusalem. The one who sat on the throne upheld by angels lay in a manger and the angels looked down on Him.

Not only did the Lord of glory come down from the platform, but in Jesus Christ, the glory of God came to the temple. And just as Ezekiel had seen in his vision that the temple needed to be cleansed, Christ saw that the temple had become a den of thieves and robbers. Christ came to the temple, and day after day He taught the things of God.

But the people did not want Him, so the glory of God left the temple, not on a flying platform, but bound and escorted by guards with swords and clubs. The glory of God left Jerusalem, bearing a cross to a place called Calvary outside the city wall, and there the Lord of glory was crucified.

Then, on the third day, He rose from the dead. It was impossible for death to keep hold of Him. For forty days, He appeared to His disciples giving "many convincing proofs that he was alive" (Acts 1:3). Then Christ went to a mountain that is east of the city, called the Mount of Olives. Christ stood on the very spot where Ezekiel had seen the glory of God hovering as the platform left the temple, and then as the disciples watched, Christ ascended into the presence of the Father. He has returned to the throne that Ezekiel saw in his vision.

Then an angel appeared to the disciples and said, "Why do you stand here looking into the sky? This same Jesus, who has been taken from you into heaven, will come back in the same way you have seen him go into heaven" (Acts 1:11).

The glory of God appeared. The glory departed from the city as He was rejected and crucified outside Jerusalem. The glory has returned to the throne in heaven, and the glory of God will come again. That is where all history is headed.

On that day we will go one better than Ezekiel. He saw the Lord descend in a vision. We will be caught up to meet Him in the air, and so we will be forever with the Lord.

UNLOCKED

God is omnipresent. That means that He is always present in every place. Nothing is hidden from Him. But the Bible also makes it clear that there is a sense in which God's presence comes to His people, and at times may be withdrawn from His people. It is possible for us to grieve the Spirit, and there may be times when God hides His presence from us. This is why Paul tells us that he exercised discipline in his personal life because, having preached to others, he did not want to become disqualified (1 Corinthians 9:27). Paul was not worried that he would lose his salvation, but he was deeply concerned about losing his usefulness in ministry.

Christ made it clear to the churches in the book of Revelation that if they refused to repent from patterns of persistent sin, a time would come when Christ would withdraw His own presence from them. That is why the church must be careful not to grieve the Spirit of God.

This is also why we should pray for revival. God can do more in us and through us than any of us have experienced. Paul prayed that the church would be filled with all the fullness of God (Ephesians 3:19). Think of what that would be like!

PAUSE FOR PRAYER

Almighty God,

I lift my heart in worship and praise to You the God who knows all things and from whom no secrets are hidden. Cleanse the hidden and secret places of my heart so that there will be no area of my life of which I would be ashamed in Your presence. Fill my life with the presence and power of Your Holy Spirit today, and guard my way so that I may not grieve You by sinning against You.

Come to Your church so that Your people may have a new sense of Your glory, majesty, and power. Revive your church, I pray.

Thank You that one day all Your people will see Your glory. Through Jesus Christ I pray. Amen.

Shepherd

EZEKIEL 34

What does

effective

leadership

look like?

*12*Shepherd

EZEKIEL 34

DISCOVER
how God evaluates ministry.

LEARN
the key indicators of a
healthy church.

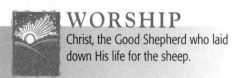

WORSHIP
Christ, the Good Shepherd who laid
down His life for the sheep.

FOR some years after we were married, my wife, Karen, worked as a teacher in a London school. The buildings were run down, there was a shortage of books and materials, and morale among the staff was low. The school principal had resigned in frustration, and the place was being run by a deputy head who was about to retire and didn't want the responsibility.

Eventually a new principal was appointed. On her first day in the school she called a staff meeting. "This school," she said, "has the reputation of being the worst in the area, and I intend to make it the best." Newer members of the staff thought this was marvelous; those who had been around a long time found it insulting, but what she said was true, and over the next years she led the school in a remarkable turnaround in standards.

The experience of any group of people will largely be determined by the quality of their leadership. So when we talk about leadership, we are looking at an issue that affects every one of our lives. The experience of every family, school, business, church, and nation will largely depend on the quality of its leadership.

It should come as no surprise that the Bible has a great deal to say about this subject. In one sense the whole of the Old Testament is a story about leadership, and most of it is about leadership failures. The story leaves us asking, "Who will lead God's people into the blessing that God wants them to enjoy?"

THREE KINDS OF LEADERS: THE PROPHET, PRIEST, AND KING

There are three distinct leadership roles in the Old Testament. The first of these was the role of the prophet who was to stand in the presence of God and hear the Word of God so that he could speak that Word to the people. The prophet gave leadership in the realm of truth.

Second, there was the role of the priests who operated in the temple. Their function was to offer the prayers and sacrifices. Their ministry related to worship; it was all about bringing people into the presence of God. You could go to a priest in the temple and he would pray with you. The priests offered a kind of pastoral counsel to people in relation to their spiritual lives. The role of the priest was the mirror image of the role of the prophet. The prophet spoke to men on behalf of God; the priest spoke to God on behalf of men.

Then there was the king, who would lead the people into battle and protect them from their enemies. He was also responsible for leading the people in right paths, so that they would continue to enjoy the blessing of God.

These three dimensions of leadership run all the way through the Bible story. The prophet was to lead the people into truth, the priest was to bring people to God, and the king was to lead the people into righteousness. The ministry of the prophet was about revealing, the ministry of the priest was about reconciling, and the ministry of the king was about ruling. These three ministries, taken together, show us God's plan for leadership.

The way in which God divided authority between the prophets, priests, and kings gave some checks and balances to leadership among God's people. The king ruled, but the prophet spoke the Word of God to the king. So you have Nathan coming to David, or Elijah coming to Ahab, or Jeremiah speaking to King Zedekiah, and telling them the Word of God.

The king ruled from the palace, but when he came to the temple, he was not allowed to offer a sacrifice. Only the priest could do that. Even the king in all his glory needed the priest to exercise that ministry of bringing him into the presence of God.

SPIRITUAL LEADERSHIP IN THE CHURCH

These three leadership roles are still essential to the health of the church today. The church needs the prophetic function of teaching the Word of God. This is not a matter of revealing some new truth received directly from God, because

God's revelation has been completed in Jesus Christ. But every church needs the ministry of the Word so that God's truth may be known among God's people.

Then there is a priestly function in the ministry of prayer and pastoral care. The church needs a ministry of prayer in which the needs of people are brought before God, and help is given to those who struggle with their consciences or need to find relief from guilt and fear. This is the heart of pastoral ministry.

Then there is a kingly function in the area of vision and direction. The church is called to fulfill a purpose, and we need leadership that will help us all to move in that direction. There must be administration, organization, and order within the church of God. And leaders must protect the flock of God from false teaching, and from sin that could hinder God's blessing on His people.

These three ministries will be a key indicator of the health of any local church. If you want to know about the spiritual state of a church, you could begin by asking questions like these?

1. Is there a strong, balanced, and sustained ministry of the Word so that the flock of God is being fed on a steady, healthy diet of truth?

2. Is there a ministry of prayer in which the needs of the people are brought before God privately and publicly, so that the wounded may be healed and the weak may be strengthened? Is the worship directed toward God, or is it primarily entertainment for the people?

3. Is there a sense of purpose and clarity of vision? Are the people protected from what is false so that God's people are guided in right paths, and protected from sin and error as the whole church pursues the purpose of God?

SPIRITUAL LEADERSHIP IN THE HOME

The ministries of prophet, priest, and king are central to leadership within the family. It is God's plan that in every home there should be a prophetic ministry of teaching God's truth to our children. Parents are also called to the priestly ministry of praying for our children and encouraging them in their knowledge of God.

In addition, parents are to perform a kingly ministry. They are to protect their children from an evil world and guide them into paths of righteousness. In any area of life, these are the foundational principles of leadership.

MINISTRIES FOR ALL GOD'S PEOPLE

The Scriptures tell us that, through Christ, the ministries of prophet, priest, and king have been opened to all the people of God. On the Day of Pentecost, Peter spoke about all God's people prophesying (Acts 2:17). That doesn't mean that all of us become preachers, but it does mean that God can use any of His people at any time to say something that God will use to penetrate someone else's life. A friend of mine used to say that every Christian is like a pilot light: always lit and always carrying within him the potential to light a larger flame.

All the people of God become priests as well (1 Peter 2:9). We can all pray for and minister to one another in the body of Christ. And all of God's people can offer worship, not just the choir or a few worship leaders on the platform.

All of God's people are kings. God has "raised us up with Christ and seated us with him in the heavenly realms" (Ephesians 2:6). We are positioned for victory over our enemies of sin, death, and hell, and are given the Spirit of God so that we may have the ability to move in right paths.

THE SHEPHERD LEADER

In the Bible, God has brought these three leadership roles of prophet, priest, and king together into one beautiful picture that encompasses all three dimensions of biblical leadership, and that is the image of a shepherd.

- The shepherd *feeds* the sheep—that is the role of the prophet, to sustain the people of God on a healthy diet of the Word of God.

- The shepherd *seeks* the sheep; when one of them is injured or lost, the shepherd is responsible for finding the sheep and doing what it takes to bring that sheep back, and that is the role of the priest.

- The shepherd *leads* the sheep—that's the role of the king, giving direction and protection to the flock.

So when God speaks about shepherds, He is speaking about all the dimensions of leadership together—revealing, reconciling, and ruling; truth, worship, and power; preaching, pastoring, and leading—everything that is involved in leadership among the people of God.

Nowhere is the shepherd role detailed more clearly than in Ezekiel 34.

THE SHEPHERD'S PERFORMANCE REVIEW

Most professions have a system of making an annual review or appraisal of the way in which employees have performed their duties. God had trusted the shepherds of Israel with the great responsibility of leading His people, and in Ezekiel 34, God gives an evaluation of their performance.

God spoke these words through Ezekiel, who was ministering to a community of ten thousand people who had been uprooted from their homes in Jerusalem and were now living as exiles by the Kebar River near Babylon. These people must have wondered why all this had happened to the people of God. So God spoke to Ezekiel, telling him that the people of God came to disaster because of a massive failure of leadership.

> *The word of the LORD came to me: "Son of man, prophesy against the shepherds of Israel; prophesy and say to them: 'This is what the Sovereign LORD says: Woe to the shepherds of Israel who only take care of themselves! Should not shepherds take care of the flock?'" (vv. 1–2)*

God brings three particular charges against the leaders of His people: They abuse their power, subvert the truth, and neglect the Lord.

LEADERS WHO ABUSE THEIR POWER

> *"You have not strengthened the weak or healed the sick or bound up the injured. You have not brought back the strays or searched for the lost. You have ruled them harshly and brutally."*
> (V. 4; EMPHASIS ADDED)

It is as if God was saying, "You kings have been given power; now what have you done with it?"

Ezekiel was not speaking about any one king, but about the whole history of the kings. The exile to Babylon did not happen because of the sins of one generation, but because of the repeated pattern of sin over many generations. God was saying that there had been a consistent pattern of abuse of power down through the entire history of the nation.

This should not surprise us because it is exactly what God said would happen before the first king was appointed. When the people asked for a king, God told them that a king would conscript their sons into the army, take their daughters into the service of the palace, and raise taxes on their crops and livestock, so that in the end, the people would "cry out for relief from the king [they had] chosen" (1 Samuel 8:18).

That is exactly what happened. Many kings were wicked, but even the best kings ended up placing great burdens upon the people. Solomon is remembered for all his glory, but his abuses of power were considerable. He built the temple, but a large part of it was done under forced labor, and the taxes on the people were almost intolerable.

When he died, the people came to his son Rehoboam and said, "Your father put a heavy yoke on us, but now lighten the harsh labor and the heavy yoke he put on us, and we will serve you" (1 Kings 12:4). But when Rehoboam made his first public policy speech, this is what he said: "My father made your yoke heavy; I will make it even heavier. My father scourged you with whips; I will scourge you with scorpions" (12:14).

This is hardly a model of exercising power in the interests of the people! But it became a pattern, and God said, "That's not being a shepherd."

LEADERS WHO SUBVERT GOD'S TRUTH

God spoke through Ezekiel to those who claimed to be prophets, but replaced the Word of God with a catalog of their own opinions.

> The word of the LORD came to me: "Son of man, prophesy against the prophets of Israel who are now prophesying. Say to those who prophesy out of their own imagination: 'Hear the word of the LORD! This is what the Sovereign LORD says: Woe to the foolish prophets who follow their own spirit and have seen nothing!'" (13:1–3)

These leaders looked at the market and discovered what people wanted to hear. Then they shaped their message to fit the felt needs of the hour. In Ezekiel's time, these prophets observed that the people wanted to hear a message of peace, so they gave the people what they wanted. They led God's people astray by saying "peace" when God had said that there would be no peace (Ezekiel 13:10). What God had said did not concern them. Their ministry was not driven by truth but by demand. But that's not feeding the sheep!

LEADERS WHO NEGLECT THE LORD

"Her priests do violence to my law and profane my holy things;

they do not distinguish between the holy and the common; they teach that there is no difference between the unclean and the clean; and they shut their eyes to the keeping of my Sabbaths, so that I am profaned among them." (22:26)

The priests were given a ministry of bringing people to God, but instead of bringing people to God, they became like secular counselors and focused on helping people to be at peace with themselves. They were not exercising a ministry of prayer or showing people how to be reconciled with God. If you had gone to one of these priests, you could have gone through a whole session without any prayer or any reference to Scripture. In fact, they said very little about God. They had lost the vertical—man to God. Their ministry focused entirely on the horizontal—man to man.

So God was giving very low marks to the shepherds of Israel. He had looked at their work and had seen terrible abuses of power, a deliberate subversion of the truth, and a neglect of God Himself so that ministry among God's people had become secularized. The effect of all this was that God's flock was malnourished, they were not cared for, and they were not protected.

TIME FOR A NEW SHEPHERD

God found the situation among His people intolerable, so He determined to intervene. But He would do so in an unexpected way. In fact, God told Ezekiel something absolutely astonishing:

> *"I myself will tend my sheep...declares the Sovereign LORD."*
> (34:15)

In effect, God said, "I will be the prophet, priest, and king to My people. I will personally bring the truth to them. I will come and care for My people Myself. I will personally protect them and lead them in the right paths. I will be the shepherd to the sheep." It must have been hard for Ezekiel to understand how God could possibly do that.

SPOTLIGHT ON CHRIST

When Jesus Christ came into the world, He saw that the people were still living under the kind of religious leadership that imposes unnecessary burdens. The shepherds of God's flock were not bringing the people into the joy of the knowledge of God, and as Jesus looked at the people, "he had compassion on them." They were "like sheep without a shepherd" (Matthew 9:36).

Christ gave an uncompromising assessment of the shepherds of God's people. "All who ever came before me were thieves and robbers," He said (John 10:8). They feathered their own nest. They used the flock for their own advantage. Then Jesus identified Himself as the Shepherd of Ezekiel 34 who would tend the sheep:

> "I am the good shepherd. The good shepherd lays down his life
> for the sheep." (JOHN 10:11)

Here was sacrificial leadership. As the Good Shepherd, Jesus would give the lost sheep everything they would need. First, He would feed the sheep with God's truth. Perhaps you have wondered how you could grow in the Christian life, or how you could be sustained in what you are facing. Christ will sustain you and He will nourish you in the truth. You will grow more than you ever thought you could as you walk with Him.

Second, Jesus Christ came to seek the sheep. He illustrated His own ministry in the story of the shepherd who left the sheep in his pen, in order to go and find one who was lost, "and when he finds it, he joyfully puts it on his shoulders and goes home" (Luke 15:5–6). Jesus is the One who will bring lost people back to God. And He does not wait for them to come to Him. Christ does the work of going out and finding lost people and bringing them back to God.

Third, Christ leads the sheep, all the while protecting them from their enemies. "My sheep...shall never perish; no one can snatch them out of my hand" (John 10:27–28). He will guard you by all means, and when death comes, He will bring you into everlasting life.

Christ said, "I am the way and the truth and the life" (John 14:6). But there were other shepherds among the people who did not like the truth He was teaching, the way He was leading, or the life He was giving. They saw the danger of losing their flocks. So they called Him in, and Christ was brought to stand before the shepherds of God's own people. The Good Shepherd became as one of the sheep.

CHRIST BEFORE THE "SHEPHERDS"

In the dramatic story of the trial and crucifixion of Jesus, several key characters filled the roles of a prophet, a priest, and a king. But they were not worthy shepherds of the people.

First, Christ was brought to the house of Annas the priest (John 18:12–13). If ever there was a priest who used his position to feather his own nest, Annas was the man. The Bazaars of Annas in the temples were infamous for their exorbitant rates of exchange, which bordered on extortion and let Annas live like royalty. You can imagine how upset Annas must have been when he heard of Christ overturning the traders' tables in the temple.

The position of high priest seems to have been kept in a tight family circle, and at this time, the position was held by Annas's son-in-law, Caiaphas.

When Christ stood before Caiaphas, surrounded by elders and teachers, one of the shepherds of Israel spat in Christ's face. Others slapped Him and struck Him with their fists (Matthew 26:67). God had given the high priest the responsibility of leading His people in worship. But in the house of Caiaphas, the one who was to lead worship stood by as they spat in the face of the Son of God.

Then Christ was sent from the priest to the king, whose name was Herod. This was the king who had abused his power by ordering the execution of John the Baptist. John was a prophet and had spoken God's Word to the king, and Herod did not like it. Herod was more like a butcher than a shepherd. The king was responsible for defending God's people, but Herod offered no defense to Christ. He simply sent Him back to Pilate.

As the governor of the land, Pilate's duty was to establish the truth and administer justice. Although not a prophet, he did receive a revelation as God spoke to his wife through a dream. Later, when Christ spoke to Pilate about the truth, the governor was not impressed. "What is truth?" he asked (John 18:38). Unlike true prophets, this judge did not believe that there was such a thing as truth regarding Jesus' identity, and so his decision about Jesus could not be based on justice, but rather on the prevailing mood of the people. Pilate washed his hands and went with the popular vote which, on that particular week, was for the crucifixion of the Son of God.

So Christ the Good Shepherd became a meek lamb. He was "led like a lamb to the slaughter" (Isaiah 53:7). He suffered as one of the sheep under the shepherds who abused power, subverted truth, and cared more for themselves than for God. At the cross, He became the sacrificial lamb who would take away the sins of the world.

THE MIGHTY SHEPHERD

Then on the third day, He rose from the dead. Death is a dark valley. But the Shepherd has already been through it. He has cleared the enemies out of the tunnel. It is still a dark place, but it is a safe place for all who belong to the Shepherd. "Though I walk through the valley of the shadow of death, I will fear no evil, for you are with me" (Psalm 23:4).

Then Christ ascended to heaven, and on the Day of Pentecost He poured out the Holy Spirit. Ever since that time, He has been giving gifts to the church. The ascended Christ gave some to be apostles, prophets, evangelists, pastors, and teachers (Ephesians 4:11). Some are gifted to give direction to God's people. Some are gifted to proclaim the truth. Some care for the flock and prepare God's people for works of service so that the body of Christ may be built up. Those who are gifted and called to leadership in the church are undershepherds of the flock of God. They serve under the Good Shepherd. There could be no greater privilege or responsibility.

SHEPHERDING THE FLOCK OF GOD

Jesus gave very clear instructions about how leadership is to be exercised in the church. "You know that the rulers of the Gentiles lord it over them, and their high officials exercise authority over them. Not so with you. Instead, whoever wants to become great among you must be your servant, and whoever wants to be first must be your slave—just as the Son of Man did not come to be served, but to serve, and to give his life as a ransom for many" (Matthew 20:25–28). Don't use your power to promote personal agendas. Use your power as a servant of the people of God.

Leaders in the church are to make sure that the flock of God are fed on the truth. There will always be pressure from people with itching ears who have their own agenda for what they want to hear from the pulpit, but pastors are to preach the Word and lay leaders are to support and encourage them in that task.

Leaders of Christ's church are not entertainers who make a living by appealing to felt needs. They are to be like priests who will reach out to lost people and bring them to God. The church is to be a kingdom of priests, a worshiping community with a heart for the lost. Christian leaders are given a great trust by the Chief Shepherd and by the flock of God. They are accountable for the way in which they exercise their ministry to the Lord Himself.

Is Christ your Shepherd? Can you say, "The Lord is my shepherd"? The apostle Peter used a beautiful phrase to describe what it means to become a real Christian. He said that we "were like sheep going astray…[who] have returned to the Shepherd…of [our] souls" (1 Peter 2:25). We return to the Shepherd when we believe that Christ is the truth, receive the reconciliation that He, as our great High Priest, has achieved through His sacrifice on the cross, and submit to His rule as King. If you are not sure that Christ is your Shepherd, you can come into His flock today by believing His truth, trusting His sacrifice, and submitting to His rule.

UNLOCKED

Shepherding God's flock involves the ministries of the prophet, priest, and king. Those who are trusted by God with the responsibility of leadership in the church must be very careful that they do not become like the shepherds in Ezekiel's day who abused their positions. It is an abuse of privilege to teach one's own opinions, to neglect the spiritual needs of God's people, or to impose unnecessary burdens on them.

Effective leaders will teach God's truth, pastor God's people, and lead God's flock in paths that are pleasing to God. They focus on these duties because they are accountable to the Great Shepherd of the sheep, Jesus Christ. Jesus gave His life for the sheep, and as the Good Shepherd, He will bring His sheep into God's fold.

Human leaders may sometimes disappoint and fail us, but the Good Shepherd cares for the sheep and will not lose a single one.

PAUSE FOR PRAYER

Gracious Father,

Pour out Your blessing on the leaders of Your church today. Help them to walk with You in integrity, and keep them from the attacks of the evil one. Give Your shepherds a deep love for Your Word and for Your people. Give them great wisdom to lead Your people in right paths and to protect them from danger.

Thank You that Your church is in the hands of the Great Shepherd who gave His life for the sheep. Feed me with Your word, renew and restore my soul, and lead me in right paths, for Jesus' sake. Amen.

Breath

EZEKIEL 37

How does God

bring life to

people who are

spiritually dead?

13 Breath

EZEKIEL 37

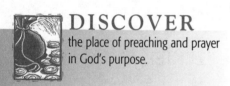

DISCOVER

the place of preaching and prayer
in God's purpose.

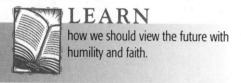

LEARN

how we should view the future with
humility and faith.

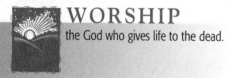

WORSHIP

the God who gives life to the dead.

THE bedraggled stranger walked into town and asked for directions to the house of the prophet. He was exhausted after his seven-hundred-mile journey, and he said that he had bad news. Ezekiel never forgot the day that the stranger arrived at his home. It was the fifth day of the tenth month in the twelfth year (Ezekiel 33:21). That meant that it had been twelve years since Ezekiel and the ten thousand other exiles had been taken captive and deported to the Kebar River.

There had been endless discussion among the exiles about what would happen next in Jerusalem. False prophets had insisted that the exile would only be for a short time, and that soon God's people would be back in God's city, but that was not what God had said. Now the bedraggled stranger arrived with the news that Ezekiel had dreaded even though he knew that it would happen: "The city has fallen!" (33:21).

It is hard for us to imagine the impact of this. Jerusalem was the city of God. God had put His name and His presence there. These people had been brought up in Sabbath school singing songs like "There is a river whose streams make glad the city of God, the holy place where the Most High dwells. God is within her, *she will not fall*" (Psalm 46:4–5; italics added).

So how could God have allowed this to happen? Did it mean that God had given up on His people? What kind of future was there now? Those were the great questions that the exiles at the Kebar River were struggling with. That was when God gave Ezekiel a vision of the future for these people.

FACING THE CREDIBILITY GAP

Before the vision, God had already made a great promise to His people: "I will give you a new heart and put a new spirit in you; I will remove from you your heart of stone and give you a heart of flesh" (Ezekiel 36:26). Despite His promise, the people said, "Our bones are dried up and our hope is gone; we are cut off" (37:11).

God was saying, "A terrible thing has happened, but I want you to know that it is not the end. My purpose continues, and I am going to fulfill My promise."

But the people were answering, "No, this is the end of the road. There is no future for us. After what has happened, our hope is gone."

The people felt that there was a credibility gap between the promises of God and the circumstances they were facing. They heard what God was saying through Ezekiel, but they were finding it very difficult to connect the Word of God with the broken reality that was all around them.

Perhaps there have been times when you have felt that in church on Sunday morning. The preacher talks about how the life of God can be poured into the church so that the truth, love, and grace of God may flow into the community. He reads from the Bible about the wonderful promises of God. But you look at the rising godlessness of our time and say, "No, we are cut off."

There are times when the broken circumstances of life make us feel that we are beyond the range of the promises of God, and that while they may be for other people, at other times, or in other places, they are somehow not for us. If you have felt that, then the vision God gave to Ezekiel is just for you.

UNDERSTANDING THE SCALE OF THE PROBLEM

The hand of the LORD was upon me, and he brought me out
by the Spirit of the LORD and set me in the middle of a valley;
it was full of bones. (37:1)

In this vision, God took Ezekiel to a rather grim valley. It was like a mass graveyard filled with human remains, as if there had been a great slaughter there hundreds of years before. God told Ezekiel that the bones he was seeing in the vision represented the whole house of Israel (v. 11). The people were complaining that "our bones are dried up," so God used the picture of a valley of dry bones to speak to them.

The first thing God did to impress upon Ezekiel the scale of the problem was to give the prophet a guided tour.

*He led me back and forth among them [the bones], and I saw
a great many bones on the floor of the valley, bones that were
very dry.* (v. 2)

I don't suppose that Ezekiel particularly enjoyed this experience. God led him back and forth over this grim valley. The longer the tour continued, the more deeply the hopelessness of the situation was impressed on Ezekiel's mind. There was not the faintest sign of life in the valley. God was saying, "I want you to take in how dead this whole situation is. You need to see how hopeless things have become." Ezekiel had to be convinced that the only hope would be through a direct intervention of God.

The only hope would be through a direct intervention of God.

Actually, this is a great way to start out in ministry! You have to begin with an honest assessment of the realities you are facing. God said to Ezekiel, "Here is what you are up against. You are called to minister in a place where there is not the slightest sign of life."

Ezekiel had remarkable gifts and abilities. He clearly had an unusual flair for creative communication. But none of that would be much use in a valley of dry bones. "Ezekiel, here is something to help with your humility. Your gifts, your talents, your resources aren't going to amount to a hill of beans in a valley of dry bones! Ezekiel, see how dry the bones are! There is no program that will fix this problem. There is nothing that you can do that will transform the reality that I am showing you right now."

The first thing that we need to understand in ministry is that what God calls us to do is impossible. If we do not grasp this principle, we will not survive in ministry for long.

Perhaps God is showing you a valley of dry bones. Maybe you have been looking for signs of hope in the spiritual condition of someone you love. You have been praying for them for a long time, but the truth is that there is not the slightest sign of life. When you try to talk with them about spiritual things, their eyes glaze over. They are as unresponsive to the things of God as the dry bones Ezekiel saw. Maybe something has happened and now the situation seems more hopeless than it ever did before. God took Ezekiel over the valley of dry bones again and again until in the end, he was absolutely convinced that the only hope would be a direct intervention of God. Do you see that?

How to Answer God's Big Question

After showing Ezekiel the desperate state of the valley, God asked the prophet the big question.

> *He asked me, "Son of man, can these bones live?"* (v. 3)

How would you have answered that question?

Ezekiel could have said yes. There are people today who are looking at the valley of dry bones and saying, "Yes, they will live." I listened to a tape recently in which a well-known Bible teacher began his message by announcing categorically that America is on the brink of the greatest outpouring of the Holy Spirit that the world has ever seen. He was absolutely certain about it. I hope he is right, but I don't know how he knows that. There is a great danger in confusing naive optimism with faith.

Alternatively, Ezekiel could have said no. It is very easy for us in a postmodern culture, where Christianity is moving to a minority position, to feel that our freedoms will be eroded, and before long the church will fade into insignificance. I have also heard this predicted. I hope that it is wrong, but how can we know what the future holds?

Ezekiel took neither of these positions, and his response gives us a model of faith.

> *"O sovereign LORD, you alone know."* (v. 3)

The prophet was saying, "Lord, there is no way that I can know what You will do in the future with these particular bones." There is great humility in Ezekiel's response.

We also need such humility. We need an attitude that says, "Lord, keep me from the arrogance that says yes. Keep me from the spirit that says, 'I know how it works; I can make it happen.' Keep me from the presumption that says we can reclaim this country for Christ."

There is also great faith in Ezekiel's response, "You alone know."

"Lord, keep me from the unbelief that says no. Keep me from the spirit that says, 'These are dark days, and the difficulties are so great that I cannot see any possibility of change.'" Ezekiel would neither despair nor presume. He found his rest in the sovereignty of God.

I am very grateful that God does know the future. Some people are questioning that today. I am glad Ezekiel was not in the position of saying, "Well, I don't know, and of course God can't know because it all depends on how people respond!" If it all depended on how people respond, there wouldn't be much hope in the valley of dry bones.

Ezekiel got the answer absolutely right. Similarly we should say, "Lord, I don't know if the future of the church in this country is revival or decline, but You do. I don't know whether those I pray for will come to Christ or whether they will remain in their hardness of heart, but You know. I do not know whether we are going to see a great missionary advance through ever-opening doors or whether we will find the doors of opportunity closing, but You know. The future of those I pray for and seek to minister to is known to You, and I will find my rest in the sovereignty of God."

God took Ezekiel on a tour in which he saw the utter hopelessness of the situation. Then God asked him a question that led him to affirm his confidence in the sovereignty of God.

WHAT TO DO WHILE YOU ARE TRUSTING GOD

Then, God called Ezekiel into action.

> *"Prophesy to these bones."* (v. 4)

Notice that believing in the sovereignty of God is never an excuse for sitting back and doing nothing. Ezekiel had trusted the future into the hands of God, but now God had something for him to do.

"Ezekiel, here is what I want you to do: Preach to the bones."

"You want me to speak to a pile of bones?"

"Yes, Ezekiel, that's right."

"Do I actually have to speak out loud? I'd feel rather stupid doing that when the audience are all dead. Can't I just think my sermon or even just say a prayer instead?"

"No, I want you to prophesy out loud."

"To the bones?"

"Yes, to the bones."

This is one of the strangest commands in the Bible. Why would God want the prophet to speak to a pile of dead bones?

Pastor Erwin Lutzer of Chicago's Moody Memorial Church once told me about a class that he holds from time to time for preachers. In the first session, he takes a group of seminarians on a field trip to a cemetery. They gather on the grass, somewhat curious at what is going on. Then Pastor Lutzer asks if someone in the group will volunteer to preach. Nobody wants to do that, of course. The whole thing seems ridiculous. What is the point of preaching in a situation where, by definition, hearing, understanding, and responding are impossible?

The point of the exercise is simple. Every time someone presents the Word of God to an unbelieving person, that is exactly the situation. The Bible says that until God makes us alive through Jesus Christ, we are spiritually dead (Ephesians 2:1–5).

God does amazing things when His truth is proclaimed.

There is something inherently absurd about preaching the gospel or sharing your faith. When we do that, we are speaking to people who are spiritually dead and, therefore, by definition, incapable of response. Maybe you have felt the pain of this. You speak to a colleague about eternal things, or about the glory of Christ, or the life-changing power of the Cross, and there is no response! Their eyes glaze over, and you know that your best efforts just didn't connect.

Ezekiel might well have objected that God was calling him to do something that had no reasonable chance of success. But God called him to preach anyway. "Prophesy to the bones, Ezekiel." So he did. Perhaps he felt rather stupid, but he began to speak the Word of God to the bones.

As he spoke, an amazing thing happened. To Ezekiel's absolute astonishment, there was some movement in the graveyard. Nothing had moved in that valley for years, but now there was the sound of movement, and as Ezekiel looked, he saw that the bones were coming together! They connected to form the intricate structure of skeletons. Ezekiel kept preaching. Something was happening as he preached, and as he continued to watch, he saw tendons sealing the connections of the bones, and then flesh, and then skin. It was incredible.

> *I looked, and tendons and flesh appeared on them and skin covered them, but there was no breath in them. (v. 8)*

Bones speak of structure. Tendons speak of unity (they hold the bones together). Flesh (which includes muscle) speaks of strength, and skin speaks of appearance. If the bodies had only been covered in flesh, they would have looked hideous, but God gave them skin. All of that was there, but there was no breath.

The church of Jesus Christ can have all these things, and still not have life. The church can have marvelous structures; people can be very united; there can be the strength of all kinds of resources, and an outward appearance that is very attractive, but still no breath.

At this point in the vision, all that had happened was that under Ezekiel's ministry, the graveyard was better organized! It was no longer a massive burial ground for dry bones; now it was a burial place of dead corpses! The miracle that God would do in the valley began as the prophet preached. God does amazing things when His truth is proclaimed. But it was clear to Ezekiel that it would take more than his preaching to bring life back to the valley of dry bones.

Charles Spurgeon said, "You may study your sermon, you may examine the original of your text, you may critically follow it out in all its bearings; you may go and preach it with great correctness of expression; but you cannot quicken a soul by that sermon. You may go up into your pulpit, you may illustrate, explain, and enforce the truth; with mighty rhetoric you may charm your hearers; you may hold them spellbound, but no eloquence of yours can raise the dead."[1]

Parents can teach their children God's truth; churches can run magnificent programs. We can pass out tracts and go on marches. All such activities are good. Yet none of these things in themselves will raise the spiritually dead. Something else has to happen.

SPEAKING TO THE BREATH
Then he said to me, "Prophesy to the breath." (v. 9)

God called Ezekiel to accompany his ministry of preaching to people who were spiritually dead with another ministry. He must prophesy to the bones, but he must also prophesy to the breath.

The Hebrew word that is translated "breath" is *Ruach*. It can mean "breath," "wind," or "spirit." Back in the book of Genesis, God made man from the dust of the ground. God formed a corpse from chemical matter. The corpse consisted of bones, tendons, flesh and skin, but he did not have life. Then God "breathed into his nostrils the breath of life, and the man became a living being" (Genesis 2:7).

Now God is about to do the same thing again in the valley of dry bones.

The prophet sees structure, unity, strength, and an attractive appearance before him, but there is no life here. So God tells Ezekiel to call on the wind of God's Spirit.

"This is what the sovereign LORD says: Come from the four winds, O breath, and breathe into these slain, that they may live." (v. 9)

So Ezekiel began to pray, and as he did, the breath of God entered the corpses. Ezekiel saw them coming to life, and then standing up, until right there, in what had been a valley of dry bones, there stood a vast army ready for action (vv. 9–10).

Never, never, never underestimate what God can do, when His Word is preached and His people pray. If the breath of the Spirit of God blows upon a situation that is completely dead, a remarkable transformation will take place.

As Ezekiel looked at the vast army in the valley, he knew that this was the work of God. But he also knew that God had done this miracle as he preached and as he prayed. He must have wondered, *What if I had not spoken? What if I had not prayed?*

Don't you long for the wind of the Spirit to accompany the preaching of God's Word so that miracles of grace will happen in the darkest and most hopeless places? Where the wind blows is in the sovereignty of God. It is not under our control. But God calls us to speak the truth and call on the Spirit of God in prayer.

So what are we to do if our children's eyes glaze over as we try to present the truth, or if a colleague seems unresponsive as we share our testimony? First, we can try to introduce them to, or keep them in, an environment where they will hear God's truth. Then we can surround them with the ministry of prayer. We are to speak the Word of God and to call on the Spirit of God. We are to proclaim the Word and to call on the wind. And God is telling us that amazing things can happen in the most unpromising places when His Word is preached and His people pray.

FROM VISION TO REALITY

Of course, all of this was simply a vision that God gave to Ezekiel. It was a wonderful vision, because it spoke directly to God's people when they felt there was no future for them. But the amazing thing is that the vision became reality. The people by the Kebar River turned out to be the key to God's purpose for His people. When Jerusalem was destroyed, God kept these people safe in Babylon. They were preserved like Noah in the ark, and through these people and their children, the unbroken line of God's purpose would continue.

Seventy years later, the children of those people, who had said, "Our hope is gone; we are cut off," returned to Jerusalem to rebuild the temple and the city walls. They established a worshiping community where God's name would be honored and His law obeyed. Through these once-discouraged people by the Kebar River God advanced His plan to bring blessing to the nations of the world.

SPOTLIGHT ON CHRIST

When Nicodemus talked with Jesus about his spiritual life, this religious leader came at night, presumably because he wanted to have a private discussion. After all, he was one of the leaders of the synagogue, and people expect their spiritual leaders to have their own spiritual lives sorted out. But Nicodemus knew that there was a dryness and a hunger in his own soul. He knew that he needed help, and so he came to Jesus.

Nicodemus was part of a group that had structure, unity, strength, and a great appearance, but somewhere deep in this man's soul, he knew that he did not have spiritual life. He felt like a corpse in a valley of dry bones.

Jesus said to him,

> "Flesh gives birth to flesh, but the Spirit gives birth to spirit. You should not be surprised at my saying, 'You must be born again.' The wind blows wherever it pleases. You hear its sound, but you cannot tell where it comes from or where it is going. So it is with everyone born of the Spirit." (JOHN 3:6–8)

Nicodemus needed the wind of the Spirit of God to blow on him and give him new life. And that is exactly what happened to him. When Christ was crucified, Nicodemus stepped forward to ask for the body of Jesus (John 19:38–39), and in this way he identified himself as a disciple of Christ.

When Jesus rose from the dead, He appeared to His disciples and showed them His scars. Then He breathed on them and said, "Receive the Holy Spirit" (John 20:22). Just as physical life was breathed into Adam by God at the creation, so now, spiritual life was breathed into the disciples by the Lord Jesus Christ. Spiritual life is the gift of God. Nothing much seemed to happen at that moment. When Jesus breathed on them, He was illustrating what would happen after His ascension, when the wind of God would blow on them, and the Spirit would come.

Forty days later, it happened. They were all gathered together in one place, in the city of Jerusalem, and they had been praying. "Suddenly a sound like the blowing of a violent wind came from heaven and filled the whole house where they were sitting" (Acts 2:2). And when that happened, Peter spoke to a vast crowd of people who were spiritually dead. He prophesied to the bones and spiritual life came to them through the Word and by the Spirit.

Three thousand people were converted on that day. They were from all over the known world, and they began to spread the good news of Jesus Christ to the nations. Spiritually dry bones came to life. Today, all who have the breath of God's Spirit breathed within, have a new, everlasting life.

When we get to the end of the Bible story, we find that God has one more thing to do involving bones. God has set a day for gathering the bones of His people. Believers who have died are taken immediately and consciously into the presence of Christ. But there is still a final miracle of grace that will not be given to any believers until it is given to all believers together.

> *The Lord himself will come down from heaven,...and the dead in Christ will rise first. After that, we who are still alive and are left will be caught up together with them in the clouds to meet the Lord in the air.* (1 THESSALONIANS 4:16–17)

Knowing this truth, we can "encourage each other with these words" (4:18).

UNLOCKED

The way in which God brings life to spiritually dead people is a great mystery and a miracle of His grace. There are many things that we do not understand, but the Scriptures do make certain things clear. Spiritual life is imparted by the Spirit of God. The Spirit is like the wind, and we do not control where, how, or when the wind blows. But God does work through people like you and me; Ezekiel's vision clearly indicates that the Spirit of God works in, through, and along with the declaring of God's truth and the prayers of God's people. This does not mean that people will be converted every time we teach the Bible and pray, but it does mean that people will not normally come to spiritual life without a ministry of the Word and prayer. These are the normal means that God uses. God's Spirit brought life to the dead bones as Ezekiel was faithful to God's call to speak His truth and pray. As we are faithful to this same calling, we may look to the Spirit of God to bring the wonderful gift of spiritual life.

PAUSE FOR PRAYER

I come to You, the author and sustainer of life, and stand amazed at Your awesome power. Thank You for giving me new life through Your Word and by the power of Your Spirit. Thank You for making me a new creation in Jesus Christ.

Breathe new life from above into your church, O Lord. Help me to feel my need and to be renewed in Your power. Cause Your people to rise up in faith and obedience so that our nation may hear Your voice and know that You are the living God.

I pray this in the name of my Lord and Savior, Jesus. Amen.

> *O Breath of Life, come sweeping through us,*
> *Revive your church with life and power.*
> *O Breath of Life, come cleanse, renew us,*
> *And fit your church to meet this hour.*
> *O wind of God, come bend us break us,*
> *Till humbly we confess our need.*
> *Then in your tenderness remake us,*
> *Revive, restore, for this we plead.*
>
> —BESSIE P. HEAD
> "O BREATH OF LIFE"

NOTE

1. Charles Spurgeon, "Come from the Four Winds, O Breath!" Metropolitan pulpit sermon 2246, as cited in "The C. H. Spurgeon Collection," CD disk (Albany, Oreg.: Ages Software, 1998). Preached in 1890.

Alien

DANIEL 1

How can I live in

the world without

being squeezed

into its mold?

14 Alien

DANIEL 1

722	End of North Kingdom
700 b.c.	
640–609	Josiah
608–598	Jeholakim
606–536	Babylonian Captivity
605	First Deportation
600	**598–597** Jehoiachin
	597 Second Deportation
	597–586 Zedekiah
	586 Fall of Jerusalem
DANIEL	
	536 First Return to Jerusalem
500	

DISCOVER
how to live a distinctively Christian life in a secular world.

LEARN
how Satan tries to subvert the Christian.

WORSHIP
because Christ has overcome the world.

MY wife, Karen, teaches kindergarten at a Christian school. On the day of the 2000 presidential election, the children were sitting on the rug talking about all that was going on. It was election day, and the children had caught the excitement. Then Karen told them that she would not be voting, and she asked them why they thought this might be.

"Is it because you are too old?" asked one confident youngster.

"Is it because you are teaching us?"

"Is it because you have a meeting to go to later?"

Eventually a bright child asked, "Is it because you come from England, Mrs. Smith?"

"Yes," said Karen, "and do you know what they call me? A resident alien."

It is amazing what sticks in a child's mind, because two weeks later, when the children were sitting on the rug for their morning prayer time, one little girl began to pray for my wife. "Dear Lord, please help people to stop calling Mrs. Smith a resident alien, because that's really not very nice!"

ALIENS WITH A HEAVENLY PASSPORT

The Bible uses the words *aliens* and *strangers* to describe God's people (1 Peter 2:11). We do not belong here in any permanent way. We are given the privilege of life in this world for a short time, but this world is not home for us. We belong to another city "whose builder and maker is God" (Hebrews 11:10 NKJV), and our time here is a preparation for taking our citizenship, which is above. You cannot understand this life or this world until you have grasped that this is not what God created you for.

If you are a Christian, you should think of yourself as a person who carries two passports. One of them will expire, because when Christ returns national identities will be relegated to history as all of God's people are united together in heaven. But your passport as a citizen of heaven will never pass away. It will remain forever.

The art of the Christian life is to live in this world without becoming consumed by it. We are to use the short time frame of our life here to prepare for the main event which is still to come. The story of Daniel is about one of God's people in an alien land, and it gives us a powerful model of how we should live in a secular and materialistic culture.

HIGH SCHOOL STUDENTS ABDUCTED!

Daniel was one of the small group of talented students who were taken to Babylon after the first siege of Jerusalem. He was taken from his home in the third year of Jehoiakim (1:1) and remained in Babylon until the first year of King Cyrus (v. 21). That is a period of sixty-five or seventy years and so, given a normal life expectancy, Daniel must have been under the age of twenty when he came to Babylon. In all probability, he was of high school age.

Try and get a picture of this high school student in your mind as we follow the story. Daniel was one of the brightest and the best. He came from a good home and was a straight-A student. He had an "aptitude for every kind of learning" (v. 4). He was also extremely fit and very good-looking. The world was at his feet.

Then one day during his junior year, Dan was sitting at his desk when there was a knock on the door. A moment later, three soldiers from the Babylonian army burst in, and Daniel was dragged off and, along with some of his school friends, marched seven hundred miles to Babylon. These prize pupils were abducted—part of the first deportation—and the parents could do nothing to stop it!

Daniel's parents must have been distraught. And who knows what must have been going through Daniel's own mind as he talked with his friends.

"What do you think they will do to us, Dan?"

"They'll probably torture us till we die."

They needn't have worried, because when they arrived in Babylon, they found that far from being abused and imprisoned, they were treated like royalty and enrolled in a topflight boarding school. They had been selected to participate in the nation's premier education program and would be fast-tracked into the king's service. If they played their cards right, they would have the opportunity of holding down some of the top jobs in the whole of the Babylonian empire. Life in captivity was turning out not to be so bad after all!

THE PRESSURE TO CONFORM

Daniel had grown up under the care of his parents and the influence of godly people. Now suddenly, he was taken out of that environment and placed in a new situation where he had to stand on his own feet…and make his own decisions. In Jerusalem many knew him. But in Babylon he was completely anonymous.

> "How can you believe that your god is the only God?"

Those who travel know all about this pressure. At home there are many people who know you, but when you get on a plane or check into a hotel, nobody knows who you are. Suddenly, it occurs to you that you can be whoever you want to be, and that brings pressure. All Satan has to do with some people is put them in a different location and their testimony is completely undermined.

This is a great test for those who leave home and head off to college. The watchful eyes of parents cannot extend to a new location, and that's when who you really are will be made known. That is exactly the situation that Daniel was confronted with. When you can be whoever you want to be, then the person you really are will be revealed. That was the first pressure Daniel faced.

Daniel was placed under the care of a tutor called Ashpenaz, who was assigned to teach these students "the language and literature of the Babylonians" (v. 4). Back in Jerusalem, Daniel would have studied Hebrew and learned the Bible. But the Bible was not on the curriculum in Babylon.

Daniel was exposed to a whole spectrum of learning, much of which would have been quite foreign to him. In fact, a great deal of it would have been in direct conflict with what he had been taught from the Bible as a child. Learning the literature of the Babylonians would have included the myths of their gods: Marduk, Bel, and Nebo.

There would have been all the usual discussions among the students over coffee. And there would have been challenges from other students and their tutor. "How can you Jewish boys seriously believe that your god is the only God?…Don't you understand that every culture has its own religious stories and that all of them point to the same spiritual reality?…How can you possibly think that you are the only ones who have the truth? Don't you understand that these Bible stories are simply a way of describing the personal beliefs of the author?" It is not very different for many Christian young people in secular universities today.

Parents are sometimes distressed over things that their children have to read or are taught in secular schools. Students are studying literature that is sometimes in direct contradiction to the truth. But this is nothing new. It is exactly the situation that Daniel faced. God has given us a model of how one godly youngster and a group of his friends stood against that pressure. Far from their secular education overwhelming them, it was actually the making of them. In the goodness of God, their Babylonian education became the anvil on which their faith was hammered out into maturity.

WHAT'S IN A NAME?
Ashpenaz gave new names to his new students (1:7). He did not want to use their Jewish names, so he gave them Babylonian names instead. Daniel's name means "God is my Judge"; *El* was one of the Hebrew names for God. Ashpenaz changed this to Belteshazzar. *Bel* was the name of one of the Babylonian gods, and Belteshazzar means keeper of the hidden treasures of Bel. At this point, the Ashpenaz plan becomes very clear. He was taking these brightest Jewish students, and he was attempting to "Babylonize" them.

By putting them in another place, and filling their minds with another learning, and calling them by another name, he was attempting to erode the roots of their distinctive faith in God, so that at the end of three years in the royal college, they would emerge with flying colors and a thoroughly Babylonian worldview. They would still be Jews, of course, but they would think, act, behave, and respond exactly like Babylonians.

MASKS OF THE ENEMY
At key points during Old Testament times, God's people lived under two very different kinds of oppression. Pharaoh's plan was to persecute God's people. He was ruthless and put them through hard labor. It was a terrible attack on God's people, but all that happened was that they multiplied and became stronger. Satan uses the same tactic today in many places where Christians are persecuted for their faith. The outcome is usually the same; God's people become stronger under persecution.

Nebuchadnezzar's plan was more subtle. He had read his history and knew that what Pharaoh had attempted didn't work. Nebuchadnezzar realized that the best way to subdue these people was not to persecute them, but to bless them. His strategy was to welcome them and absorb them into the culture of Babylon. He opened doors of opportunity for them and placed them on the fast track to Babylonian success. He was convinced that they would find it so intoxicating that they would quickly forget all about their distinctive calling as the people of God, and it would not be long before they would lose every trace of what made them different.

This story speaks powerfully to the church in America today. There are some places in the world where the enemy of our souls is using the crude tactics of Pharaoh. But he is increasingly using the tactics of Nebuchadnezzar, and they are proving very effective in his warfare against the church. The strategy is very simple. Intoxicate the people of God with the sheer fascination and splendor of this world. Spread the assumption that what they believe could not actually be true. Gradually erode their distinctive practices and values, and it will not be long before they are so assimilated into the culture that their distinctive calling to live for the glory of God will simply be overwhelmed. There are some believers who might be heroes under the persecutions of Egypt, but are unable to resist the seductions of Babylon.

A TASTE OF THE HIGH LIFE

The king assigned them a daily amount of food and wine from the king's table. They were to be trained for three years, and after that they were to enter the king's service. (v. 5)

This was heady stuff for a group of high schoolers. They were eating from the same menu as the king of Babylon. Every mealtime the same message was getting through to these students: "The king's palace is the place to be. This is where the doors of opportunity are. This is the fast track to success and all that success offers." The king knew that once they got a taste for the high life, they would find it difficult to settle for anything else.

But Daniel decided that he would not eat from the king's table. He "resolved not to defile himself with the royal food" (v. 8). There are different opinions about why this was. Some suggest that it was to do with Jewish food laws. Others suggest that it was because the king's meat had been offered to idols before it was cooked. I am convinced that there is a much larger issue here. Daniel abstained from the king's table, not because of some scruples of conscience, but because he was absolutely realistic about the pressure of the culture that could so easily suck him in.

He understood what was happening. He realized that Nebuchadnezzar wanted to overwhelm him with the opportunities of life in Babylon, and Daniel was determined that this would never happen. He would live, serve, and prosper in Babylon, but he would never allow Babylon to consume his heart. He would always remember that he served a greater King, and he would never forget that he belonged to another place.

But he needed some way of keeping that fixed in his mind. So he chose to establish a discipline for himself. He turned down the offer of a daily visit to the top restaurant in town and ate a brown bag lunch of vegetables instead. He did not do this because of some external law, but because of an internal desire. It was an act of freedom, a voluntary discipline, designed to remind him of his distinctive calling and to increase his spiritual strength.

Daniel did this because he knew that if he did not exercise some restraint, he would be gradually sucked in until he was completely consumed by the values of the culture. He was determined that he would not let his soul get hooked on the things of this world; he knew that if that happened, he would lose his freedom to be an effective servant of God.

Are you being realistic about the pressure that the world places on you? Every day you are bombarded by a view of life that is self-centered and has no room for God. The message of the culture is clear, powerful, and attractive: "Nothing matters more than you do, so pursue your own pleasure." Once we have identified the pressures we face, it's time to develop a strategy for resistance.

CULTIVATING THE ABILITY TO SAY NO

The greatest significance of Daniel's decision to abstain from the king's table was that he was cultivating the ability to say no. This is critical to an effective Christian life. "The grace of God…teaches us to say …'No' to ungodliness" (Titus 2:11–12).

Daniel made a great decision. One day a future king would remove freedom of worship and call on everyone to pray in the name of the king, or else face death in a den of lions. When that day came, Daniel would be able to stand firm.

If you do not develop that ability to say no on smaller issues, you will not be able to say no when larger tests and temptations come. This is why it is so important to develop the ability to withstand peer pressure, and why there is great value in following Daniel's example of exercising voluntary restraint over some legitimate pleasures and opportunities.

Daniel was at liberty to eat from the king's table, but he perceived that the habit of the king's table would exert a drawing power in his life that could subvert his loyalty to the Lord, and so he used his freedom to exercise restraint. He would not allow himself to get into a position where the good things of this life consumed his heart.

This is full of practical significance for us today. Some Christians operate as if there was only one question to be answered in the practical decisions of life. We ask, "Is it right or wrong?" and unless it's illegal, immoral, or it makes us fat, we eagerly affirm our liberty to enjoy. But there is another question to ask of things that come within our area of freedom: "Is it wise?"

What films should you watch? How large a mortgage should you take? What parties should you go to? What company should you keep? On what should you spend your money? Daniel's example reminds us that as we make these decisions, we need to consider the long-term potential for being sucked into the values and lifestyles of the world.

THE SPIRIT OF FASTING

Daniel could not change what they taught him at school. He could not change what Ashpenaz and the others chose to call him. But he could create a space in his life that was a daily reminder to him that he was a servant of God. He chose to exercise restraint and it strengthened him.

Terry Waite was for some years the special envoy of the Archbishop of Canterbury in England. He was seeking to negotiate the release of hostages in Lebanon when he was taken hostage by terrorists himself. In His book, *Taken on Trust*, he describes the first thing that he did after being taken captive.

> Unless it's illegal, immoral, or it makes us fat, we eagerly affirm our liberty to enjoy.

What would be the first thing that you would do if you were chained, blindfolded, and locked in a concrete building with no idea of what lay ahead? Terry Waite decided to fast, because he knew that he needed to build his inner strength for the challenges ahead.

There are more ways of fasting than going without food. If we embrace every legitimate thing that the world offers, on the basis that "there's nothing wrong with it," we may find that we have naively missed the bigger picture, and that we have been seduced into adopting values of the world. The big issue for Daniel in

Babylon was to make sure that his soul was not consumed with the abundance of opportunity that surrounded him so that his distinctive allegiance to God became nothing more than a memory.

God does not call us to a life of austerity, but a life of undisciplined indulgence will eventually erode all that distinguished the people of God from your life. Daniel was determined that his success in Babylon would never do this to him.

FAITHFUL AND SUCCESSFUL

God gave Daniel and his friends great success in their studies:

> *To these four young men God gave knowledge and under-standing of all kinds of literature and learning.* (v. 17)

Their gifts blossomed and flourished. So when they came to their finals, which would have been in the form of an oral exam before the king, they passed with flying colors, and Daniel found himself appointed to a premier position of influence within the most powerful government of his day. Faithfulness and success need not be alternatives; they are natural partners.

Daniel had proved faithful in small things, and so God trusted him with greater things. That's always the pattern. Never imagine that faithfulness to Christ means being second rate or settling for small things. Daniel proved that he could be trusted, so God increased Daniel's gifts and abilities and opened the door of opportunity. Daniel would have influence beyond what he had ever dreamed, becoming second in command to the king.

In the darkest hour for God's people, the light of faith burned brightly in a teenager who refused to be overcome by the world and learned to live a distinctive life of faith in an alien culture.

SPOTLIGHT ON CHRIST

All this points us toward our Lord Jesus Christ. He came into this world from another place. He took our flesh and came among us as a stranger, and yet as a friend.

Satan wanted Him to buy into the thinking and values of this world. "Use your powers to benefit yourself. With your ability, you could make a name for yourself and increase your ministry." And so Satan three times tempted Jesus: "Turn these stones into bread....Jump from the pinnacle of the temple....Worship me and all these kingdoms of the world will be yours" (See Matthew 4:1–9).

But Christ refused. He chose to live by the Word of God, and for the glory of God. He said, "My food is to do the will of him who sent me" (John 4:34; see also Matthew 4:4). He cultivated His walk with the Father as he prayed and soaked His mind in the Word of God. Christ was ready to do whatever it took to be obedient to the Father, and it cost Him everything. For such obedience, "God exalted him…and gave him the name that is above every name, that at the name of Jesus every knee should bow" (Philippians 2:9–10).

Satan used Nebuchadnezzar-type (assimilation) tactics in his first assault on Jesus and failed completely. He was left with no other option but to use the tactics of Pharaoh (persecution) in a ferocious assault unleashed at the cross. Christ faced the seductive enticements of the world in the temptations and the open hostility of the world on the cross. He triumphed over both and was able to say to His disciples, "Take heart! I have overcome the world" (John 16:33).

Christ warned His disciples about the conflict they would experience. There are times when Christians face the direct hatred and open hostility of the world. Jesus said, "If the world hates you, keep in mind that it hated me first" (John 15:18). At other times, Satan tries to subvert Christians through the enticements and pleasures of the world. Paul urges us not to "conform any longer to the pattern of this world, but be transformed by the renewing of your mind" (Romans 12:2).

> When you know yourself to be an alien, you become free to serve.

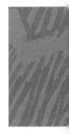

One scene in Jesus' life best reflects the message of the book of Daniel. On the night when He was betrayed, Christ washed the feet of the disciples. None of them had felt that they wanted to serve the others in that way, but Jesus was different.

> *Jesus knew that the Father had put all things under his power, and that he had come from God and was returning to God; so he got up from the meal, took off his outer clothing, and wrapped a towel around his waist.* (JOHN 13:3–4; EMPHASIS ADDED)

Do you see the secret? Christ knew who He was and where He was going. The other disciples were worried about who was first in the pecking order. But when you know that you belong to God and that you are destined for eternity, what does that matter?

We are aliens. And knowing that our destiny is to be with the Lord, we are free to pour out our lives in service that fulfills the will of God and brings blessing to others. Jesus knew that He was returning to God, so He got up, put a towel around His waist, and washed the disciples' feet.

When you know yourself to be an alien, you become free to serve.

Daniel spent most of his life in Babylon, but he knew that he did not belong there. Christ knew that He had come from the Father and that He was returning to the Father. Does your life reflect the values of someone who knows that while you live here, your true home and your destiny is in heaven?

UNLOCKED

Daniel was faced with the powerful seductions of the world, but he overcame them. He maintained and developed a godly and successful life in an affluent and ungodly culture. He was realistic about the subtle pressure that he faced and exercised voluntary restraint that enabled him to develop the ability to say no. He nourished his love for God so that it was stronger than any of the attractions and pleasures of the world.

Daniel knew that he belonged to God and that he was an alien in Babylon. Those who know that their true home is in heaven will be free to live for the glory of God on earth.

PAUSE FOR PRAYER

Gracious Father,

I confess that the things of this world have often consumed my heart. The attractions of wealth, power, and pleasure are strong. Give me a love for You that is stronger. Help me to be different—not only in what I believe but also in how I live—from those who do not know You. Show me where I can practice voluntary restraint. Help me to rise above drifting with the crowd.

Save me from the power of coveting, and help me to live for Your glory, so that at the end of my life I may hear You say, "Well done, good and faithful servant, enter into your master's joy."

May I do this all through Jesus Christ my Lord, in whose name I pray. Amen.

Love

HOSEA 11

What is love?

 *15* Love

HOSEA 11

 # DISCOVER
four amazing dimensions of the love of God.

 # LEARN
how to love when your feelings run dry.

 # WORSHIP
because God is faithful even when we have been faithless.

THE reflected light of the moon danced on the water as Robert slipped an arm around Kelly's shoulder and shifted a little closer. It was only their second date, and the movie wasn't all that much. But now they had driven to the lake to enjoy the view. After he turned off the engine, there was a kind of silence. Neither of them knew what to say.

Then, rather nervously, Robert said, "I think...I love you." It seemed like the right thing to say, but when he spoke, the words seemed to fall flat. He wasn't sure why he said it, and he wasn't really sure what he meant.

Kelly didn't know how to answer. She thought about saying, "I love you too," but it seemed a bit early in their relationship, and anyway, she wasn't entirely sure where the conversation—if that's how it should be described—was heading. So she shifted nervously in her seat and said nothing.

What do those deceptively simple words "I love you" mean? Robert didn't know, and neither did Kelly. Indeed, what does that phrase, spoken to our sons and daughters, future fiancés and spouses, really mean?

The answer is that it all depends! The Greeks had four words for love. They distinguished *eros* (sexual love), *phileo* (brotherly love and friendship), and *storge* (kinship) love. In our impoverished English language, all of these are lumped together in the one word *love*, so it's little wonder that we sometimes get confused. But the Bible uses a fourth Greek word, *agape*, to describe God's love for us and the love that He calls us to show to one another.

The best way to learn the real meaning of *agape* is through the story of Hosea. God used Hosea's personal experience of a broken heart and wrecked marriage to speak to His people—and to demonstrate the true meaning of real love.

A TWO-TIMING RELATIONSHIP

When God made His covenant with the nation of Israel, He said, "I will…be your God, and you will be my people" (Leviticus 26:12). You shall have no other gods before me." The covenant was exclusive. "If I am to be your God," the Lord was saying, "I must be your only God." The best picture we have of this exclusive covenant is marriage. In the Old Testament, God pictures Himself as being the husband of Israel, and in the New Testament, the church is the bride of Christ.

Hosea's ministry was during the reigns of Uzziah, Jotham, Ahaz, and Hezekiah (Hosea 1:1). This was the same time as Isaiah. Uzziah, Jotham, and Ahaz all failed to remove the pagan altars in the land, and it was not until late in Hosea's life that King Hezekiah tore them down (2 Kings 18:3–4). So throughout most of Hosea's life, God's people were "two-timing." They had a covenant relationship with God, but they had also made room for other gods on the side. That was as offensive and as painful to God as an unfaithful wife would be to her husband. Hosea's painful marriage became a mirror in which the love of God for His people is wonderfully revealed.

The book of Hosea is a real-life drama played out in four scenes.

SCENE 1: THE WEDDING—LOVE'S CHOICE

> When the LORD began to speak through Hosea, the LORD said to him, "Go, take to yourself an adulterous wife and children of unfaithfulness, because the land is guilty of the vilest adultery in departing from the LORD." (HOSEA 1:2)

We are not to think that the Lord was telling Hosea to phone up a dating agency and find the profile of the worst woman in town. We may reasonably assume that Hosea had already come to know a lady by the name of Gomer, that he had fallen in love with her, and that he was planning to marry her (see verse 3). But now, shortly before the wedding, God told Hosea what the future would hold.

Try to imagine what this must have been like for Hosea as he was preparing for his wedding. One night he had a dream, but it was not an ordinary dream. He knew that God was speaking to him. In his dream, he saw Gomer, the woman he loved. Then, to his horror, Hosea saw his fiancée with another man, and then another.

As the dream became a nightmare, he saw Gomer looking back and laughing at him. It was a disturbing and horrible laugh.

Hosea woke up in a cold sweat. Surely this could not be the future! And yet, somehow he knew that God was revealing what lay ahead: Gomer would become an adulterous wife. Hosea was absolutely horrified, and yet at the same time, he knew that God was telling him to go ahead with the wedding.

So he married Gomer daughter of Diblaim. (HOSEA 1:3)

Hosea chose to marry in the full knowledge of the pain that lay ahead.

Can you picture the wedding service? The minister begins by welcoming everybody to the service. "We are gathered here today," he says, "to join Hosea and Gomer in marriage. If anyone knows of any reason why they may not be lawfully joined together in marriage, let them speak now, or else keep silent forever." Then he turns to Diblaim, the bride's father. "Who gives this woman to be married to this man?" Diblaim speaks his two famous words with style: "I do." If Gomer had been as difficult at home as she turned out to be after she was married, I imagine that he must have been very relieved to get her to the altar!

The minister continues. "Hosea, will you take Gomer to be your wife, to have and to hold from this day forward, for better, for worse?" Hosea has a lump in his throat. He knows that there would be a lot of "worse" in the days that lay ahead. But without hesitation he says, "I will."

Then the minister turns to Gomer. "Will you have Hosea to be your husband? Will you love him, honor and obey him, and forsaking all others, keep only to him as long as you both shall live?"

Hosea looks deep into Gomer's eyes in that moment while everybody waits for her response. "I will," she says. Hosea knows she won't, but he chooses to marry her anyway. Would you have done that?

Over the years a number of folks have told me, with great sadness, that if they had known the pain that the future would hold they would never have gone through with the wedding. Of course, none of us who has made a marriage vow knew, when we said "for better or worse," what the future would hold. But Hosea did know, and his extraordinary decision to marry a woman who he already knew would repeatedly break his heart gives us an extraordinary insight into the love of God. God is telling us, "This is what I have done: I have made a covenant with My people in the full knowledge that they would be unfaithful and that they would bring Me indescribable pain."

God knew before the beginning of time that men and women would choose the knowledge of evil, and that delivering us from it would involve God Himself taking human flesh, entering our world, and being rejected by it. It would lead to indescribable suffering and pain in the heart of God, but He went ahead and did it anyway.

God knew from the beginning that Israel would turn to idols, and yet He set His love on these people. He said to them, "I will be your God and you will be My people." He invited them into an exclusive covenant relationship with Him, knowing that they would be hard-hearted, stubborn, and faithless.

God has shown the same love to us. Does it not strike you as amazing that God should pledge His love to you in Christ in the full knowledge of what you would be like? He knew how slow, selfish, and stubborn we would be, and yet He loved us still.

> [God] knew how slow, selfish, and stubborn we would be, and yet He loved us still.

Christ took you on in the full knowledge of what you would be like. That is why there is a profound sense in which it is never possible to disappoint God. He loved you in the full knowledge of the deepest and most consistent failure of your life. "While we were still sinners, Christ died for us" (Romans 5:8). God does not wait for us to sort out our lives before He takes us on. He commits Himself to sinners, in the full knowledge of all the pain that this will involve.

SCENE 2: THE HOME—LOVE'S PAIN

It appears that Hosea and Gomer enjoyed some good years after the wedding. They had three children—two boys and a girl—but the names given to the children are rather disturbing and seem to indicate that there were some serious problems beneath the surface. The children were called Jezreel, which was the place of a massacre (see 2 Kings 10:1–11); Lo-Ruhamah, which means "not loved"; and Lo-Ammi, which means "not my people" (1:4–9).

Try to picture Hosea at home with the children. It is late at night, and Gomer has been gone for hours. She has been evasive about where she is going and what she is doing, but Hosea is not naive. He knows what is going on. He has confronted his wife, but nothing has changed. So Hosea is pacing the floor in his own home, a man distraught with the pain of wounded love.

Over the years, Gomer's absences become longer and more frequent. She will walk in and she will walk out. The whole situation is absolutely intolerable. Hosea is in an agony of soul. God had told him that he would experience this pain, but now he is thrust into it.

Hosea's pain is a window into the heart of God. God's own people were as faithless to Him as Gomer was to Hosea, and their love of other gods brought the same kind of pain to the heart of God as Hosea experienced when his wife went off with another man. Thus in Hosea 6:4, God asked: "What can I do with you, Ephraim? What can I do with you, Judah? Your love is like the morning mist, like the early dew that disappears."

> Every time we pursue self-interest over God's interest, we are inflicting a wound in the heart of God.

"One minute you say you love Me, but the next minute, your love has faded away! What am I to do with you?" Anyone who has experienced the pain of a broken home will know exactly what is pouring from the heart of God.

Gomer's behavior helps us to understand that sin is a deeply painful and personal offense against God. Every time we lie, cheat, steal, swear, lust, or blaspheme; every time we pursue self-interest over God's interest, we are inflicting a wound in the heart of God. If sin were merely breaking some principle or regulation, it would be much less serious. But sin is wounding the heart of God.

There is a great poem by John Masefield called "The Everlasting Mercy." It tells the story of Saul Kane, who came to faith in Christ through the work of a Quaker missionary called Miss Bourne, who used to go around some of the worst inner-city pubs in England. She was a woman of unusual courage. On one occasion Saul Kane was in a terrible state, leading a group of others in foul language and all that goes with it.

Then he spotted Miss Bourne standing at the bar. This courageous woman had entered "men-only territory" in the name of Christ. Amid the cigarette butts and matches she walked up to Kane, her eyes wide and her heart breaking. She told him that his next drink, his next dirty word was like another crown of thorns pressed on the head of Christ.

It was the turning point of his life. Saul Kane couldn't continue doing what he was doing to Christ.[1]

SCENE 3: THE CITY—LOVE'S INITIATIVE

The Old Testament Law set out the death penalty for both parties involved in an act of adultery (Leviticus 20:10). That is why Christ allows the possibility of divorce following adultery (Matthew 19:9). Adultery created a unique set of circumstances because if the full penalty of the Old Testament Law was exacted, the unfaithful partner would be stoned to death, and therefore, by definition, the innocent party would be free to remarry. So divorce was a legitimate option for Hosea.

God had made an exclusive covenant relationship with His people "I will...be your God, and you will be my people." (Leviticus 26:12). But God's people had violated the core of that covenant. They had turned to other gods. It seems clear that, under these circumstances, the appropriate course of action would be for God to terminate the covenant He had made with these people and find another people for Himself.

Clearly the situation was intolerable and could not be allowed to continue, so God determined that He must act. He could not allow His people walking in and out of an exclusive covenant relationship in this way. Something had to be done. God's people would face the full consequences of their sins. They would be cut off.

> "Will not Assyria rule over them because they refuse to repent?
> Swords will flash in their cities, will destroy the bars of their
> gates and put an end to their plans." (11:5–6)

It appears that God's mind was made up. It was too late for the people to say they were sorry. Actions have consequences, and this was the end of the road. "Even if they call to the Most High, he will by no means exalt them" (v. 7).

But then, it seems that God cannot live with this conclusion. He just cannot let judgment be the last word for His own people.

> "How can I give you up, Ephraim? How can I hand you over,
> Israel?...My heart is changed within me; all my compassion
> is aroused." (v. 8)

God's justice says, "I have to bring this to a close," but His love says, "I simply cannot give up the people I love." Can you sense the tearing of the heart of God here? All the way through the Old Testament story you have these two themes: God in His awesome holiness, and God in His incomparable love. It seems as if they are pulling in opposite directions.

It is like Hosea saying, "I can't stand what Gomer is doing any longer!" But at the same time, he is saying, "I can't stop loving her." His mind goes back and forth. At night he says, "I have to see a lawyer," but when the morning comes, he can't bring himself to go. If this dilemma is painfully close to home for you, then you have a unique insight into the heart of God.

God told Hosea what he was to do about his estranged and unfaithful wife. It is a wonderful picture of how God has chosen to deal with us.

> The LORD said to me, "Go, show your love to your wife again, though she is loved by another and is an adulteress. Love her as the LORD loves the Israelites." (3:1)

So Hosea went into the city to find his wife. She was not in a pleasant part of town. He looked for her, and when he eventually found her, she was in a desperate state. Hosea describes how he "bought her for fifteen shekels of silver" (3:2). Can you imagine what this must have been like for Hosea?

SCENE 4: HOME AGAIN—LOVE'S JOY

We are not given scene four within the book of Hosea, but it is clearly promised. There's a clear parallel running between Hosea's marriage and God's relationship with His people; that's the whole point of the book. If Hosea illustrates God's pain, we may reasonably assume that the ultimate outcome of God's story would be reflected in the ending of Hosea's story.

God tells us how the story of His relationship with His people will end.

> "I am now going to allure her; I will lead her into the desert and speak tenderly to her." (2:14)

The desert, of course, is the place where the couple can be alone. God is going to win back His bride. He is talking about a new honeymoon alone together. Later, speaking of the whole nation, God says,

> "I will heal their waywardness and love them freely, for my anger has turned away from them." (14:4)

Gomer is home again. The nation Israel is home again, reconciled with God.

Hosea must have written all of this down at the end of his life. I admit to some imagination here, but I picture him as an old man sitting at his desk with his cane beside him. As he looks across the room, he sees an old lady sitting in her rocking chair, and he thinks to himself, "I love her now more than I ever did."

Hosea's story had a happy ending. The broken relationship was restored. It was the story of love's choice, love's pain, love's initiative, and love's joy. Hosea's traumatic and yet triumphant experience is a picture of God's story.

God has chosen to love sinners. He knows all about love's pain and its cost. Nowhere is this truth clearer than in His sending of His Son to earth for wayward, undeserving man. As the apostle Paul wrote, "God demonstrates his own love for us in this: While we were still sinners, Christ died for us" (Romans 5:8).

God has taken love's initiative in Jesus Christ, and for all eternity God will share love's joy with His people.

We did not deserve such love. Justice demanded something else. But the Cross brings God's love and justice together. Picture a mound of explosives. Two long fuses extend from the mound, for miles into the distance, one going to the right, the other to the left. At the end of the one fuse a sign points toward the explosives, with one word written on it, "Justice." At the end of the other fuse a second sign also points toward the explosives, bearing on it the word "Love."

The two fuses are lit simultaneously. Over on the one side, someone spots the slow-burning fuse. He says, "This is terrifying; when that fuse gets to the explosive of justice there will be hell to pay!" On the other side, someone else spots the fuse as it burns. He says, "This is wonderful; when the fuse gets to the explosive of love, heaven will be opened."

The fuses burn their way forward until they burn into each other, and when they do, there is an explosion that shakes the whole earth. Justice and love collide together at the Cross.

That's the story of the Bible. On the day Adam sinned, God told him that he would die. At the same time, God promised victory over the curse. There would be someone born of the woman who would crush the head of the serpent and deliver man from death.

God lit two long fuses. With justice and love God would destroy sin's curse and deliver sinners. Justice and mercy. These two themes burn their way through the Old Testament story, until they meet together at Calvary. Justice and mercy reach their fullest expression at the Cross. Love met God's requirement for justice, as a perfect sacrifice was offered for our sins.

Why would you turn away from love like this?

Were the whole realm of nature mine,
That were an offering far too small.
Love so amazing, so divine,
Demands my life, my soul, my all.

—ISAAC WATTS
"WHEN I SURVEY THE WONDROUS CROSS" [ADAPTED]

UNLOCKED

True love is neither an urge nor a feeling, but a decision. It is a steady commitment to act in the interests of the one who is loved, irrespective of the cost. Hosea demonstrated the true meaning of love in his actions towards Gomer. Hosea made a decision that he would act in her best interests irrespective of the cost. That is why he married her even though he knew the pain and sorrow that lay ahead. That is why he remained committed to her through the dark years when he would have been quite justified in ending the relationship. And that is why, when she came to the lowest point, he paid a price and brought her home.

Hosea loved Gomer "as the LORD loves the Israelites" (Hosea 3:1), and through his extraordinary love for his wife under desperate circumstances, he has given us a snapshot of the heart of God.

The Bible tells us "God so loved the world that he gave his one and only Son" (John 3:16). This does not mean that God was overcome with warm feelings about us. In fact, quite the opposite is the case. God sees our sin and it is repulsive to Him, just as Gomer's behavior was repulsive to Hosea. But God has made a choice to act in our best interests without regard to the cost, even if that meant sacrificing His Son.

The love of God for us has been decisively demonstrated in history through the death of Jesus, but it does not end there. Paul also tells us that "God has poured out his love into our hearts by the Holy Spirit, whom he has given us" (Romans 5:5). The words "poured out" speak of abundance, gushing out, saturation. The Holy Spirit pours this love into our hearts so that the love of God is not only historically demonstrated on the cross, but also personally experienced in our lives today. When we have discovered this love, then, by the power of the Spirit we can also choose to act in the best interests of another person without regard to the cost.

PAUSE FOR PRAYER

Almighty God.

I bow in Your presence, humbled and in awe of Your amazing love. I cannot fathom why You should commit Yourself to me in the full knowledge of my sin, but I thank You that you did. I cannot grasp why You should remain faithful when I have been so faithless, but I praise You that You have. I cannot know why You should send Your Son at immeasurable cost to rescue me and bring me back to Yourself, but with awe and wonder I confess that this is what You have done.

Give me a greater ability to grasp the dimensions of Your amazing love for me, and fill my heart with this redeeming love so that something of Your nature may be reflected in me, through Jesus Christ. Amen.

NOTE

1. John Masefield, "The Everlasting Mercy" in the *Collected Poems of John Masefield* (New York: Heineman, 1942).

Faith

HABAKKUK 2

What are we to

make of the evil

God allows in the

world today?

*16*Faith

HABAKKUK 2

DISCOVER
the amazing way in which God uses
evil within His own purpose.

LEARN
why faith is better than sight.

WORSHIP
as you see how God will ultimately
destroy all evil.

THE news was not encouraging during the week I wrote the first draft of this chapter, but it was not unusual either. Violence in the Middle East, atrocities in the Balkans, and a family wiped out in a multiple murder in California. I pointed out the persistent pattern of events like these and wrote, "By the time you are reading this, the headlines will be different, but the themes will be the same: violence, destruction, and death."

Now, as I complete the final revisions, the point seems more poignant than before. The headlines are filled with the aftermath of America's greatest disaster to date: the terrorist attack on the World Trade Center and the Pentagon, leaving more than 4,000 civilians dead. The themes are the same: violence, destruction, and death.

I cannot predict the headlines today, as you hold this book in your hands, but I am sadly confident that the themes will not have changed. Sometimes we wonder how long the depressing catalog of evils in the world will continue.

That was the question that faced the prophet Habakkuk. His prophecy reads rather like the book of Job, with one important difference. Job was concerned with the question of personal suffering, but Habakkuk was concerned with the evil that God allows in the world.

The major role of a prophet was to speak to men from God. But Habakkuk was different in that he also spoke to God on behalf of men. A large part of this book is taken up with Habakkuk's complaints against God. He raises some profound questions. He was deeply disturbed about why God allows things to be as they are in this world. Perhaps you are too.

That is the great issue of the Bible story. The Bible does not begin with you and me. It begins with God and the world. "In the beginning God." That is the first thing. "In the beginning God created the heavens and the earth." That is the second thing.

There is a great danger of Christians becoming narrow-minded people who treat the Bible like a kind of handbook on personal salvation and largely ignore all the rest. The Bible is the revelation of God, and it tells us about His plan for the world. The Bible tells us that the world belongs to God, and that He has His own reasons for tolerating evil for a time. God tells us that in the end, evil will be brought to nothing, and the whole earth will be filled with God's glory.

The Bible gives us what some people call a *worldview*, a way of making sense of the world in which we live, a way of understanding the things that are going on around us. Nowhere in the Bible is this more clearly present than in the book of Habakkuk.

"WHY DO YOU ALLOW IT, GOD?"

We are not told precisely when Habakkuk lived. The one clue we are given is that God says, "I am raising up the Babylonians" (Habakkuk 1:6). The Babylonians destroyed the city of Jerusalem in 586 B.C., so it is reasonable to assume that Habakkuk spoke the Word of God about a generation before that time.

Habakkuk begins with the prophet asking a profound question:

> How long, O LORD, must I call for help, but you do not listen?
> Or cry out to you, "Violence!" but you do not save? Why do you
> make me look at injustice? Why do you tolerate wrong? (1:2–3)

Imagine Habakkuk at home in the city of Jerusalem, with his head in his hands. He cannot read his *Jerusalem Tribune* newspaper without seeing something about a shooting or a killing or some kind of violence and destruction. When he looks around the city, he says, "Destruction and violence are before me; there is strife, and conflict abounds" (1:3). Everywhere he looks, in business, government, between neighbors, or even in the temple, there are disputes and arguments. You might have expected at least a basic neighborliness among God's people, and it had once been so. But now it seems to be every man for himself, and Habakkuk finds himself in a litigious society.

The result was, of course, that "the law is paralyzed" (v. 4). The courts were jammed with litigation, but when all is said and done, justice did not prevail. The reason for this was that "the wicked hem in the righteous, so that justice is perverted" (v. 4). More and more cases were being decided on the basis of money and power than truth and justice, and as a result, the whole legal system was coming apart at the seams. Does this sound like another world or does it sound strangely familiar?

The thing that made this so painful for Habakkuk was that all this was happening among God's people! God had called these people to be a light to other nations. Jerusalem was supposed to be the city where God's name was honored and people lived according to His law. Habakkuk's heart was heavy because of the rampant injustice in the city of God. He wondered how long God would allow this to go on and longed for God to do something about the sins of His own people.

Why does God tolerate wrong? How are we to understand what is happening in our day? Habakkuk raises the great questions that believers in a fallen world face in every generation. Why is the world as it is? Why does God allow the evils that stalk the world today?

YOU WON'T BELIEVE THIS!

"Look at the nations and watch—and be utterly amazed. For I am going to do something in your days that you would not believe, even if you were told." (1:5).

Habakkuk had been waiting for God to act, and now God was ready to move. Perhaps the prophet thought, *Great. Tell me what this unbelievable thing is, Lord! Are You going to bring a national revival? Will there be a vast turning to faith in the next generation?*

What God said next must have left Habakkuk speechless.

"I am raising up the Babylonians." (1:6)

I imagine Habakkuk doing a double take at this point.

"The Babylonians?!"

"Yes, Habakkuk; the Babylonians."

If you want to know how Habakkuk must have felt about this, put in a more contemporary name. This would be like God saying, "Yes, I know that there are terrible things going on among My people, so here is My answer: I am going to raise up Saddam Hussein."

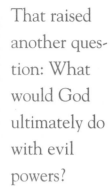

That raised another question: What would God ultimately do with evil powers?

"But You can't do that, God! Things are in a pretty desperate state among the people of God, but nothing like what's going on among the Babylonians. They are the denial of everything that You stand for. You can't possibly raise *them* up, can You?"

The cure seemed worse than the condition. But God's answer was quite clear. God would use the Babylonians to deal with the sins of His own people. He would use their evil to accomplish His own purpose.

That does take some believing! It seems to raise more questions than it does answers, and so it is not surprising that Habakkuk asked a second question.

> O LORD, you have appointed them [the Babylonians] to execute judgment....You have ordained them to punish. Your eyes are too pure to look on evil; you cannot tolerate wrong. Why then do you tolerate the treacherous? Why are you silent while the wicked swallow up those more righteous than themselves? (1:12–13)

Habakkuk's first question was about the sins of God's people. His second question was about the wider evil in the world. Habakkuk seemed to have accepted that God could use an evil power like Babylon to bring judgment to His own people, but that raised another question: What would God ultimately do with evil powers?

WHERE HISTORY IS HEADING

There seems to be a pause in the conversation, and we have to wait until Habakkuk 2 before we come to God's answer. When God finally speaks, He makes a major announcement.

> Then the LORD replied: "Write down the revelation and make it plain on tablets so that a herald may run with it. For the revelation awaits an appointed time; it speaks of the end and will not prove false. Though it linger, wait for it; it will certainly come and will not delay." (2:2–3)

God was saying, "Habakkuk, I want you to write down what I am about to say, because this is something that everybody needs to know. It needs to be a permanent record, because what I am about to tell you will not happen until the appointed time. I am going to unveil what will happen in the end." So Habakkuk pulled out a pen and a tablet and recorded God's five statements. Each one began with the word *woe*, which indicated that something would be stopped.

"*Woe to him* who piles up stolen goods and makes himself wealthy by extortion!" (2:6, all italics added). This is a person who has accumulated wealth without integrity.

"*Woe to him* who builds his realm by unjust gain" (v. 9). This person has lost sight of truth and justice and will do anything to build his power and achieve his own ends.

"*Woe to him* who builds a city with bloodshed" (v. 12). This person has placed a low value on human life.

"*Woe to him* who gives drink to his neighbors, pouring it from the wineskin till they are drunk, so that he can gaze on their naked bodies" (v. 15). Here is the abuser of drugs, the abuser of women.

"*Woe to him* who says to wood, 'Come to life!' Or to lifeless stone, 'Wake up!'" (v. 19). This person is an idolater. The greatest thing in his life is his own achievement. What he has made has been put in the place of God.

God is promising that all the dimensions of evil in the world will finally be stopped. Their destruction is assured. God will completely overthrow all evil, and "the earth will be filled with the knowledge of the glory of the LORD, as the waters cover the sea" (2:14). That is where human history is heading.

LIVING BY FAITH

Right in the middle of this struggle with the problem of evil, God tells Habakkuk—and us—that

> "*The righteous will live by his faith.*" (v. 4)

These are the words that the apostle Paul quoted as a summary of the gospel. "The gospel....is the power of God for the salvation of everyone who believes....For in the gospel a righteousness from God is revealed, a righteousness that is by faith from first to last, just as it is written: 'The righteous will live by faith'" (Romans 1:16–17).

The righteous living by faith was not a new idea concocted by the apostle Paul in the New Testament. The righteous have always lived by faith. The Bible is one story, and God's people have always had to operate on the basis of faith and will do so until Christ returns.

Now when Habakkuk talks about "the righteous," he does not mean that there are some people who are absolutely in the right in every respect. The Bible is absolutely clear that "there is no one righteous, not even one" (Romans 3:10). But there are clearly people who desire righteousness in their own lives and in the world. Jesus spoke about these people when He said, "Blessed are those who hunger and thirst for righteousness, for they will be filled" (Matthew 5:6).

How are these people, like Habakkuk, who hunger and thirst after righteousness to make sense of this confusing world? How are we to navigate our way through the uncertain and unpredictable events in our world? How are we to hold our course in the face of the great evils that arise in the course of history? The answer is *faith*. "The righteous shall live by faith."

FAITH IS BETTER THAN SIGHT

Sight is a wonderful gift, but it has a very limited capacity. It cannot look around corners, it can look in one direction at a time, and when it turns to look another way, it loses the capacity to view what it saw before!

For as long as we are living in this fallen world, faith is much better than sight. Sight looks at evidence, forms opinions, and draws conclusions. The problem with sight is that it is only capable of looking at the observable realities; it does not have the capacity to perceive any further.

Sight never reckons on the invisible power of God, and that is why sight is hopelessly inadequate when it comes to making sense of this world in which we live. By definition sight must leave the invisible God out of the picture. So if you try to make sense of your life or of events in this world purely on the basis of sight, you will be very discouraged.

Faith sees beyond the difficulties and counts on God.

God was telling Habakkuk that he would see the rise of Babylon. He would live through things that seemed utterly overwhelming. The level of evil in the world would stagger him. But God also told Habakkuk that he must not operate on the basis of what he saw around him.

This does not mean that the person who exercises faith goes through life with his eyes closed. His eyes should be wide open to the problems. But faith goes beyond sight. Faith sees beyond the difficulties and counts on God.

If we operate on the basis of sight, we will soon be pretty discouraged. We will see the abuse of power in high places, the weakness and worldliness of the church, appalling acts of violence, and terrible abuse. We will see "Babylon" rampant. If we are longing for righteousness and are operating on the basis of sight, we will soon be overwhelmed with darkness and despair.

Of course, when we are in the presence of Christ, sight will be altogether different. Then we will see Him. Sight will then have the capacity of apprehending God, but it does not have that capacity now. The joy of heaven will be that *we will behold Him*. Until then, we must walk by faith.

FAITH RESTS ON GOD'S PROMISE

That was what God was inviting Habakkuk to do. God Almighty would prosper Babylon, and Jerusalem would be crushed. The apparent triumph of evil would make it seem that God's purpose was being overturned, but God was saying, "My purpose will be achieved; in the end, evil will be completely destroyed. That is My Word, and this will be My work. Now trust Me."

Faith rests in the Word and the work of God. It trusts what God says and finds rest in what God does. That's what Abraham did. God had promised to make Abraham's descendants like the stars of the heavens (Genesis 15:5). The only problem was that Abraham was a hundred years old, and his wife was nearly ninety! The statistical probability of Isaac being born was around about zero!

Sight said, "There isn't a lot of hope here," but faith went beyond sight and found rest in the Word of God. God had said, "Your descendants will be like the stars in the skies," and Abraham trusted what God said and rested in what only God could do. Paul said that Abraham "faced the fact that his body was as good as dead" (Romans 4:19), yet he gave glory to God being fully persuaded that God had the power to do what He had promised (v. 21).

That is how faith operates. It looks beyond the observable realities and counts on God's promise. You may be looking at a pretty discouraging situation in your own life. The observable reality is not good. Perhaps there isn't any basis for hope in what you see. God calls you to operate on the basis of faith. Faith recognizes the realities, but it rests in the promises of God.

FAITH OPENS THE DOOR TO LASTING JOY

The book of Habakkuk ends with worship. The prophet has asked his questions; God has given His promise and called the prophet to faith. Then in chapter 3 Habakkuk begins to worship as he remembers the faithfulness of God, and it leads him to one of the great confessions of faith in the Old Testament.

Habakkuk looks up to God, and he prays, ending with a confession of complete confidence:

> Though the fig tree does not bud and there are no grapes on the vines, though the olive crop fails and the fields produce no food, though there are no sheep in the pen and no cattle in the stalls, yet I will rejoice in the LORD, I will be joyful in God my Savior. (3:17–18)

This confession of faith from a prophet who has struggled to make sense of the evils around him reminds us of Job's worship on the day of his suffering. It is one of the high-water marks of Old Testament faith.

Habakkuk discovered a joy that did not depend on what was happening around him. He described the worst of all imaginable circumstances, and then told God, "Even if everything goes wrong and all hell breaks loose, here is my position: I will not operate on the basis of sight, but on the basis of faith. I will rest in Your promise, and I will find my joy in knowing that You are my Savior."

Habakkuk's joy was based on the assurance that even when the Babylonians overwhelmed the city of God, the Lord was in control. He had grasped that history moves under the plan of God and is heading for the day when all evil will be overthrown and brought to nothing.

This joy does not depend on what is happening in the market or who is in the White House. We should pray for fig trees to bud and grapes on the vine and sheep in the pen and cattle in the stall, but our joy does not depend on these unpredictable things. Habakkuk discovered a joy that is rooted in God and in the certainty that His purpose will be fulfilled. That gave him stability, and he was able to worship God with joy at a time when evil was advancing in the world!

What do you know about this kind of faith?

SPOTLIGHT ON CHRIST

Six hundred years later Jerusalem, the same city where Habakkuk had once agonized over the evil around him and which the Babylonians later destroyed, had been rebuilt—just as God had promised. By the time of Jesus' birth, it was a bustling metropolis; the Babylonian Empire was long gone. However, another empire, based in Rome, had risen to usurp Jerusalem's autonomy. The evil of the one did not seem very different from the evil of the other.

Rome seemed like Babylon by another name. In Christ's day, it was still hard to get justice, which was now in the hands of a politically motivated judge named Pontius Pilate.

Watch the scene: A couple of false witnesses take the stand in court and tell lies to an already prejudiced jury. Why would God allow that? Soldiers stand in a circle around a man whose hands are tied. They strike Him and spit upon Him and place a crown of thorns on His head. It looks rather like the violence and destruction that Habakkuk saw. Why would God allow that?

Come and see an innocent man nailed to a cross. As He dies in agony, He cries out, "My God, my God, why...?" God allowed evil to have its day and used that evil to accomplish His own purposes.

In his book *Making Sense out of Suffering*, Peter Kreeft says, "Calvary is judo; the enemy's own power is used to defeat him."[1] That is a brilliant analogy. God takes the power of evil and uses its own momentum to bring about its own downfall. Satan's end becomes God's means.

> Satan's end becomes God's means. Of course, sight would never tell you that.

Of course, sight would never tell you that. Even the disciples operated on the basis of sight, and so all they could perceive was the Son of God agonizing in death. They all forsook Him and fled. The women did better and stayed, along with John by the cross, but all they saw was the death of their hopes and the end of their joy.

But when faith looks at the cross, it sees more than a terrible evil. Faith sees God at work and believes His promise. Faith sees that this was why Christ came into the world. Faith reckons that if God has said Christ will save His people from their sins, then even His death must be for that purpose.

At the most personal level, I have to say that faith is better than sight. Here's why: If I do a careful analysis of my life in the light of the Law of God, sight says that I have sinned and fall short of the glory of God. That fact is not only observable to me, but also to my wife and to everybody who knows me well. It is the truth about all of us. There is no one righteous, not even one.

But faith goes deeper than sight. Faith rests on the promise of God. Faith says "Christ died for my sins" and believes God's promise that "there is...no condemnation for those who are in Christ Jesus" (Romans 8:1) because on the cross, He took our sin so that we could be forgiven and reconciled to God. This faith in Christ brings lasting joy. I can say with Habakkuk, "I will rejoice in God my Savior."

That's why Paul took up the words of Habakkuk, "the righteous shall live by faith." In the light of the Cross, this means not just that faith is the way for people who long for righteousness to get through this life, but that faith is the way in which those who long for righteousness will enter the life to come.

If you follow the Bible story to its end, you will discover that Babylon appears again in the book of Revelation. The old Babylonian Empire collapsed centuries before the birth of Christ. Since then, history has seen a whole line of great powers rise and fall. They all seem like Babylon by another name. The Bible uses the name Babylon to sum up the rising and falling powers of this world in their arrogance and defiance of God.

During the final years of John's life, while the apostle was in solitary confinement on the Isle of Patmos, God gave him a glimpse of things to come. In Revelation, John tells us what he saw: "Fallen! Fallen is Babylon the Great!" (Revelation 18:2). Gone! Finished! John glimpsed what God had promised to Habakkuk!

Then, John saw Christ descend from heaven in all His glory, and he heard what sounded like a great crowd shouting, "Hallelujah! For our Lord God Almighty reigns. Let us rejoice and be glad and give him glory!" (Revelation 19:6–7).

UNLOCKED

The Bible teaches us that there is such a thing as evil. It is ugly and destructive; it always brings pain and sorrow. The power of evil was unleashed in the world when Adam and Eve chose to disobey God in the Garden of Eden. Ever since that time, man has tried to shake free from its grip, but deliverance from evil is beyond our power. Governments may and must restrain it, but we cannot get free from it. Only God can deliver us from evil.

But we live in a world that has rejected the God of the Bible. Even in our own society, there are many attempts to remove God from public life. We ask the Deliverer to leave, and then when evil is unleashed, we wonder why He seems so far away.

God will destroy all evil. In the end it will not stand. That was God's promise on the day sin entered the world (Genesis 3:15), and it is the great hope that is presented in the gospel. But God gives us the freedom to choose whether we want to live in a world without evil. If we do, we must be delivered from the evil within us as well as the evil around us.

Christ has come to deliver us from evil. He breaks its power in our lives when we come to Him in faith, but He allows its power to remain in the world that rejects Him. That tension makes us long for the day when Christ will return and evil will be no more.

Until that day, God calls us to walk by faith and not by sight. We are to look beyond the latest disaster or atrocity. The Cross reminds us that even the greatest evil cannot thwart the purpose of God, and faith anticipates the day of God's final victory.

PAUSE FOR PRAYER

Almighty God,

I come to You in grief and sadness because of the evil that I see at work in the world. Help me to hate what is evil and cling to what is good. Help me to be vigorous in fighting against evil wherever I see its presence in my thoughts, words, actions, or intentions.

Help me to operate on the basis of faith and not on the basis of what I see around me. Thank You that Christ has come into the world to deliver us from evil. Help me always to place my confidence and my trust in Him. Amen.

NOTE

1. Peter Kreeft, *Making Sense out of Suffering* (Ann Arbor, Mich.: Servant, 1986), 132.

Hope

MALACHI 4

Is there

any hope?

17 Hope

MALACHI 4

DISCOVER

why no religion can lead you to God.

LEARN

why the Old Testament cannot be God's final word.

WORSHIP

as you see how the whole Bible story points us to Jesus Christ.

A UDIENCES who enjoy live theater go for several reasons, including the actors, the directors, and even the music. Some like good storytelling, as the plot and characters unfold over time. If the Bible were presented as a condensed drama, it would unfold in two parts, like a two-act play.

Act one of this great drama would be the Old Testament. In real time, it spans more than a millennium—about 1,600 years from Abraham to Malachi. So by the end of the long story of act one, we are quite ready to spill out into the foyer for an intermission, before we come back to see what happens in act two.

As we look back over act one, the whole of the story has been about a problem and a promise. The problem was presented to us at the beginning of the story, when the first man and woman—created by a loving God who surrounded them with good things—wanted something else. Adam and Eve had no experience of evil, and they felt that their lives would be more complete if they knew something about it.

There wasn't much opportunity for evil in the paradise of God, but God gave them one command, and disobeying that was their first experience of evil.

LIFE OUTSIDE THE GARDEN

Their sin had immediate consequences. First it changed the nature of their relationship with God. God had appeared to them, taking a form in which He could walk with them in the garden. They had enjoyed fellowship with God and entered into conversation with Him.

But after the first sin, Adam and Eve hid from the Lord when He came into the garden; they did not want to be near Him. The Lord had to call to Adam and draw him out of hiding, and by the end of the day, Adam found himself outside of the garden. God no longer appeared to him. Adam knew God, but he could not see God or hear His voice. He was alienated from God.

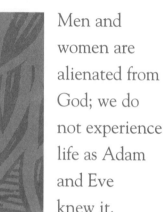

> Men and women are alienated from God; we do not experience life as Adam and Eve knew it.

Adam and Eve's experience of life changed that day. God had given them a beautiful relationship. They had been the perfect match. Their love for each other was a mirror of the love of God for them. They were at ease together, and their trust in each other was complete. But the knowledge of evil changed all that. Adam blamed his wife for what had gone wrong, his wife blamed the serpent and the serpent didn't have a leg to stand on! For the first time, suspicion developed between the man and the woman. They discovered that the knowledge of evil was not a onetime event, it was now a power within them.

God told them what the future would hold. There would be a great battle with this evil. It would run through every generation and across every culture. Life in this world would never be as it had been in the paradise of God.

Sin changed their prospects for the future. There was this terrible matter of the curse. God said to the serpent, "Cursed are you." God was saying, "You will be utterly destroyed. All that you have done will be brought to nothing."

Then God turned to the man. But (as we saw in chapter 2 of volume 1 of *Unlocking the Bible Story*) God immediately deflected the curse from Adam and onto the ground: "Cursed is *the ground* because of you" (Genesis 3:17, italics added). Adam must have wondered what the ground had done! What he deserved, the ground sustained.

God diverted the curse away from the man so that his life could be spared and room made for him to be reconciled to God. But the point of the curse was clear. Evil would ultimately be destroyed, and the great problem for Adam and his children was that this evil was now within them.

Adam and Eve were driven out of the garden and cherubim guarded the way back into the paradise of God, along with a flaming sword that represented the judgment of God. There was no way back into the presence and the blessing of God except through this judgment in which they would be utterly destroyed.

This is the great problem that runs right through the Bible story. Men and women are alienated from God; we do not experience life as Adam and Eve knew it in the garden, and there is this dreadful curse that hangs over every person born into the world.

That was all back at the beginning of act one of this great drama of the Bible story. Now we come to Malachi, the last book of the Old Testament. Malachi was the last of the Old Testament prophets. He spoke the Word of God around the time when Nehemiah led a small community of people back to Jerusalem to rebuild the city walls. Malachi gives us a fascinating insight into what life was like in that community.

After Malachi, there was an intermission. Nothing significant happened in God's story for four hundred years and the next prophet to appear on the scene was John the Baptist. So as we come to the end of the Old Testament story, it's worth asking for an update: Where are we with regard to the problem that was presented at the beginning of the Bible story?

AN ARGUMENT THAT IS GOING NOWHERE

The question is where do things stand in the relationship between God and His people after all these years of alienation from God? Malachi does not give us an encouraging answer.

There is a pattern that runs through the book in which God makes a statement, but His people will not accept what He says. It is as if an argument develops between God and His people, rather like a counseling session in which one rather petulant person is unwilling to accept the truth of anything that the other person says.

The book of Malachi opens with God affirming His love for His people.

> *"I have loved you," says the LORD. (1:2)*

That seems a reasonable statement when you think that He brought them out of Egypt, gave the promises, and restored them from exile, but God's people will not accept that. It is as if they fold their arms in defiance and say, "How have you loved us?" (1:2).

As you read through the book of Malachi, it is clear that there is an argument going on between God and His people. God is seeking to restore the relationship with His people, and so He raises the issues that have caused the relationship to break down. That is the only way in which a relationship can be restored: The issues that have caused offense must be brought to light and dealt with honestly. But God's people are in denial about the problem.

Have you ever seen an argument in which one person digs in and will not admit any responsibility for what's wrong? Those who have attempted to restore a broken relationship will know what this is like. If you have one party who is reaching out to make peace and the other party is unresponsive and in denial about the problem, then you face an uphill struggle. That's what is happening here.

DENIAL, DENIAL, DENIAL

God raises an issue with the priests. They were supposed to order the worship of God and supervise the sacrifices. God says that they show contempt for His name. But the priests won't accept this. Instead, they wanted to know, 'How have we shown contempt for your name?' (v. 6). God explains the problem. He is raising the issue because He wants to bring resolution and to restore the relationship. "You place defiled food on my altar." But the priests will not accept this either. Instead they ask, "How have we defiled you?" (v. 7).

This has all the marks of a discussion that is getting nowhere, but the pattern runs right through the book. Denial, denial, denial. God raises the issue of repentance with the people. " 'Ever since the time of your forefathers you have turned away from my decrees and have not kept them. Return to me, and I will return to you,' says the LORD Almighty." The response has the note of petulance about it: "How are we to return?" (3:7).

God raises the issue of tithes. "Will a man rob God? Yet you rob me." The response is predictable: "How do we rob you?" (3:8).

Then God points out that the people speak about Him harshly. " 'You have said harsh things against me,' says the LORD. 'Yet you ask, "What have we said against you?" ' " (3:13).

Over the years, I have sat through some pretty sad conversations, but this one just about takes the cake! God is reaching out to His people. He tells them that He loves them. He wants to restore the relationship with His people, and so He raises the issues so that they can be resolved, but time after time, His people take the posture of denial and fold their arms in defiance toward God, and that's where the Old Testament ends!

This story that began with a man and a woman in fellowship with God ends with men and women alienated from God, in denial of the problem, unwilling to take any responsibility, and unable to do anything about it.

THE PAIN OF A BROKEN HOME

If that was the story of man and woman's relationship with God, what about the story of their relationship with each other in marriage? In the Old Testament, that story began with joy, but it ends in tears. In the garden, Adam and Eve had enjoyed perfect happiness, but at the end of the Old Testament, Malachi says,

> The LORD is acting as the witness between you and the wife of your youth, because you have broken faith with her, though she is your partner, the wife of your marriage covenant…."I hate divorce," says the LORD God. (2:14–16)

I never met a person who, on their wedding day, thought or hoped that they would one day stand in a divorce court. It must be one of the most painful experiences in all the world. But as God spoke to the culture of Malachi's time, it was clear that marriages were breaking and tearing apart. The joy of shared hopes and dreams for the future were ending in the tears of broken promises.

That is the story of the Old Testament. It began with a man and a woman sharing the joy of a perfect life together in the garden, and it ends with men and women in the divorce court, unable to sustain a relationship of faithfulness and love. That's the tragedy of our world.

The breaking of marriages had devastating effects on the children. That's why in Malachi 4 God spoke about a day when the hearts of the fathers will be turned to the children and the children to their fathers (v. 6). The fact that God says this tells us that the whole family unit was falling apart. Dads had lost heart for their children. Sons and daughters didn't care about their parents. Families lived without love. Long stories of accumulated wrongs developed without forgiveness penetrating. What began with joy, ended in tears.

PROSPECTS FOR THE FUTURE

While the key word of Malachi is hope, the last word in the Old Testament is not nearly so encouraging. God speaks about someone who will come and "turn the hearts of the fathers to their children, and the hearts of the children to their fathers; or else I will come and strike the land with a *curse*" (4:6; italics added).

God's curse on evil hangs over over the whole book of Malachi. Consider just these two verses: "I will send a curse upon you, and I will curse your blessings" (2:2). "You are under a curse—the whole nation of you—because you are robbing me" (3:9). God's curse is on all evil.

So when we come to the end of the Old Testament, we have not come very far in dealing with the problem of alienation from God, the hardness of the human heart, or the curse that hangs over men and women. The problems that began in the garden are written all over the book of Malachi, right up to the last word.

> God never goes back on a promise, and after seventy years in exile, a small group of people [rebuilt]… Jerusalem.

THE UNFULFILLED PROMISE

Though the problem of sin's curse pervades the Old Testament, the Bible story is also about a promise. Remember, on the very day when evil entered into the world, God promised that someone would be born of a woman who would crush the serpent's head. He would destroy the evil one and all his works. This victory would come at great cost. While this person would crush the serpent's head, the serpent would bite His heel (Genesis 3:15). So deliverance from evil would involve great pain and suffering.

Right from the beginning of this great drama, then, we are looking for someone who will overcome the power of evil and deliver the human race from our predicament.

In the course of time God appeared to Abraham and said, "I will bless you and through you all the nations of the earth will be blessed." Isaac was born, and then Jacob (later renamed Israel), and from them, God raised up a great nation. These people were oppressed by great evil in Egypt, but God brought them out and made a covenant with them. "I will be your God and you will be My people."

Moses led them out of Egypt and Joshua led them into Canaan, but no deliverer had appeared to save them from their sinful selves. Then God gave a special promise to David, the second king of Israel. A king one day would be born into David's line whose kingdom and reign would last forever (2 Samuel 7:13). But after the time of David, most of the kings were a great disappointment. One king after another led the people down the wrong track. Instead of worshiping the Lord, God's people imitated the worship and the lifestyle of people around them, and the result was that evil became rampant even among the people of God.

So God drew a line in the sand. Nebuchadnezzar took the brightest and best of God's people into exile in Babylon, and the city of Jerusalem with its temple and its palace was utterly destroyed.

Where was hope? It was there all the time. God never goes back on a promise, and after seventy years in exile, a small group of people went back to rebuild the city of Jerusalem. God sent Malachi the prophet to remind them, not only of the problem, but also of the promise.

> "The sun of righteousness will rise with healing in its wings. And
> you will go out and leap like calves released from the stall." (4:2)

God was telling the people that there would be healing for the problem that had run all the way through human history. Evil had gained a grip on the world. Even God's people were imprisoned by it. But the day would come when God's people would experience the freedom that calves enjoy when they are released from the stall. But at the end of the Old Testament, we are still looking for that promise to be fulfilled.

TIME FOR THE INTERMISSION

So the great drama of act one is complete, and it is time for the intermission. What a first act! The relationship with God that began with fellowship ends in alienation. The experience of life that was filled with joy is now marked with tears. The prospect of everlasting life, which was there in the garden, has now been eclipsed by a curse that hangs over men and women on account of sin. A great promise has been given, but it has not yet been fulfilled, and that is where the Old Testament ends.

So the intermission comes, and we all spill into the foyer to reflect on the first half. We sidle up to a large group of people standing in the foyer as they talk about what they have seen in act one.

"Some of that was a bit heavy," says a large man as he lights up his pipe.

"Some of it made me want to cry," says a delicate lady with a glass in her hand.

"I hope that act two has a happier ending than this," adds a third.

"Well, it must," says someone else in the group. "All the way through there have been promises and pointers; something's going to happen soon, I'm telling you."

"Well, whatever it is, it ain't happened yet," says Bob, rather impatiently. "Nothing has happened in the whole of act one that has dealt with the basic problem."

"What do you mean nothing has happened? We've had the Law, and the sacrifices; we've had kings and priests; we've seen the cloud of God's presence in the temple ..."

"Yes, but the main problem in the story has not been solved," Bob replies. "They are alienated from God, their whole experience of life is spoiled, and they have this dreadful curse hanging over them. The story won't have a happy ending unless that problem is solved!"

The bell rings for the end of the intermission, and the group all file back to their seats in the theater for act two.

DON'T MISS ACT TWO!

Suppose that someone in the audience leaves the theater during the intermission. They have seen act one, but they never see act two. They leave the theater with an unsolved problem and an unfulfilled promise.

When you come to the end of the Old Testament, with all its laws, priests, and sacrifices, you are left asking, "What will it take to end this alienation from God? What will it take to change the human heart? And what will it take to remove the dreadful curse that hangs over every person born into the world?"

There are many people today who think that "all religions lead to God." But the Old Testament says precisely the opposite. It teaches that no religion can bring us to God, including the Old Testament religion itself! Today, many people miss the second act. They embrace the Old Testament but they do not know how God has dealt with sin's curse by a final sacrifice.

As we close Malachi and the Old Testament, it should be obvious that we have a major problem. We have sinned against God. We have broken His laws. We have become alienated from Him, and the curse of evil hangs over us.

SPOTLIGHT ON CHRIST

That is why Jesus Christ had to come into the world. He came to do what no religion could ever do. He came to solve the problem and fulfill the promise. You could go to church, say your prayers, and try to live a moral life, but without Christ you cannot be reconciled to God. That is why His coming into the world is the greatest thing in all human history. He can change your heart, He can take away the curse that hangs over you, and He can reconcile you to God. The Old Testament is an unfinished story. It shows us our need of Christ.

No wonder heaven erupted with joy when Jesus was born into the world. It was the greatest event in all of human history. Christ came into the world in order to give His life as a sacrifice for sin. By His death, He bridged the gap of alienation between man and God. Since He is God in human flesh, Jesus Christ is the meeting place of man and God in His own nature, and through His death, He opened the way in which our sins can be forgiven and we can be reconciled to God.

Christ also bore the curse. Just as God diverted the curse away from Adam, He is ready to divert the curse away from you. But the curse is real and it has to go somewhere. So Jesus came, and as the apostle Paul explained, Christ

> redeemed us from the curse of the law by becoming a curse for us, for it is written: "Cursed is everyone who is hung on a tree." (GALATIANS 3:13)

Jesus bore the curse of God. The Son of God did what nobody else could do: "He himself bore our sins in his body on the tree, so that we might die to sins and live for righteousness" (1 Peter 2:24). His death exhausted the punishment for sin, and on the third day, He rose from the dead so that we may enter into everlasting life.

Thanks to Christ's sacrifice, those who turn to Him will never experience the wrath of God, because He has taken it for them. He has reconciled men and women to God, and He will bring them to everlasting life.

The story that began in the garden will not end in tears. It will end with more joy than Adam and Eve could ever have known in the garden. It will end with a city populated by all those who have been redeemed by Christ. It will be more than the paradise Adam and Eve knew, because we will be free not only from the presence of sin but also from the possibility of sin. We will see God and enter into life in all its fullness forevermore.

UNLOCKED

This chapter has addressed a huge question. Is there any hope for broken lives and for a fallen world? The Old Testament story makes it clear that there is no hope in religion or in laws or in any kind of human structure or program. God demonstrated that through the story of His people over a period of sixteen hundred years.

But all of that was to prepare us for Christ. God destroys false hopes so that we may find our true hope in His Son, who answers the problem of sin and fulfills the promise of God.

In this chapter, I have asked you to think about the story of the Bible as a great drama and to imagine yourself in the audience. But you are also in the play. The Bible is the great drama of the human race. It is our story, and your life is caught up in it. You are not a spectator; you are one of the reasons Christ came into the world.

PAUSE FOR PRAYER

Gracious Lord,

Thank You for showing me my need of Christ and for sending Your Son into the world. Thank You that through His death I am reconciled to You. Thank You that He bore the curse that otherwise would have fallen on me because of my sin. Thank You that He is changing my heart.

I praise You for Your grace and power, and I thank You that I can see them at work in my life.

Through Jesus Christ. Amen.

You Can Do It!

Can you imagine the insight and joy gained from reading the entire Bible? In as little as 15 minutes a day, *The One Year Bible* will guide you through God's Word with daily readings from the Old Testament, New Testament, Psalms, and Proverbs.

Begin reading *The One Year Bible* from cover to cover and experience the spiritual growth and communion with God that come from daily Bible reading. Available in the clear, accurate New Living Translation. Also available in the NIV and King James Version.

Available wherever Bibles are sold.

TYNDALE

for those who thirst.

□ January 1
Genesis 1:1–2:25
Matthew 1:1–2:12
Psalm 1:1-6
Proverbs 1:1-6

□ January 2
Genesis 3:1–4:26
Matthew 2:13–3:6
Psalm 2:1-12
Proverbs 1:7-9

□ January 3
Genesis 5:1–7:24
Matthew 3:7–4:11
Psalm 3:1-8
Proverbs 1:10-19

□ January 4
Genesis 8:1–10:32
Matthew 4:12-25
Psalm 4:1-8
Proverbs 1:20-23

□ January 5
Genesis 11:1–13:4
Matthew 5:1-26
Psalm 5:1-12
Proverbs 1:24-28

□ January 6
Genesis 13:5–15:21
Matthew 5:27-48
Psalm 6:1-10
Proverbs 1:29-33

□ January 7
Genesis 16:1–18:15
Matthew 6:1-24
Psalm 7:1-17
Proverbs 2:1-5

□ January 8
Genesis 18:16–19:38
Matthew 6:25–7:14
Psalm 8:1-9
Proverbs 2:6-15

□ January 9
Genesis 20:1–22:24
Matthew 7:15-29
Psalm 9:1-12
Proverbs 2:16-22

□ January 10
Genesis 23:1–24:51
Matthew 8:1-17
Psalm 9:13-20
Proverbs 3:1-6

□ January 11
Genesis 24:52–26:16
Matthew 8:18-34
Psalm 10:1-15
Proverbs 3:7-8

□ January 12
Genesis 26:17–27:46
Matthew 9:1-17
Psalm 10:16-18
Proverbs 3:9-10

□ January 13
Genesis 28:1–29:35
Matthew 9:18-38
Psalm 11:1-7
Proverbs 3:11-12

□ January 14
Genesis 30:1–31:16
Matthew 10:1-23
Psalm 12:1-8
Proverbs 3:13-15

□ January 15
Genesis 31:17–32:12
Matthew 10:24–11:6
Psalm 13:1-6
Proverbs 3:16-18

□ January 16
Genesis 32:13–34:31
Matthew 11:7-30
Psalm 14:1-7
Proverbs 3:19-20

□ January 17
Genesis 35:1–36:43
Matthew 12:1-21
Psalm 15:1-5
Proverbs 3:21-26

□ January 18
Genesis 37:1–38:30
Matthew 12:22-45
Psalm 16:1-11
Proverbs 3:27-32

□ January 19
Genesis 39:1–41:16
Matthew 12:46–13:23
Psalm 17:1-15
Proverbs 3:33-35

□ January 20
Genesis 41:17–42:17
Matthew 13:24-46
Psalm 18:1-15
Proverbs 4:1-6

□ January 21
Genesis 42:18–43:34
Matthew 13:47–14:12
Psalm 18:16-36
Proverbs 4:7-10

□ January 22
Genesis 44:1–45:28
Matthew 14:13-36
Psalm 18:37-50
Proverbs 4:11-13

□ January 23
Genesis 46:1–47:31
Matthew 15:1-28
Psalm 19:1-14
Proverbs 4:14-19

□ January 24
Genesis 48:1–49:33
Matthew 15:29–16:12
Psalm 20:1-9
Proverbs 4:20-27

□ January 25
Genesis 50:1—Exodus 2:10
Matthew 16:13–17:9
Psalm 21:1-13
Proverbs 5:1-6

□ January 26
Exodus 2:11–3:22
Matthew 17:10-27
Psalm 22:1-18
Proverbs 5:7-14

□ January 27
Exodus 4:1–5:21
Matthew 18:1-22
Psalm 22:19-31
Proverbs 5:15-21

□ January 28
Exodus 5:22–7:25
Matthew 18:23–19:12
Psalm 23:1-6
Proverbs 5:22-23

□ January 29
Exodus 8:1–9:35
Matthew 19:13-30
Psalm 24:1-10
Proverbs 6:1-5

□ January 30
Exodus 10:1–12:13
Matthew 20:1-28
Psalm 25:1-15
Proverbs 6:6-11

□ January 31
Exodus 12:14–13:16
Matthew 20:29–21:22
Psalm 25:16-22
Proverbs 6:12-15

□ February 1
Exodus 13:17–15:18
Matthew 21:23-46
Psalm 26:1-12
Proverbs 6:16-19

□ February 2
Exodus 15:19–17:7
Matthew 22:1-33
Psalm 27:1-6
Proverbs 6:20-26

□ February 3
Exodus 17:8–19:15
Matthew 22:34–23:12
Psalm 27:7-14
Proverbs 6:27-35

□ February 4
Exodus 19:16–21:21
Matthew 23:13-39
Psalm 28:1-9
Proverbs 7:1-5

□ February 5
Exodus 21:22–23:13
Matthew 24:1-28
Psalm 29:1-11
Proverbs 7:6-23

□ February 6
Exodus 23:14–25:40
Matthew 24:29-51
Psalm 30:1-12
Proverbs 7:24-27

□ February 7
Exodus 26:1–27:21
Matthew 25:1-30
Psalm 31:1-8
Proverbs 8:1-11

□ February 8
Exodus 28:1-43
Matthew 25:31–26:13
Psalm 31:9-18
Proverbs 8:12-13

□ February 9
Exodus 29:1–30:10
Matthew 26:14-46
Psalm 31:19-24
Proverbs 8:14-26

□ February 10
Exodus 30:11–31:18
Matthew 26:47-68
Psalm 32:1-11
Proverbs 8:27-32

□ February 11
Exodus 32:1–33:23
Matthew 26:69–27:14
Psalm 33:1-11
Proverbs 8:33-36

☐ February 12
Exodus 34:1–35:9
Matthew 27:15-31
Psalm 33:12-22
Proverbs 9:1-6

☐ February 13
Exodus 35:10–36:38
Matthew 27:32-66
Psalm 34:1-10
Proverbs 9:7-8

☐ February 14
Exodus 37:1–38:31
Matthew 28:1-20
Psalm 34:11-22
Proverbs 9:9-10

☐ February 15
Exodus 39:1–40:38
Mark 1:1-28
Psalm 35:1-16
Proverbs 9:11-12

☐ February 16
Leviticus 1:1–3:17
Mark 1:29–2:12
Psalm 35:17-28
Proverbs 9:13-18

☐ February 17
Leviticus 4:1–5:19
Mark 2:13–3:6
Psalm 36:1-12
Proverbs 10:1-2

☐ February 18
Leviticus 6:1–7:27
Mark 3:7-30
Psalm 37:1-11
Proverbs 10:3-4

☐ February 19
Leviticus 7:28–9:6
Mark 3:31–4:25
Psalm 37:12-29
Proverbs 10:5

☐ February 20
Leviticus 9:7–10:20
Mark 4:26–5:20
Psalm 37:30-40
Proverbs 10:6-7

☐ February 21
Leviticus 11:1–12:8 ·
Mark 5:21-43
Psalm 38:1-22
Proverbs 10:8-9

☐ February 22
Leviticus 13:1-59
Mark 6:1-29
Psalm 39:1-13
Proverbs 10:10

☐ February 23
Leviticus 14:1-57
Mark 6:30-56
Psalm 40:1-10
Proverbs 10:11-12

☐ February 24
Leviticus 15:1–16:28
Mark 7:1-23
Psalm 40:11-17
Proverbs 10:13-14

☐ February 25
Leviticus 16:29–18:30
Mark 7:24–8:10
Psalm 41:1-13
Proverbs 10:15-16

☐ February 26
Leviticus 19:1–20:21
Mark 8:11-38
Psalm 42:1-11
Proverbs 10:17

☐ February 27
Leviticus 20:22–22:16
Mark 9:1-29
Psalm 43:1-5
Proverbs 10:18

☐ February 28
Leviticus 22:17–23:44
Mark 9:30–10:12
Psalm 44:1-8
Proverbs 10:19

☐ March 1
Leviticus 24:1–25:46
Mark 10:13-31
Psalm 44:9-26
Proverbs 10:20-21

☐ March 2
Leviticus 25:47–27:13
Mark 10:32-52
Psalm 45:1-17
Proverbs 10:22

☐ March 3
Leviticus 27:14—Numbers 1:54
Mark 11:1-25
Psalm 46:1-11
Proverbs 10:23

☐ March 4
Numbers 2:1–3:51
Mark 11:27–12:17
Psalm 47:1-9
Proverbs 10:24-25

☐ March 5
Numbers 4:1–5:31
Mark 12:18-37
Psalm 48:1-14
Proverbs 10:26

☐ March 6
Numbers 6:1–7:89
Mark 12:38–13:13
Psalm 49:1-20
Proverbs 10:27-28

☐ March 7
Numbers 8:1–9:23
Mark 13:14-37
Psalm 50:1-23
Proverbs 10:29-30

☐ March 8
Numbers 10:1–11:23
Mark 14:1-21
Psalm 51:1-19
Proverbs 10:31-32

☐ March 9
Numbers 11:24–13:33
Mark 14:22-52
Psalm 52:1-9
Proverbs 11:1-3

☐ March 10
Numbers 14:1–15:16
Mark 14:53-72
Psalm 53:1-6
Proverbs 11:4

☐ March 11
Numbers 15:17–16:40
Mark 15:1-47
Psalm 54:1-7
Proverbs 11:5-6

☐ March 12
Numbers 16:41–18:32
Mark 16:1-20
Psalm 55:1-23
Proverbs 11:7

☐ March 13
Numbers 19:1–20:29
Luke 1:1-25
Psalm 56:1-13
Proverbs 11:8

☐ March 14
Numbers 21:1–22:20
Luke 1:26-56
Psalm 57:1-11
Proverbs 11:9-11

☐ March 15
Numbers 22:21–23:30
Luke 1:57-80
Psalm 58:1-11
Proverbs 11:12-13

☐ March 16
Numbers 24:1–25:18
Luke 2:1-35
Psalm 59:1-17
Proverbs 11:14

☐ March 17
Numbers 26:1-51
Luke 2:36-52
Psalm 60:1-12
Proverbs 11:15

☐ March 18
Numbers 26:52–28:15
Luke 3:1-22
Psalm 61:1-8
Proverbs 11:16-17

☐ March 19
Numbers 28:16–29:40
Luke 3:23-38
Psalm 62:1-12
Proverbs 11:18-19

☐ March 20
Numbers 30:1–31:54
Luke 4:1-30
Psalm 63:1-11
Proverbs 11:20-21

☐ March 21
Numbers 32:1–33:39
Luke 4:31–5:11
Psalm 64:1-10
Proverbs 11:22

☐ March 22
Numbers 33:40–35:34
Luke 5:12-28
Psalm 65:1-13
Proverbs 11:23

☐ March 23
Numbers 36:1—Deuteronomy 1:46
Luke 5:29–6:11
Psalm 66:1-20
Proverbs 11:24-26

☐ March 24
Deuteronomy 2:1–3:29
Luke 6:12-38
Psalm 67:1-7
Proverbs 11:27

☐ March 25
Deuteronomy 4:1-49
Luke 6:39–7:10
Psalm 68:1-18
Proverbs 11:28

☐ March 26
Deuteronomy 5:1–6:25
Luke 7:11-35
Psalm 68:19-35
Proverbs 11:29-31

☐ March 27
Deuteronomy 7:1–8:20
Luke 7:36–8:3
Psalm 69:1-18
Proverbs 12:1

☐ March 28
Deuteronomy 9:1–10:22
Luke 8:4-21
Psalm 69:19-36
Proverbs 12:2-3

☐ March 29
Deuteronomy 11:1–12:32
Luke 8:22-39
Psalm 70:1-5
Proverbs 12:4

☐ March 30
Deuteronomy 13:1–15:23
Luke 8:40–9:6
Psalm 71:1-24
Proverbs 12:5-7

☐ March 31
Deuteronomy 16:1–17:20
Luke 9:7-27
Psalm 72:1-20
Proverbs 12:8-9

☐ April 1
Deuteronomy 18:1–20:20
Luke 9:28-50
Psalm 73:1-28
Proverbs 12:10

☐ April 2
Deuteronomy 21:1–22:30
Luke 9:51–10:12
Psalm 74:1-23
Proverbs 12:11

☐ April 3
Deuteronomy 23:1–25:19
Luke 10:13-37
Psalm 75:1-10
Proverbs 12:12-14

☐ April 4
Deuteronomy 26:1–27:26
Luke 10:38–11:13
Psalm 76:1-12
Proverbs 12:15-17

☐ April 5
Deuteronomy 28:1-68
Luke 11:14-36
Psalm 77:1-20
Proverbs 12:18

☐ April 6
Deuteronomy 29:1–30:20
Luke 11:37–12:7
Psalm 78:1-31
Proverbs 12:19-20

☐ April 7
Deuteronomy 31:1–32:27
Luke 12:8-34
Psalm 78:32-55
Proverbs 12:21-23

☐ April 8
Deuteronomy 32:28-52
Luke 12:35-59
Psalm 78:56-64
Proverbs 12:24

☐ April 9
Deuteronomy 33:1-29
Luke 13:1-21
Psalm 78:65-72
Proverbs 12:25

☐ April 10
Deuteronomy 34:1—Joshua 2:24
Luke 13:22–14:6
Psalm 79:1-13
Proverbs 12:26

☐ April 11
Joshua 3:1–4:24
Luke 14:7-35
Psalm 80:1-19
Proverbs 12:27-28

☐ April 12
Joshua 5:1–7:15
Luke 15:1-32
Psalm 81:1-16
Proverbs 13:1

☐ April 13
Joshua 7:16–9:2
Luke 16:1-18
Psalm 82:1-8
Proverbs 13:2-3

☐ April 14
Joshua 9:3–10:43
Luke 16:19–17:10
Psalm 83:1-18
Proverbs 13:4

☐ April 15
Joshua 11:1–12:24
Luke 17:11-37
Psalm 84:1-12
Proverbs 13:5-6

☐ April 16
Joshua 13:1–14:15
Luke 18:1-17
Psalm 85:1-13
Proverbs 13:7-8

☐ April 17
Joshua 15:1-63
Luke 18:18-43
Psalm 86:1-17
Proverbs 13:9-10

☐ April 18
Joshua 16:1–18:28
Luke 19:1-27
Psalm 87:1-7
Proverbs 13:11

☐ April 19
Joshua 19:1–20:9
Luke 19:28-48
Psalm 88:1-18
Proverbs 13:12-14

☐ April 20
Joshua 21:1–22:20
Luke 20:1-26
Psalm 89:1-13
Proverbs 13:15-16

☐ April 21
Joshua 22:21–23:16
Luke 20:27-47
Psalm 89:14-37
Proverbs 13:17-19

☐ April 22
Joshua 24:1-33
Luke 21:1-28
Psalm 89:38-52
Proverbs 13:20-23

☐ April 23
Judges 1:1–2:9
Luke 21:29–22:13
Psalm 90:1–91:16
Proverbs 13:24-25

☐ April 24
Judges 2:10–3:31
Luke 22:14-34
Psalm 92:1–93:5
Proverbs 14:1-2

☐ April 25
Judges 4:1–5:31
Luke 22:35-53
Psalm 94:1-23
Proverbs 14:3-4

☐ April 26
Judges 6:1-40
Luke 22:54–23:12
Psalm 95:1–96:13
Proverbs 14:5-6

☐ April 27
Judges 7:1–8:17
Luke 23:13-43
Psalm 97:1–98:9
Proverbs 14:7-8

☐ April 28
Judges 8:18–9:21
Luke 23:44–24:12
Psalm 99:1-9
Proverbs 14:9-10

☐ April 29
Judges 9:22–10:18
Luke 24:13-53
Psalm 100:1-5
Proverbs 14:11-12

☐ April 30
Judges 11:1–12:15
John 1:1-28
Psalm 101:1-8
Proverbs 14:13-14

☐ May 1
Judges 13:1–14:20
John 1:29-51
Psalm 102:1-28
Proverbs 14:15-16

☐ May 2
Judges 15:1–16:31
John 2:1-25
Psalm 103:1-22
Proverbs 14:17-19

☐ May 3
Judges 17:1–18:31
John 3:1-21
Psalm 104:1-23
Proverbs 14:20-21

☐ May 4
Judges 19:1–20:48
John 3:22–4:3
Psalm 104:24-35
Proverbs 14:22-24

☐ May 5
Judges 21:1—Ruth 1:22
John 4:4-42
Psalm 105:1-15
Proverbs 14:25

☐ May 6
Ruth 2:1–4:22
John 4:43-54
Psalm 105:16-36
Proverbs 14:26-27

☐ May 7
1 Samuel 1:1–2:21
John 5:1-23
Psalm 105:37-45
Proverbs 14:28-29

☐ May 8
1 Samuel 2:22–4:22
John 5:24-47
Psalm 106:1-12
Proverbs 14:30-31

☐ May 9
1 Samuel 5:1–7:17
John 6:1-21
Psalm 106:13-31
Proverbs 14:32-33

☐ May 10
1 Samuel 8:1–9:27
John 6:22-42
Psalm 106:32-48
Proverbs 14:34-35

☐ May 11
1 Samuel 10:1–11:15
John 6:43-71
Psalm 107:1-43
Proverbs 15:1-3

☐ May 12
1 Samuel 12:1–13:23
John 7:1-30
Psalm 108:1-13
Proverbs 15:4

☐ May 13
1 Samuel 14:1–14:52
John 7:31-53
Psalm 109:1-31
Proverbs 15:5-7

☐ May 14
1 Samuel 15:1–16:23
John 8:1-20
Psalm 110:1-7
Proverbs 15:8-10

☐ May 15
1 Samuel 17:1–18:4
John 8:21-30
Psalm 111:1-10
Proverbs 15:11

☐ May 16
1 Samuel 18:5–19:24
John 8:31-59
Psalm 112:1-10
Proverbs 15:12-14

☐ May 17
1 Samuel 20:1–21:15
John 9:1-41
Psalm 113:1–114:8
Proverbs 15:15-17

☐ May 18
1 Samuel 22:1–23:29
John 10:1-21
Psalm 115:1-18
Proverbs 15:18-19

☐ May 19
1 Samuel 24:1–25:44
John 10:22-42
Psalm 116:1-19
Proverbs 15:20-21

☐ May 20
1 Samuel 26:1–28:25
John 11:1-54
Psalm 117:1-2
Proverbs 15:22-23

☐ May 21
1 Samuel 29:1–31:13
John 11:55–12:19
Psalm 118:1-18
Proverbs 15:24-26

☐ May 22
2 Samuel 1:1–2:11
John 12:20-50
Psalm 118:19-29
Proverbs 15:27-28

☐ May 23
2 Samuel 2:12–3:39
John 13:1-30
Psalm 119:1-16
Proverbs 15:29-30

☐ May 24
2 Samuel 4:1–6:23
John 13:31–14:14
Psalm 119:17-32
Proverbs 15:31-32

☐ May 25
2 Samuel 7:1–8:18
John 14:15-31
Psalm 119:33-48
Proverbs 15:33

☐ May 26
2 Samuel 9:1–11:27
John 15:1-27
Psalm 119:49-64
Proverbs 16:1-3

☐ May 27
2 Samuel 12:1-31
John 16:1-33
Psalm 119:65-80
Proverbs 16:4-5

☐ May 28
2 Samuel 13:1-39
John 17:1-26
Psalm 119:81-96
Proverbs 16:6-7

☐ May 29
2 Samuel 14:1–15:22
John 18:1-24
Psalm 119:97-112
Proverbs 16:8-9

☐ May 30
2 Samuel 15:23–16:23
John 18:25–19:22
Psalm 119:113-128
Proverbs 16:10-11

☐ May 31
2 Samuel 17:1-29
John 19:23-42
Psalm 119:129-152
Proverbs 16:12-13

☐ June 1
2 Samuel 18:1–19:10
John 20:1-31
Psalm 119:153-176
Proverbs 16:14-15

☐ June 2
2 Samuel 19:11–20:13
John 21:1-25
Psalm 120:1-7 |
Proverbs 16:16-17

☐ June 3
2 Samuel 20:14–21:22
Acts 1:1-26
Psalm 121:1-8
Proverbs 16:18

☐ June 4
2 Samuel 22:1–23:23
Acts 2:1-47
Psalm 122:1-9
Proverbs 16:19-20

☐ June 5
2 Samuel 23:24–24:25
Acts 3:1-26
Psalm 123:1-4
Proverbs 16:21-23

☐ June 6
1 Kings 1:1-53
Acts 4:1-37
Psalm 124:1-8
Proverbs 16:24

☐ June 7
1 Kings 2:1–3:2
Acts 5:1-42
Psalm 125:1-5
Proverbs 16:25

☐ June 8
1 Kings 3:3–4:34
Acts 6:1-15
Psalm 126:1-6
Proverbs 16:26-27

☐ June 9
1 Kings 5:1–6:38
Acts 7:1-29
Psalm 127:1-5
Proverbs 16:28-30

☐ June 10
1 Kings 7:1-51
Acts 7:30-50
Psalm 128:1-6
Proverbs 16:31-33

☐ June 11
1 Kings 8:1-66
Acts 7:51–8:13
Psalm 129:1-8
Proverbs 17:1

☐ June 12
1 Kings 9:1–10:29
Acts 8:14-40
Psalm 130:1-8
Proverbs 17:2-3

☐ June 13
1 Kings 11:1–12:19
Acts 9:1-25
Psalm 131:1-3
Proverbs 17:4-5

☐ June 14
1 Kings 12:20–13:34
Acts 9:26-43
Psalm 132:1-18
Proverbs 17:6

☐ June 15
1 Kings 14:1–15:24
Acts 10:1-23
Psalm 133:1-3
Proverbs 17:7-8

☐ June 16
1 Kings 15:25–17:24
Acts 10:24-48
Psalm 134:1-3
Proverbs 17:9-11

☐ June 17
1 Kings 18:1-46
Acts 11:1-30
Psalm 135:1-21
Proverbs 17:12-13

☐ June 18
1 Kings 19:1-21
Acts 12:1-23
Psalm 136:1-26
Proverbs 17:14-15

☐ June 19
1 Kings 20:1–21:29
Acts 12:24–13:15
Psalm 137:1-9
Proverbs 17:16

☐ June 20
1 Kings 22:1-53
Acts 13:16-41
Psalm 138:1-8
Proverbs 17:17-18

☐ June 21
2 Kings 1:1–2:25
Acts 13:42–14:7
Psalm 139:1-24
Proverbs 17:19-21

☐ June 22
2 Kings 3:1–4:17
Acts 14:8-28
Psalm 140:1-13
Proverbs 17:22

☐ June 23
2 Kings 4:18–5:27
Acts 15:1-35
Psalm 141:1-10
Proverbs 17:23

☐ June 24
2 Kings 6:1–7:20
Acts 15:36–16:15
Psalm 142:1-7
Proverbs 17:24-25

☐ June 25
2 Kings 8:1–9:13
Acts 16:16-40
Psalm 143:1-12
Proverbs 17:26

☐ June 26
2 Kings 9:14–10:31
Acts 17:1-34
Psalm 144:1-15
Proverbs 17:27-28

☐ June 27
2 Kings 10:32–12:21
Acts 18:1-22
Psalm 145:1-21
Proverbs 18:1

☐ June 28
2 Kings 13:1–14:29
Acts 18:23–19:12
Psalm 146:1-10
Proverbs 18:2-3

☐ June 29
2 Kings 15:1–16:20
Acts 19:13-41
Psalm 147:1-20
Proverbs 18:4-5

☐ June 30
2 Kings 17:1–18:12
Acts 20:1-38
Psalm 148:1-14
Proverbs 18:6-7

☐ July 1
2 Kings 18:13–19:37
Acts 21:1-17
Psalm 149:1-9
Proverbs 18:8

□ July 2
2 Kings 20:1–22:2
Acts 21:18-36
Psalm 150:1-6
Proverbs 18:9-10

□ July 3
2 Kings 22:3–23:30
Acts 21:37–22:16
Psalm 1:1-6
Proverbs 18:11-12

□ July 4
2 Kings 23:31–25:30
Acts 22:17–23:10
Psalm 2:1-12
Proverbs 18:13

□ July 5
1 Chronicles 1:1–2:17
Acts 23:11-35
Psalm 3:1-8
Proverbs 18:14-15

□ July 6
1 Chronicles 2:18–4:4
Acts 24:1-27
Psalm 4:1-8
Proverbs 18:16-18

□ July 7
1 Chronicles 4:5–5:17
Acts 25:1-27
Psalm 5:1-12
Proverbs 18:19

□ July 8
1 Chronicles 5:18–6:81
Acts 26:1-32
Psalm 6:1-10
Proverbs 18:20-21

□ July 9
1 Chronicles 7:1–8:40
Acts 27:1-20
Psalm 7:1-17
Proverbs 18:22

□ July 10
1 Chronicles 9:1–10:14
Acts 27:21-44
Psalm 8:1-9
Proverbs 18:23-24

□ July 11
1 Chronicles 11:1–12:18
Acts 28:1-31
Psalm 9:1-12
Proverbs 19:1-3

□ July 12
1 Chronicles 12:19–14:17
Romans 1:1-17
Psalm 9:13-20
Proverbs 19:4-5

□ July 13
1 Chronicles 15:1–16:36
Romans 1:18-32
Psalm 10:1-15
Proverbs 19:6-7

□ July 14
1 Chronicles 16:37–18:17
Romans 2:1-24
Psalm 10:16-18
Proverbs 19:8-9

□ July 15
1 Chronicles 19:1–21:30
Romans 2:25–3:8
Psalm 11:1-7
Proverbs 19:10-12

☐ July 16
1 Chronicles 22:1–23:32
Romans 3:9-31
Psalm 12:1-8
Proverbs 19:13-14

☐ July 17
1 Chronicles 24:1–26:11
Romans 4:1-12
Psalm 13:1-6
Proverbs 19:15-16

☐ July 18
1 Chronicles 26:12–27:34
Romans 4:13–5:5
Psalm 14:1-7
Proverbs 19:17

☐ July 19
1 Chronicles 28:1–29:30
Romans 5:6-21
Psalm 15:1-5
Proverbs 19:18-19

☐ July 20
2 Chronicles 1:1–3:17
Romans 6:1-23
Psalm 16:1-11
Proverbs 19:20-21

☐ July 21
2 Chronicles 4:1–6:11
Romans 7:1-13
Psalm 17:1-15
Proverbs 19:22-23

☐ July 22
2 Chronicles 6:12–8:10
Romans 7:14–8:8
Psalm 18:1-15
Proverbs 19:24-25

☐ July 23
2 Chronicles 8:11–10:19
Romans 8:9-25
Psalm 18:16-36
Proverbs 19:26

☐ July 24
2 Chronicles 11:1–13:22
Romans 8:26-39
Psalm 18:37-50
Proverbs 19:27-29

☐ July 25
2 Chronicles 14:1–16:14
Romans 9:1-24
Psalm 19:1-14
Proverbs 20:1

☐ July 26
2 Chronicles 17:1–18:34
Romans 9:25–10:13
Psalm 20:1-9
Proverbs 20:2-3

☐ July 27
2 Chronicles 19:1–20:37
Romans 10:14–11:12
Psalm 21:1-13
Proverbs 20:4-6

☐ July 28
2 Chronicles 21:1–23:21
Romans 11:13-36
Psalm 22:1-18
Proverbs 20:7

☐ July 29
2 Chronicles 24:1–25:28
Romans 12:1-21
Psalm 22:19-31
Proverbs 20:8-10

☐ July 30
2 Chronicles 26:1–28:27
Romans 13:1-14
Psalm 23:1-6
Proverbs 20:11

☐ July 31
2 Chronicles 29:1-36
Romans 14:1-23
Psalm 24:1-10
Proverbs 20:12

☐ August 1
2 Chronicles 30:1–31:21
Romans 15:1-22
Psalm 25:1-15
Proverbs 20:13-15

☐ August 2
2 Chronicles 32:1–33:13
Romans 15:23–16:9
Psalm 25:16-22
Proverbs 20:16-18

☐ August 3
2 Chronicles 33:14–34:33
Romans 16:10-27
Psalm 26:1-12
Proverbs 20:19

☐ August 4
2 Chronicles 35:1–36:23
1 Corinthians 1:1-17
Psalm 27:1-6
Proverbs 20:20-21

☐ August 5
Ezra 1:1–2:70
1 Corinthians
Psalm 27:7-14
Proverbs 20:22-23

☐ August 6
Ezra 3:1–4:24
1 Corinthians 2:6–3:4
Psalm 28:1-9
Proverbs 20:24-25

☐ August 7
Ezra 5:1–6:22
1 Corinthians 3:5-23
Psalm 29:1-11
Proverbs 20:26-27

☐ August 8
Ezra 7:1–8:20
1 Corinthians 4:1-21
Psalm 30:1-12
Proverbs 20:28-30

☐ August 9
Ezra 8:21–9:15
1 Corinthians 5:1-13
Psalm 31:1-8
Proverbs 21:1-2

☐ August 10
Ezra 10:1-44
1 Corinthians 6:1-20
Psalm 31:9-18
Proverbs 21:3

☐ August 11
Nehemiah 1:1–3:14
1 Corinthians 7:1-24
Psalm 31:19-24
Proverbs 21:4

☐ August 12
Nehemiah 3:15–5:13
1 Corinthians 7:25-40
Psalm 32:1-11
Proverbs 21:5-7

☐ August 13
Nehemiah 5:14–7:60
1 Corinthians 8:1-13
Psalm 33:1-11
Proverbs 21:8-10

☐ August 14
Nehemiah 7:61–9:21
1 Corinthians 9:1-18
Psalm 33:12-22
Proverbs 21:11-12

☐ August 15
Nehemiah 9:22–10:39
1 Corinthians 9:19–10:13
Psalm 34:1-10
Proverbs 21:13

☐ August 16
Nehemiah 11:1–12:26
1 Corinthians 10:14-33
Psalm 34:11-22
Proverbs 21:14-16

☐ August 17
Nehemiah 12:27–13:31
1 Corinthians 11:1-16
Psalm 35:1-16
Proverbs 21:17-18

☐ August 18
Esther 1:1–3:15
1 Corinthians 11:17-34
Psalm 35:17-28
Proverbs 21:19-20

☐ August 19
Esther 4:1–7:10
1 Corinthians 12:1-26
Psalm 36:1-12
Proverbs 21:21-22

☐ August 20
Esther 8:1–10:3
1 Corinthians 12:27–13:13
Psalm 37:1-11
Proverbs 21:23-24

☐ August 21
Job 1:1–3:26
1 Corinthians 14:1-17
Psalm 37:12-29
Proverbs 21:25-26

☐ August 22
Job 4:1–7:21
1 Corinthians 14:18-40
Psalm 37:30-40
Proverbs 21:27

☐ August 23
Job 8:1–11:20
1 Corinthians 15:1-28
Psalm 38:1-22
Proverbs 21:28-29

☐ August 24
Job 12:1–15:35
1 Corinthians 15:29-58
Psalm 39:1-13
Proverbs 21:30-31

☐ August 25
Job 16:1–19:29
1 Corinthians 16:1-24
Psalm 40:1-10
Proverbs 22:1

☐ August 26
Job 20:1–22:30
2 Corinthians 1:1-11
Psalm 40:11-17
Proverbs 22:2-4

□ August 27
Job 23:1–27:23
2 Corinthians 1:12–2:11
Psalm 41:1-13
Proverbs 22:5-6

□ August 28
Job 28:1–30:31
2 Corinthians 2:12-17
Psalm 42:1-11
Proverbs 22:7

□ August 29
Job 31:1–33:33
2 Corinthians 3:1-18
Psalm 43:1-5
Proverbs 22:8-9

□ August 30
Job 34:1–36:33
2 Corinthians 4:1-12
Psalm 44:1-8
Proverbs 22:10-12

□ August 31
Job 37:1–39:30
2 Corinthians 4:13–5:10
Psalm 44:9-26
Proverbs 22:13

□ September 1
Job 40:1–42:17
2 Corinthians 5:11-21
Psalm 45:1-17
Proverbs 22:14

□ September 2
Ecclesiastes 1:1–3:22
2 Corinthians 6:1-13
Psalm 46:1-11
Proverbs 22:15

□ September 3
Ecclesiastes 4:1–6:12
2 Corinthians 6:14–7:7
Psalm 47:1-9
Proverbs 22:16

□ September 4
Ecclesiastes 7:1–9:18
2 Corinthians 7:8-16
Psalm 48:1-14
Proverbs 22:17-19

□ September 5
Ecclesiastes 10:1–12:14
2 Corinthians 8:1-15
Psalm 49:1-20
Proverbs 22:20-21

□ September 6
Song of songs 1:1–4:16
2 Corinthians 8:16-24
Psalm 50:1-23
Proverbs 22:22-23

□ September 7
Song of songs 5:1–8:14
2 Corinthians 9:1-15
Psalm 51:1-19
Proverbs 22:24-25

□ September 8
Isaiah 1:1–2:22
2 Corinthians 10:1-18
Psalm 52:1-9
Proverbs 22:26-27

□ September 9
Isaiah 3:1–5:30
2 Corinthians 11:1-15
Psalm 53:1-6
Proverbs 22:28-29

☐ September 10
Isaiah 6:1–7:25
2 Corinthians 11:16-33
Psalm 54:1-7
Proverbs 23:1-3

☐ September 11
Isaiah 8:1–9:21
2 Corinthians 12:1-10
Psalm 55:1-23
Proverbs 23:4-5

☐ September 12
Isaiah 10:1–11:16
2 Corinthians 12:11-21
Psalm 56:1-13
Proverbs 23:6-8

☐ September 13
Isaiah 12:1–14:32
2 Corinthians 13:1-13
Psalm 57:1-11
Proverbs 23:9-11

☐ September 14
Isaiah 15:1–18:7
Galatians 1:1-24
Psalm 58:1-11
Proverbs 23:12

☐ September 15
Isaiah 19:1–21:17
Galatians 2:1-16
Psalm 59:1-17
Proverbs 23:13-14

☐ September 16
Isaiah 22:1–24:23
Galatians 2:17–3:9
Psalm 60:1-12
Proverbs 23:15-16

☐ September 17
Isaiah 25:1–28:13
Galatians 3:10-22
Psalm 61:1-8
Proverbs 23:17-18

☐ September 18
Isaiah 28:14–30:11
Galatians 3:23–4:31
Psalm 62:1-12
Proverbs 23:19-21

☐ September 19
Isaiah 30:12–33:9
Galatians 5:1-12
Psalm 63:1-11
Proverbs 23:22

☐ September 20
Isaiah 33:10–36:22
Galatians 5:13-26
Psalm 64:1-10
Proverbs 23:23

☐ September 21
Isaiah 37:1–38:22
Galatians 6:1-18
Psalm 65:1-13
Proverbs 23:24

☐ September 22
Isaiah 39:1–41:16
Ephesians 1:1-23
Psalm 66:1-20
Proverbs 23:25-28

☐ September 23
Isaiah 41:17–43:13
Ephesians 2:1-22
Psalm 67:1-7
Proverbs 23:29-35

☐ September 24
Isaiah 43:14–45:10
Ephesians 3:1-21
Psalm 68:1-18
Proverbs 24:1-2

☐ September 25
Isaiah 45:11–48:11
Ephesians 4:1-16
Psalm 68:19-35
Proverbs 24:3-4

☐ September 26
Isaiah 48:12–50:11
Ephesians 4:17-32
Psalm 69:1-18
Proverbs 24:5-6

☐ September 27
Isaiah 51:1–53:12
Ephesians 5:1-33
Psalm 69:19-36
Proverbs 24:7

☐ September 28
Isaiah 54:1–57:14
Ephesians 6:1-24
Psalm 70:1-5
Proverbs 24:8

☐ September 29
Isaiah 57:15–59:21
Philippians 1:1-26
Psalm 71:1-24
Proverbs 24:9-10

☐ September 30
Isaiah 60:1–62:5
Philippians 1:27–2:18
Psalm 72:1-20
Proverbs 24:11-12

☐ October 1
Isaiah 62:6–65:25
Philippians 2:19–3:3
Psalm 73:1-28
Proverbs 24:13-14

☐ October 2
Isaiah 66:1-24
Philippians 3:4-21
Psalm 74:1-23
Proverbs 24:15-16

☐ October 3
Jeremiah 1:1–2:30
Philippians 4:1-23
Psalm 75:1-10
Proverbs 24:17-20

☐ October 4
Jeremiah 2:31–4:18
Colossians 1:1-17
Psalm 76:1-12 |
Proverbs 24:21-22

☐ October 5
Jeremiah 4:19–6:15
Colossians 1:18–2:7
Psalm 77:1-20
Proverbs 24:23-25

☐ October 6
Jeremiah 6:16–8:7
Colossians 2:8-23
Psalm 78:1-31
Proverbs 24:26

☐ October 7
Jeremiah 8:8–9:26
Colossians 3:1-17
Psalm 78:32-55
Proverbs 24:27

☐ October 8
Jeremiah 10:1–11:23
Colossians 3:18–4:18
Psalm 78:56-72
Proverbs 24:28-29

☐ October 9
Jeremiah 12:1–14:10
1 Thessalonians 1:1–2:8
Psalm 79:1-13
Proverbs 24:30-34

☐ October 10
Jeremiah 14:11–16:15
1 Thessalonians 2:9–3:13
Psalm 80:1-19
Proverbs 25:1-5

☐ October 11
Jeremiah 16:16–18:23
1 Thessalonians 4:1–5:3
Psalm 81:1-16
Proverbs 25:6-8

☐ October 12
Jeremiah 19:1–21:14
1 Thessalonians 5:4-28
Psalm 82:1-8
Proverbs 25:9-10

☐ October 13
Jeremiah 22:1–23:20
2 Thessalonians 1:1-12
Psalm 83:1-18
Proverbs 25:11-14

☐ October 14
Jeremiah 23:21–25:38
2 Thessalonians 2:1-17
Psalm 84:1-12
Proverbs 25:15

☐ October 15
Jeremiah 26:1–27:22
2 Thessalonians 3:1-18
Psalm 85:1-13
Proverbs 25:16

☐ October 16
Jeremiah 28:1–29:32
1 Timothy 1:1-20
Psalm 86:1-17
Proverbs 25:17

☐ October 17
Jeremiah 30:1–31:26
1 Timothy 2:1-15
Psalm 87:1-7
Proverbs 25:18-19

☐ October 18
Jeremiah 31:27–32:44
1 Timothy 3:1-16
Psalm 88:1-18
Proverbs 25:20-22

☐ October 19
Jeremiah 33:1–34:22
1 Timothy 4:1-16
Psalm 89:1-13
Proverbs 25:23-24

☐ October 20
Jeremiah 35:1–36:32
1 Timothy 5:1-25
Psalm 89:14-37
Proverbs 25:25-27

☐ October 21
Jeremiah 37:1–38:28
1 Timothy 6:1-21
Psalm 89:38-52
Proverbs 25:28

☐ October 22
Jeremiah 39:1–41:18
2 Timothy 1:1-18
Psalm 90:1–91:16
Proverbs 26:1-2

☐ October 23
Jeremiah 42:1–44:23
2 Timothy 2:1-21
Psalm 92:1–93:5
Proverbs 26:3-5

☐ October 24
Jeremiah 44:24–47:7
2 Timothy 2:22–3:17
Psalm 94:1-23
Proverbs 26:6-8

☐ October 25
Jeremiah 48:1–49:22
2 Timothy 4:1-22
Psalm 95:1–96:13
Proverbs 26:9-12

☐ October 26
Jeremiah 49:23–50:46
Titus 1:1-16
Psalm 97:1–98:9
Proverbs 26:13-16

☐ October 27
Jeremiah 51:1-53
Titus 2:1-15
Psalm 99:1-9
Proverbs 26:17

☐ October 28
Jeremiah 51:54–52:34
Titus 3:1-15
Psalm 100:1-5
Proverbs 26:18-19

☐ October 29
Lamentations 1:1–2:19
Philippians 1:1-25
Psalm 101:1-8
Proverbs 26:20

☐ October 30
Lamentations 2:20–3:66
Hebrews 1:1-14
Psalm 102:1-28
Proverbs 26:21-22

☐ October 31
Lamentations 4:1–5:22
Hebrews 2:1-18
Psalm 103:1-22
Proverbs 26:23

☐ November 1
Ezekiel 1:1–3:15
Hebrews 3:1-19
Psalm 104:1-23
Proverbs 26:24-26

☐ November 2
Ezekiel 3:16–6:14
Hebrews 4:1-16
Psalm 104:24-35
Proverbs 26:27

☐ November 3
Ezekiel 7:1–9:11
Hebrews 5:1-14
Psalm 105:1-15
Proverbs 26:28

☐ November 4
Ezekiel 10:1–11:25
Hebrews 6:1-20
Psalm 105:16-36
Proverbs 27:1-2

☐ November 5
Ezekiel 12:1–14:11
Hebrews 7:1-17
Psalm 105:37-45
Proverbs 27:3

☐ November 6
Ezekiel 14:12–16:41
Hebrews 7:18-28
Psalm 106:1-12
Proverbs 27:4-6

☐ November 7
Ezekiel 16:42–17:24
Hebrews 8:1-13
Psalm 106:13-31
Proverbs 27:7-9

☐ November 8
Ezekiel 18:1–19:14
Hebrews 9:1-10
Psalm 106:32-48
Proverbs 27:10

☐ November 9
Ezekiel 20:1-49
Hebrews 9:11-28
Psalm 107:1-43
Proverbs 27:11

☐ November 10
Ezekiel 21:1–22:31
Hebrews 10:1-17
Psalm 108:1-13
Proverbs 27:12

☐ November 11
Ezekiel 23:1-49
Hebrews 10:18-39
Psalm 109:1-31
Proverbs 27:13

☐ November 12
Ezekiel 24:1–26:21
Hebrews 11:1-16
Psalm 110:1-7
Proverbs 27:14

☐ November 13
Ezekiel 27:1–28:26
Hebrews 11:17-31
Psalm 111:1-10
Proverbs 27:15-16

☐ November 14
Ezekiel 29:1–30:26
Hebrews 11:32–12:13
Psalm 112:1-10
Proverbs 27:17

☐ November 15
Ezekiel 31:1–32:32
Hebrews 12:14-29
Psalm 113:1–114:8
Proverbs 27:18-20

☐ November 16
Ezekiel 33:1–34:31
Hebrews 13:1-25
Psalm 115:1-18
Proverbs 27:21-22

☐ November 17
Ezekiel 35:1–36:38
James 1:1-18
Psalm 116:1-19
Proverbs 27:23-27

☐ November 18
Ezekiel 37:1–38:23
James 1:19–2:17
Psalm 117:1-2 |
Proverbs 28:1

□ 19
Ezekiel 39:1–40:27
James 2:18–3:18
Psalm 118:1-18
Proverbs 28:2

□ November 20
Ezekiel 40:28–41:26
James 4:1-17
Psalm 118:19-29
Proverbs 28:3-5

□ November 21
Ezekiel 42:1–43:27
James 5:1-20
Psalm 119:1-16
Proverbs 28:6-7

□ November 22
Ezekiel 44:1–45:12
1 Peter 1:1-12
Psalm 119:17-32
Proverbs 28:8-10

□ November 23
Ezekiel 45:13–46:24
1 Peter 1:13–2:10
Psalm 119:33-48
Proverbs 28:11

□ November 24
Ezekiel 47:1–48:35
1 Peter 2:11–3:7
Psalm 119:49-64
Proverbs 28:12-13

□ November 25
Daniel 1:1–2:23
1 Peter 3:8–4:6
Psalm 119:65-80
Proverbs 28:14

□ November 26
Daniel 2:24–3:30
1 Peter 4:7–5:14
Psalm 119:81-96
Proverbs 28:15-16

□ November 27
Daniel 4:1-37
2 Peter 1:1-21
Psalm 119:97-112
Proverbs 28:17-18

□ November 28
Daniel 5:1-31
2 Peter 2:1-22
Psalm 119:113-128
Proverbs 28:19-20

□ November 29
Daniel 6:1-28
2 Peter 3:1-18
Psalm 119:129-152
Proverbs 28:21-22

□ November 30
Daniel 7:1-28
1 John 1:1-10
Psalm 119:153-176
Proverbs 28:23-24

□ December 1
Daniel 8:1-27
1 John 2:1-17
Psalm 120:1-7
Proverbs 28:25-26

□ December 2
Daniel 9:1–11:1
1 John 2:18–3:6
Psalm 121:1-8
Proverbs 28:27-28

☐ December 3
Daniel 11:2-35
1 John 3:7-24
Psalm 122:1-9
Proverbs 29:1

☐ December 4
Daniel 11:36–12:13
1 John 4:1-21
Psalm 123:1-4
Proverbs 29:2-4

☐ December 5
Hosea 1:1–3:5
1 John 5:1-21
Psalm 124:1-8
Proverbs 29:5-8

☐ December 6
Hosea 4:1–5:15
2 John 1:1-13
Psalm 125:1-5
Proverbs 29:9-11

☐ December 7
Hosea 6:1–9:17
3 John 1:1-15
Psalm 126:1-6
Proverbs 29:12-14

☐ December 8
Hosea 10:1–14:9
Jude 1:1-25
Psalm 127:1-5
Proverbs 29:15-17

☐ December 9
Joel 1:1–3:21
Revelation 1:1-20
Psalm 128:1-6
Proverbs 29:18

☐ December 10
Amos 1:1–3:15
Revelation 2:1-17
Psalm 129:1-8
Proverbs 29:19-20

☐ December 11
Amos 4:1–6:14
Revelation 2:18–3:6
Psalm 130:1-8
Proverbs 29:21-22

☐ December 12
Amos 7:1–9:15
Revelation 3:7-22
Psalm 131:1-3
Proverbs 29:23

☐ December 13
Obadiah 1:1-21
Revelation 4:1-11
Psalm 132:1-18
Proverbs 29:24-25

☐ December 14
Jonah 1:1–4:11
Revelation 5:1-14
Psalm 133:1-3
Proverbs 29:26-27

☐ December 15
Micah 1:1–4:13
Revelation 6:1-17
Psalm 134:1-3
Proverbs 30:1-4

☐ December 16
Micah 5:1–7:20
Revelation 7:1-17
Psalm 135:1-21
Proverbs 30:5-6

☐ December 17
Nahum 1:1–3:19
Revelation 8:1-13
Psalm 136:1-26
Proverbs 30:7-9

☐ December 18
Habakkuk 1:1–3:19
Revelation 9:1-21
Psalm 137:1-9
Proverbs 30:10

☐ December 19
Zephaniah 1:1–3:20
Revelation 10:1-11
Psalm 138:1-8
Proverbs 30:11-14

☐ December 20
Haggai 1:1–2:23
Revelation 11:1-19
Psalm 139:1-24
Proverbs 30:15-16

☐ December 21
Zechariah 1:1-21
Revelation 12:1-17
Psalm 140:1-13
Proverbs 30:17

☐ December 22
Zechariah 2:1–3:10
Revelation 12:18-3:18
Psalm 141:1-10
Proverbs 30:18-20

☐ December 23
Zechariah 4:1–5:11
Revelation 14:1-20
Psalm 142:1-7
Proverbs 30:21-23

☐ December 24
Zechariah 6:1–7:14
Revelation 15:1-8
Psalm 143:1-12
Proverbs 30:24-28

☐ December 25
Zechariah 8:1-23
Revelation 16:1-21
Psalm 144:1-15
Proverbs 30:29-31

☐ December 26
Zechariah 9:1-17
Revelation 17:1-18
Psalm 145:1-21
Proverbs 30:32

☐ December 27
Zechariah 10:1–11:17
Revelation 18:1-24
Psalm 146:1-10
Proverbs 30:33

☐ December 28
Zechariah 12:1–13:9
Revelation 19:1-21
Psalm 147:1-20
Proverbs 31:1-7

☐ December 29
Zechariah 14:1-21
Revelation 20:1-15
Psalm 148:1-14
Proverbs 31:8-9

☐ December 30
Malachi 1:1–2:17
Revelation 21:1-27
Psalm 149:1-9
Proverbs 31:10-24

☐ December 31
Malachi 3:1–4:6
Revelation 22:1-21
Psalm 150:1-6
Proverbs 31:25-31

Moody Press, a ministry of Moody Bible Institute, is designed for education, evangelization, and edification. If we may assist you in knowing more about Christ and the Christian life, please write us without obligation: Moody Press, c/o MLM, Chicago, Illinois 60610.